Corporate Responsibility and Labour Rights

Codes of Conduct in the Global Economy

Edited by
Rhys Jenkins, Ruth Pearson
and
Gill Seyfang

EARTHSCAN

Earthscan Publications Ltd
London • Sterling, VA

First published in the UK and USA in 2002
by Earthscan Publications Ltd

Copyright © Rhys Jenkins, Ruth Pearson and Gill Seyfang, 2002

ISBN: 1 85383 931 0 paperback
      1 85383 930 2 hardback

Typesetting by PCS Mapping & DTP, Gateshead
Printed and bound in the UK by Creative Print and Design Wales, Ebbw Vale
Cover design by Danny Gillespie

For a full list of publications please contact:

Earthscan Publications Ltd
120 Pentonville Road, London, N1 9JN, UK
Tel: +44 (0)20 7278 0433
Fax: +44 (0)20 7278 1142
Email: earthinfo@earthscan.co.uk
Web: **www.earthscan.co.uk**

22883 Quicksilver Drive, Sterling, VA 20166-2012, USA

A catalogue record for this book is available from the British Library

Library of Congress Cataloging-in-Publication Data

Corporate responsibility and labour rights : codes of conduct in the global economy /
edited by Rhys Jenkins, Ruth Pearson and Gill Seyfang.
         p. cm.
Includes bibliographical references and index.
    ISBN 1-85383-931-0 (pbk.) – ISBN 1-85383-930-2 (hardback)
    1. Social responsibility of business. 2. Industries–Self-regulation. 3. Industrial
relations. 4. Employee rights. I. Title: Corporate responsibility and labour rights. II
Jenkins, Rhys Owen, 1948- III. Pearson, Ruth, 1945- iV. Seyfang, Gill, 1969-

HD60 .C639 2002
331.25'98–dc21

                                                                    2002011681

Earthscan is an editorially independent subsidiary of Kogan Page Ltd and publishes in
association with WWF-UK and the International Institute for Environment and
Development

This book is printed on elemental chlorine-free paper

Contents

PART ONE: CODES OF CONDUCT AND GLOBAL DEREGULATION

PART TWO: CODES OF CONDUCT – PERSPECTIVES FROM STAKEHOLDERS IN THE GLOBAL PRODUCTION CHAINS

Acronyms and abbreviations

AFL-CIO	American Federation of Labor-Congress of Industrial Organizations
AIP	Apparel Industry Partnership (US)
AMRC	Asia Monitor Resource Center
ANAPROBAN	Asociación Nacional de Productores Bananeros (Costa Rica)
ASEPROLA	Asociación de Servicios de Promoción Laboral (Costa Rica)
BOI	Board of Investment (Sri Lanka)
BTHA	British Toy and Hobby Association
BVQI	Bureau Veritas Quality International
CAWN	Central America Women's Network
CCC	Clean Clothes Campaign
CEFT	Committee on Ethics and Fair Trade
CIPAF	Centro de Investigación para la Acción Femenina (Dominican Republic)
CODEMUH	Colectiva de Mujeres Hondureñas
COLEACP	Liaison Committee Europe-Africa-Caribbean-Pacific
COLSIBA	Coordinadora Latinoamericana de Sindicatos Bananeros
CORBANA	Corporación Bananera Nacional (Costa Rica)
COVERCO	Commission for the Verification of Corporate Codes of Conduct (Guatemala)
CRRID	Centre for Research in Rural and Industrial Development (India)
CSR	corporate social responsibility
CTA	China Toy Association
CWS	Co-operative Wholesale Society (UK)
DFID	Department for International Development (UK)
DLSE	Department of Labor Standards Enforcement (US)
DOL	Department of Labor (US)
EC	European Commission
ECCR	Ecumenical Committee for Corporate Responsibility (UK)
EMI	Equipo de Monitoreo Independiente (Honduras)
ESCOR	Economic and Social Committee for Overseas Research
ETI	Ethical Trade Initiative (UK)
EUROTEX	European Textile and Garment Employers
FAWU	Food and Agricultural Workers Union (South Africa)
FDI	foreign direct investment

FIFA	International Federation of Football Associations
FLA	Fair Labor Association (US)
FLSA	Fair Labor Standards Act (US)
FTZ	free trade zone
FTZWU	Free Trade Zone Workers Unions (Sri Lanka)
GAPWUZ	General Agricultural and Plantation Workers Union (Zimbabwe)
GATT	General Agreement on Tariffs and Trade
GMB	General, Municipal and Boilermakers Union (UK)
GMIES	Grupo de Monitoreo Independiente El Salvador
GMP	global manufacturing principles
GWA	General Workers Association (South Africa)
HKCIC	Hong Kong Christian Industrial Committee
HRCP	Human Rights Commission of Pakistan
IBLF	International Business Leaders' Forum (UK, formerly PWBLF)
ICCR	Interfaith Centre for Global Corporate Responsibility (US)
ICEM	International Chemical Energy and Mining
ICFTU	International Confederation of Free Trade Unions
ICTI	International Council of Toy Industries
IFAT	International Federation of Alternative Trade
IFBWW	International Federation of Building and Wood Workers
ILO	International Labour Organization
IMF	International Monetary Fund
IPEC	International Programme for the Elimination of Child Labour (ILO)
ITGLWF	International Textile, Garments and Leather Workers Federation
ITGWU	Industrial Transport and General Workers Union
ITO	International Trade Organisation
ITS	International Trade Secretariats
ITS	Intertek Testing Services
IUF	International Union of Food, Agricultural, Hotel, Restaurant, Catering, Tobacco and Allied Workers' Associations
IUI	Independent University Initiative (US)
MAI	Multilateral Agreement on Investments
MAM	Movimiento de Mujeres Mélida Anaya Montes (El Salvador)
MEC	Movimiento de Mujeres Trabajadoras y Desempleadas María Elena Cuadra (Nicaragua)
MFA	Multi-Fibre Arrangement
MIMCO	Mattel Independent Monitoring Council
MNC	multinational company
MNE	multinational enterprise
NGO	non-governmental organization

NICWJ	National Interfaith Committee for Worker Justice (US)
NOVIB	Oxfam Netherlands
NRET	Natural Resources and Ethical Trade Programme
OECD	Organisation for Economic Co-operation and Development
OPEC	Organization of Petroleum Exporting Countries
Pekerti	Indonesian People's Folk-Art and Handicraft Foundation
PWBLF	Prince of Wales Business Leaders' Forum (UK, now IBLF)
PwC	PricewaterhouseCoopers
SBSI	Indonesian Prosperity Trade Union
SCF	Save the Children Fund
SEWA	Self Employed Womens' Association (India)
SGFI	Sporting Goods Federation of India
SGS	Société Général de Surveillance
SITRAP	Sindicato de Trabajadores de Plantaciones Agrícolas (Costa Rica)
SOMO	Centre for Research on Multinational Corporation (Netherlands)
TCCR	Task Force on the Churches and Corporate Responsibility (Canada)
TCFUA	Textile, Clothing and Footwear Union of Australia
TGWU	Transport and General Workers Union (UK)
TIE-Asia	Transnationals Information Exchange-Asia
TIPP	Targeted Industries Partnership Program (US)
TMA	Toy Manufacturers of America
TNC	transnational corporation
TUAC	Trade Union Advisory Committee (OECD)
TUC	Trades Union Congress (UK)
UN	United Nations
UNCTAD	United Nations Conference on Trade and Development
UNCTC	United Nations Centre on Transnational Corporations
UNI	Union Network International
UNICEF	United Nations Children Fund
UNITE	Union of Needletrades, Industrial and Textile Employees (US)
USAS	United Students Against Sweatshops (US)
VCC	voluntary code of conduct
WBCSD	World Business Council for Sustainable Development
WFSGI	World Federation of the Sporting Goods Industry
WIEGO	Women in the Informal Economy: Globalizing and Organizing
WRAP	Worldwide Responsible Apparel Production (US)
WRC	Workers Rights Consortium (US)
WTO	World Trade Organization
WWW	Women Working Worldwide (UK)

List of figures, tables and boxes

FIGURES

TABLES

BOXES

Contributors

Nina Ascoly works on the Clean Clothes Campaign's (CCC) monitoring and verification activities and is coordinator of the CCC's Urgent Appeal Network.

Stephanie Barrientos is a Fellow at the Institute of Development Studies. Her main research areas are female employment in agribusiness in Latin America and Africa, gender and ethical trade, globalization and international labour standards.

Mick Blowfield was, at the time of writing, Research and Information Programme Manager at ETI. He has three decades of experience of working with companies, NGOs and trade unions on diverse aspects of corporate responsibility, particularly in developing countries.

Lucy Brill has been working with HomeNet since 1999. She is also a research student at Bradford University, writing a thesis on home-based workers and their organizations in the UK and Chile.

Kelly Dent has been a labour activist for the past 18 years and is currently the Coordinator of TIE-Asia, a regional labour organization. In Australia she worked in the trade union movement and the community services industry.

Laura Dubinsky formerly spent five years working as an organizer for UNITE, the Union of Needletrades, Industrial and Textile Employees, in the United States and in Canada. She now lives in the UK.

Stephen Frost is the research coordinator at the Asia Monitor Resource Center (AMRC) in Hong Kong.

Angela Hadjipateras is a founder member of the Central America Women's Network. Since 1994, she has been employed as a researcher for ACORD, an international development agency working in Africa, and her current focus is on gender and HIV/AIDS.

Angela Hale is Director of Women Working Worldwide, a small NGO based at Manchester Metropolitan University where she used to lecture.

Rhys Jenkins is Professor in the School of Development Studies, University of East Anglia, Norwich.

Dwight W Justice has worked for the ICFTU since 1990 on multinational companies, industrial relations and trade union organizing. He is a member of the Board of the Ethical Trading Initiative and involved in the Global Reporting Initiative.

Alice Kwan was until July 2001 a senior researcher with the Hong Kong Christian Industrial Committee.

Jill Murray works in the Centre for Employment and Labour Relations, Law School, University of Melbourne in Australia. She is currently examining the impact of codes of conduct in the Asia-Pacific region. Jill also advises the ILO's Business and Decent Work project on codes of conduct in the international footwear and apparel industries.

Dara O'Rourke is an Assistant Professor in the Department of Urban Studies and Planning at the Massachusetts Institute of Technology (MIT). His research focuses on industrial environmental issues and strategies for preventing pollution and workplace health problems.

Ruth Pearson is Professor of Development Studies in the Institute of Politics and International Studies and Director of the Centre for Development Studies at the University of Leeds.

Marina Prieto has been an active member of the Central America Women's Network (CAWN) since 1996, specializing in women workers in export processing zones and corporate social responsibility in the region.

Lesley Roberts, Group Business Standards Manager, has been with Pentland since 1996, developing programmes and systems to improve working conditions in the factories. Previously she was Director of Anti-Slavery International.

Gill Seyfang is a Senior Research Associate at the Centre for Social and Economic Research on the Global Environment (CSERGE) in the University of East Anglia, studying sustainable consumption and fair trade policies. She has previously worked on codes of conduct and women workers' experiences.

Linda Shaw works in adult and continuing education at the Cooperative College. She has been an active member of Women Working Worldwide for over ten years.

Jane Turner is coordinator of the Central America Women's Network (CAWN), principally involved in developing CAWN's work on labour rights in the export processing zones. She is also Gender Information Officer for Action Aid, an international development agency working in Africa, Asia and Latin America.

Rachel Wilshaw is the Ethical Purchasing Manager for Oxfam GB; she previously developed a system to monitor suppliers against fair trade principles which, unusually in code monitoring, was based on a participatory approach.

Ineke Zeldenrust is coordinator of the International Secretariat of the Clean Clothes Campaign and is responsible for the Campaign's activities regarding codes, monitoring and verification.

Preface

Richard Howitt MEP

Suddenly everyone is talking about corporate social responsibility.

This was true back in the 1970s when corporate America's role in the overthrow of Allende in Chile concentrated public concern on the increasingly unaccountable power of multinational companies (MNCs). Both the International Labour Organization (ILO) and the Organisation for Economic Co-operation and Development (OECD) developed voluntary principles and guidelines, respectively, and the United Nations (UN) was charged with responsibility for developing an international code of conduct to govern MNC behaviour. But the oil price rises of the 1970s, global recession and the imposition of Reaganomics on both sides of the Atlantic altered the political focus. In the UN, careful American manoeuvring defeated the proposal altogether.

However, corporate social irresponsibility would not go away. The early 1990s saw a stream of exposés of sweatshop conditions within the supply chains of major US clothing suppliers, in particular in Central America. Royal Dutch Shell was attacked relentlessly in Europe for its role – or lack of it – in relation to the killing of Ken Saro-Wiwa and oppression of the Ogoni people in, then, non-democratic Nigeria. The 1998 Soccer World Cup was skilfully exploited by activists to highlight child labour in South Asia's sportswear industry. Within the last year, international pharmaceutical companies have been forced on to the retreat in the face of public revulsion at the over-pricing of essential medicines for poor countries to combat the appalling Aids pandemic.

In an era when reputation began to exceed all other factors in determining company sales and value, executives could not afford to wait for a change in the political wind. The more enlightened ones began to admit to the problem, and say only they could do something about it. The company code of conduct was born.

Today, I have more than 500 examples of such codes in my office. It is clear that the best represent a sincere attempt to raise standards for workers in the production process. It is also clear that many represent no more than a glossy piece of public relations – worth quite literally no more than the paper on which they are written. And it always has to be noted that such codes emanate almost exclusively from large MNCs. The vast majority of companies, and thus employees, remain untouched. Yet one would have to be shrouded in the sort of political ideology that has also changed, to deny that something of interest is going on.

Non-governmental organizations (NGOs) have seen an opportunity to construct new North–South relationships in the war against global poverty. Trade unionists, initially fearful of what they saw as the privatization of labour laws, have increasingly begun to work with codes – although deep suspicions remain. And, don't speak too loud: some companies themselves have begun to see ethical trade not in a defensive manner, but as a source of competitive advantage to be plastered across web sites, annual meetings and international conferences everywhere.

Indeed it is the very proliferation of codes, the bewildering choice between competing standards and standards agencies, and the conference-fatigue afflicting code practitioners, which makes this publication so timely. Codes are here, are probably here to stay and have been around long enough to enable a proper analysis of what is happening, in a fast-changing field.

The volume draws on some of the most credible examples of code initiatives. Our own Ethical Trading Initiative (ETI) in the UK (see Chapter 15) was deliberately painstaking in the process of drawing up and applying standards, learning from pilots with a genuine sense of experiment. It is an approach which has managed to keep together parties at each end of the spectrum in their attitude towards corporate responsibility. Meanwhile, the Clean Clothes Campaign (CCC) (see Chapter 14) has succeeded in engaging clothing suppliers across six European countries, without jettisoning its essential campaigning role.

Indeed it is refreshing to see a range of contributors, not simply drawn from all stakeholders in the debate, but representing grassroots practitioners, which distinguishes this volume from a sometimes over-theoretical approach elsewhere in the literature. It is good to see the fair trade movement represented, some of whom have justly seen the ethical label sought by multinationals as a threat to their hard-won market niche.

The hard questions are not left out. Are codes inherently self-contradictory? Do they reach far enough down the supply chain to embrace homeworkers and non-unionized staff in deregulated export processing zones (EPZs)? Is there a gender bias or do they represent a new way of empowering women workers? Do the calls for independent monitoring and verification obscure the fact that this just does not exist? How can there be genuine involvement by those who stand to gain most in the South? I have yet to see an example of a code which describes a worker's right to go to the toilet. Yet as Kelly Dent shows (see Chapter 11) all the standards in the world mean nothing if this is the level at which rights are abused.

The book also takes as its focus consumer goods and standards for workers' rights. However, it is important that we employ the lessons learnt to raw materials, the service sector and other sectors, where the leverage of individual consumer pressure cannot be as strong. The debate about the impact of mining and oil industries on indigenous peoples and in conflict situations in developing countries, for example, can also enable us to tackle equally important questions about corporate impact on the environment and on wider human rights.

But readers should be wary of thinking that the only answer lies in making codes more comprehensive, putting mettle into monitoring, veracity into verification. The political debate continues. Activists are not simply targeting individual companies. The defeat of negotiations for a Multilateral Agreement on Investment (MAI) represented a sea change in attitudes against corporations acquiring rights, without accepting consequent responsibilities. The colourful events at Seattle brought together not just those who seek to crush globalization – they encompassed others who argue for the construction of an international legal framework which will engender genuine accountability for corporate behaviour.

It is in this context that the European Parliament voted in 1999 for just such a framework at the European level – the first time an international institution had voted for binding regulation of MNCs in 20 years. The report voted upon, for which I was spokesperson or rapporteur, made clear that good voluntary initiatives did have a contribution to make. It argued that corporate social responsibility (CSR) required action at a number of levels, from development assistance and changes to legal jurisdiction, through new rules for company disclosure and public procurement, to action in a range of global institutions. But ultimately voluntary action on its own would not be enough.

Full implementation of the ideas will inevitably come gradually but in response, for the first time, real European monies have been invested to spawn ETI-type ('ETI' standing for Ethical Trade Initiative, see Chapter 15) projects across all of the EU's Member States, without suggesting or relying on any one blueprint. When a European-wide business-led initiative, CSR-Europe, was launched in November 2000 the event was addressed by two prime ministers, and company attendance closed at 600. It proved the lie that CSR is purely an Anglo-Saxon concern.

As I write, work is being completed on a technical study of how a European Code and Monitoring Platform would operate, whilst the European Commission (EC) has published a Green Paper on Corporate Social Responsibility, fostering a mass consultation, which will set the framework for future legislative action at the European level.

As this volume shows, action in individual states, not least from companies and workers within developing countries, is equally important. The revised OECD guidelines have attracted unprecedented interest from non-member countries and, together with an inter-governmental mechanism for dispute resolution, will provide an acid test for the voluntary approach in future years.

Where all of this will leave us on the continuum between voluntary action and regulation remains to be seen. But the argument for inaction has already been lost.

Richard Howitt MEP
European Parliament Rapporteur, Corporate Social Responsibility
October 2001

Chapter 1

Introduction

Rhys Jenkins, Ruth Pearson and Gill Seyfang

THE RISE OF VOLUNTARY CODES OF CONDUCT

Since the early 1990s there has been a spectacular growth of voluntary corporate codes of conduct dealing with labour conditions. This has been part of a more general shift away from state regulation of transnational corporations (TNCs) towards an emphasis on corporate self-regulation in the areas of labour and environmental standards and human rights. Instead of the social and environmental impacts of big business being seen as a matter primarily for governments to deal with, they are now regarded as matters of corporate responsibility for which companies themselves, or their business associations, should set standards.

The emergence of voluntary corporate codes is both a manifestation of, and a response to, the process of globalization. During the first three post-war decades, developing countries were involved in the world economy primarily as producers of raw materials and as markets for manufactured goods. Transnational corporations' activities were mainly in the extractive sector (mining and oil) and increasingly in manufacturing production for the local market. The post-independence period in many developing countries saw the state play an active role in the economy and the promotion of import substituting industrialization.

After an initial period when foreign direct investment (FDI) was welcomed, many countries became increasingly critical of the activities of TNCs. Because the prevailing climate was generally favourable towards state intervention, and because TNC activity was largely nationally based,[1] the main response to the problems created by TNCs was national state regulation. In the late 1960s and 1970s some 22 developing countries passed legislation controlling TNC activities (Hepple, 1999). There were also numerous cases of nationalization of foreign corporations, which reached a peak in the mid-1970s (Jenkins, 1999).

It was in this context that a number of international efforts to establish codes of conduct for the activities of TNCs emerged in the 1970s. The most comprehensive of these was the UN Draft Code of Conduct on TNCs which was developed by the UN Centre on Transnational Corporations (UNCTC) set up in 1974. Several specialized UN agencies also developed codes covering particular aspects of TNC behaviour. These included the International Labour Organization's (ILO) *Tripartite Declaration of Principles concerning Multinational Enterprises and Social Policy* (1977) and the United Nations Conference on Trade and Development's (UNCTAD) proposed codes on Restrictive Business Practices and on the Transfer of Technology.

These international codes were seen as supporting the efforts of developing-country governments to regulate TNCs at the national level. They emerged from a perception that the growth of giant international companies posed a threat to the sovereignty of small, poor states and were an attempt to redress the balance between the growing power of TNCs and the nation states, particularly in the South.[2]

The continuing process of globalization and the political changes of the 1980s led to a shift away from the social democratic and Keynesian interventionism of the post-war period in the North, and from import substituting industrialization and statism in the South. The emphasis on monetarist policies and increased integration of international markets for goods and finance, the massive privatization of state assets and the shift in developing countries to trade liberalization and export promotion, all served to redefine the economic role of the state. These trends were reflected in government policies towards TNCs, which shifted dramatically from regulation of their activities to intense competition to attract FDI.

It is against this background that the emergence of voluntary corporate codes of conduct in the 1990s has to be understood. A number of changes in the global economy contributed to the growing interest in corporate social responsibility (CSR) and codes of conduct. The growth of global 'value chains', in which Northern buyers control a web of suppliers in the South, has led to calls for them to take responsibility not only for aspects such as quality and delivery dates but also for working conditions and environmental impacts.[3] At the same time the increased significance of brands and corporate reputation makes leading companies particularly vulnerable to bad publicity (Klein, 2000). Changing public attitudes are also an important part of the context in which corporate codes of conduct have been adopted. Companies in the North can no longer ignore the impact of their activities on the environment with impunity. The developments in global communications which have enabled corporations to control production activities on an ever widening scale have also facilitated the international transmission of information about working conditions in their overseas suppliers, contributing to increased public awareness and facilitating campaigning activities.

Experience suggests that the adoption of corporate codes of conduct is often a response to bad publicity as a result of previous activities. Prior to the recent wave of codes, there was an earlier phase of intense corporate activity around codes, particularly in the United States, in the late 1970s. These were a response to the negative publicity received by TNCs, as a result of the ITT scandal and revelations about bribery and questionable payments by many leading US companies (Kline, 1985, pp23-5). Ninety per cent of the codes studied by Kline were formulated after the Securities and Exchange Commission began to investigate questionable payments, and the passage by the US Congress of the Foreign Corrupt Practices Act of 1977 gave further impetus to this movement (Kline, 1985, p103). By the mid-1980s, however, public pressure for the adoption of codes had decreased (Kline, 1985, p108).

The second wave of corporate codes, which emerged in the early 1990s, focused on labour conditions. As with the first wave in the 1970s, the new trend for companies to adopt codes was prompted by scandals about corporate practices. Levi Strauss, with its Business Partner Terms of Engagement adopted in 1992, was one of the first companies to establish this type of code, after its overseas contractors were accused of treating their workers as indentured slaves. The mid-1990s saw further revelations concerning the use of sweatshops and child labour by leading US brands such as Gap, Kathie Lee Gifford, Nike, Disney and others. The period 1995–1996 has been described as 'the Year of the Sweatshop' in the United States as activists campaigned around these issues and highlighted the practices of the market leaders (Klein, 2000, pp327–9).

The efforts at state regulation of TNCs in the 1970s and the international codes of conduct designed to support these efforts were primarily initiatives which emanated from the South, and particularly from Southern governments. In contrast, the support for voluntary corporate codes since the 1990s has come largely from the North. Here international trade union organizations, development non-governmental organizations (NGOs), human rights organizations and the corporate sector itself have all contributed to the demand for some form of code of conduct for international business.

THE CODES DEBATE

The various stakeholders in the coalitions which have promoted voluntary codes of conduct have, inevitably, different motivations.[4] Transnational corporations, quite understandably, have responded to political and consumer pressure primarily from the perspective of defending their reputations and thus their market position, only latterly incorporating a generalized concern for social responsibility into their corporate portfolios. Consumer groups have extended their concern for information on and inputs into what is sold in Western markets to a related responsibility for the conditions and quality of the workforce involved in production. Development NGOs have responded to the global reach of production and information by extending their remit from micro interventions and macro development assistance – much of which was implemented in parallel to labour markets – to a direct relationship with workers in the global workplace. Trade unions, faced with the reality that global production implies deregulated, flexible and often informal labour, are exploring new opportunities to protect working conditions and support minimum labour standards. Women's groups, in both the South and the North, have had a long-standing concern with issues surrounding workplace conditions since research in the 1970s revealed that over 80 per cent of the workforce in consumer export industries was female.

Given this range of players and motives, how are we to evaluate the current development of voluntary codes of conduct? As the title of a recent study asks, are they a *Workers' Tool or PR Ploy?* (Wick, 2001). The positive view is that codes represent a wide range of players positioned in very different locations in the global production system, and thus offer an opportunity for initiatives which will be successful in driving up expectations and standards, because of their broad base of support. Some analysts argue that their development represents the positive multi-dimensional aspects of globalization which provide access to information allowing the global consumer and political subject to connect with issues and individuals previously too remote to feature on their horizon. Moreover, it has breathed new life into international organizations such as the ILO, which were founded on models of work rooted in single nations and assuming formal workforces, which were becoming ineffective in an increasingly informalized and unregulated workforce. Moreover the articulation of universal labour standards for the whole of a globalized production system chimes harmoniously with the current political practice of utilizing human rights treaties and discourse to argue for social and economic as well as political and civil rights – that is to couch development aspirations in human rights discourse.

However, it also has to be acknowledged that, to date, their record of achievement, as opposed to rhetoric, is strictly limited. The analysis of codes in this volume and elsewhere (Kolk et al, 1999; Seyfang, 1999) indicates that those which are most likely to reflect the real concerns and conditions of workers in world market factories are more likely to have been drawn up by labour advocates, pressure groups and NGOs and least likely to have been developed or to be owned by individual companies or industry organizations. The research findings that are available indicate that even the well-publicized codes from major retail brands in leisurewear or garments are honoured more frequently in the breach than in compliance, in spite of the development of a new 'industry' of monitors and verifiers, and the dissemination of international standards such as SA 8000 (NLC, 2000).

Many codes of conduct declare an adherence to some or all of the ILO's core labour standards on child labour, forced labour, non-discrimination, freedom of association and collective bargaining. In doing so, they legislate for the workforce in a way that often makes workers the objects of regulation rather than partners or political subjects in determining what is appropriate in their context. For, in spite of the desirability of a broad base of stakeholders in drawing up voluntary codes, the central paradox of 'cheap labour' engaged in transnational production chains is the desperate need of the workers to preserve their employment opportunities. In such situations it is imperative that the workforce is in a position to determine what the core labour standards should be for that particular workforce in that particular company/factory/country, rather than have it pre-determined by an international body. This implies that international actors (TNCs, international trade unions and NGOs) need to subordinate their notion of 'universal' labour rights to the careful appraisal of local organizations (women's groups, workers' councils, trade unions, etc) whose strategic judgement about which issues to foreground may well determine whether the workers concerned are able to retain their jobs as well as progress their grievances.

There is a danger that voluntary codes are seen as a substitute for self-organization by workers and that they may even be implemented by companies in parallel with efforts to prevent workers joining trade unions (see Chapter 13 by Dubinsky). In the case of Sri Lanka, workers have been dismissed for attempting to organize trade unions in factories supplying major brand names, many of which have codes of conduct (see Chapter 11 by Dent).

This is not to say that voluntary codes of conduct cannot provide an important arena for developing the framework for a more positive regime of labour relations under the new conditions of global production and trade. One of the problems in advancing this agenda is both the internationalization of norms of de-protection for labour under international *trade* regulations, and the separation of negotiations about international trade and investment conditions (within, for example, the World Trade Organization – WTO) from those governing labour conditions and rewards, dealt with by the ILO. Voluntary codes of conduct which cover a range of labour related issues and conditions in which transnational investors and traders are major stakeholders could become a useful negotiating platform for breaking down the artificial and injurious separation between the (de)regulation of international capital and labour.

Critics of the voluntaristic turn in labour regulation represented by corporate codes of conduct rightly raise the objection that voluntary regulation serves both as a *substitute* for statutory regulation (by governments and international bodies) and at the same time *legitimizes* the absence of statutory regulations by governments and international bodies. However this question also needs to be seen in historical context. Given the currently dominant view that globalization, defined in terms of free trade and flexible labour, offers the most positive avenue out of poverty and exclusion for developing countries, there is at present no clear platform for the re-regulation of labour nor for the strengthening of the power of labour organizations. The growth of the current global networks of voluntary codes of conduct involve major companies in forms of linkage and cooperation even while they are major competitors in the global market. If for example Nike, Reebok and Timberland all contract with the same Korean- or Taiwanese-owned footwear producer operating in mainland China or Indonesia, both company and sectoral codes of conduct provide a framework which could counteract the competitive 'race to the bottom' tactics, and lock key suppliers into a commitment to raise rather than lower labour standards.[5]

The contributions in this volume indicate that there are a number of evolving and unresolved questions about how to take codes of conduct forward in the interests of those they purport to represent. Representation of workers, and particularly of women workers, is an important issue which several chapters discuss (particularly those by Pearson and Seyfang, Shaw and Hale, and Prieto, Hadjipateras and Turner). The content of codes and the priorities given to different issues in different contexts is problematic within a general acceptance that codes should be based on universalistic and generalized practice.

A related issue is the complexity of global supply chains and the difficulties of applying a single uniform code to workers involved in different stages of production and/or working under different relations of production. Brill's chapter (Chapter 9) on homeworkers raises the significance of home-based workers' involvement in global supply chains and the dangers of either ignoring their involvement or of limiting codes to provisions which cannot apply to them, such as the abolition of piece work, provision for minimum shifts and restrictions on overtime.

The centrality – and the difficulties – of monitoring and verification are also highlighted here (see Chapter 14 by Ascoly and Zeldenrust and Chapter 16 by O'Rourke). Should private and voluntary codes of conduct be monitored by public or private organizations, and if private, should it be by commercial or not-for-profit bodies? Should the stakeholders in the codes themselves – the trade unions, the women's groups, the companies – be involved in monitoring and if so which ones? How should workers be involved in the process of monitoring and in making the process accountable and transparent? What protection can be given to workers who report transgressions of codes to monitors? Should systems of positive monitoring be developed – in terms of ensuring that suppliers comply with benchmarked 'best practice' – rather than utilizing negative monitoring aimed at discovering breaches in code provisions?

It is also important to signal that although corporate codes of conduct have generally been advocated as avenues to improve workers' pay and conditions in global export production, they could be profitably linked to other campaigns. There are many parallels between codes of conduct focused on labour rights and those which deal with company environmental performance. Demands from consumer groups for labelling agricultural products as 'organic' or 'GM free' also have parallels with labels concerning the labour conditions under which products are produced. It is also important to link these campaigns with initiatives concerning working conditions and to recognize that polluting processes and additives affect workers' bodies as well as those of consumers and local communities (Theobald, 1999).

Similarly, most consumer goods production in developing counties destined for First World markets takes place in economies which make little universal provision for unemployment benefits, pensions or other social entitlements such as universal health care and education and this fact is reflected in the limited coverage of such issues in corporate codes. However, as argued elsewhere (Pearson and Seyfang, 2001), in the absence of universally agreed commitments by states and corporations to meeting the needs and demands of labour – that they are able to work for a fair reward, with dignity, in a context where their ongoing entitlements as citizens are supported by the state and by private corporations – codes may well represent an important framework both for achieving workplace justice and for extending the global responsibilities of all major stakeholders beyond the moment of production of goods and services to the production and reproduction of labour power in the global economy.

THE STRUCTURE OF THE BOOK

The debate on voluntary codes of conduct has been going on between the various stakeholders for a number of years and has recently been joined by academics. This volume brings together contributions from both practitioners with experience of developing and implementing codes and academics who have analysed the growth of and impacts of codes.

The book is structured into two main parts. Part One considers the political economy, development and implications of codes of conduct within global manufacturing chains from an analytical standpoint, while Part Two presents the perspectives of a range of groups working directly with codes. This second group of chapters is divided into three subsections: *stakeholder perspectives* (including international trade unions, corporations, women workers and homeworkers); *regional perspectives* (focusing on China, Sri Lanka, Central America and North America); and *practical issues in developing and implementing codes* (covering the development of model codes, working with multi-stakeholder codes, and monitoring and verification in both the corporate and informal fair trade sectors).

In Chapter 2, Jenkins discusses the political economy of codes of conduct, identifying the interests of the stakeholders who have influenced their development. Based on an analysis of the content of different codes and the experience of the US garment industry, he concludes that codes are a 'contested terrain' where different interests seek to dominate the agenda. Murray takes a closer look at the ILO standards in Chapter 3, pointing out that, while they are commonly taken as core elements of voluntary codes, the ILO conventions are in fact addressed to states rather than corporations. She argues that in order to be applicable to companies, core labour standards need to be elaborated upon and extended.

The concerns and demands of women workers in export manufacturing are the starting point for Pearson and Seyfang's discussion of the relevance of codes in Chapter 4. They identify the issues workers complain about as being quite different to those commonly included in codes, yet at the same time even those conditions guaranteed by codes are regularly breached. In such a situation, the potential of codes is as a mechanism to galvanize workers' organization and promote international solidarity. In the final chapter in this part, Barrientos describes the process of investigating codes of conduct through complex international value chains. She presents resources and practical advice, and highlights the pitfalls for anyone attempting to conduct research into global commodity chains.

In Chapter 6, Roberts describes the Pentland Group's experience of codes, as a pioneering corporation in the development of codes in its sporting goods subcontracting chains that aimed to eliminate child labour in football stitching. The trade union perspective is presented in Chapter 7, where Justice gives an account of the International Confederation of Free Trade Union's (ICFTU) involvement with codes of conduct, discussing self-regulation and their alternatives. Women Working Worldwide's development and education work with women garment workers is presented in Chapter 8, where Shaw and Hale argue that, while codes have usefully put corporate responsibility on the boardroom agenda, they are but one tool available to workers in their struggle to gain union recognition and improvements in working conditions. In Chapter 9, Brill discusses the special situation of homeworkers and how codes could be adapted to help this group of unprotected workers. She presents examples of innovative practices in this area and weighs up the advantages and disadvantages of codes in this context.

Kwan and Frost of the Asia Monitor Resource Centre (AMRC) and Hong Kong Christian Industrial Committee (HKCIC) assess the impact of codes in the Chinese toy sector in Chapter 10, and conclude that while codes are made in Northern boardrooms or campaign offices, the rules that really matter are the factory rules, which are made in China and are based firmly in local industrial practices. The Sri Lankan experience is described by Dent in Chapter 11. She presents evidence gathered by Transnational Information Exchange-Asia (TIE-Asia) that the impact of codes is not unambiguous, and that they may help worsen rather than improve working conditions, with the implication that the right to organize is of greater benefit to workers, and should be prioritized. In Chapter 12, Prieto, Hadjipateras and Turner of the Central America Women's Network (CAWN) discuss the development of codes from the South, assessing the growth of autonomous women's organizations for organizing maquila women workers in Central America, and describing the Nicaraguan Ethical Code and its impacts.[6] Dubinsky's chapter shows that the issues which voluntary codes of conduct address arise not only in the South, but are also relevant in the North. She analyses the effectiveness of corporate self-regulation in garment production in Los Angeles through a case study of Guess. She raises a number of issues around their code and associated monitoring programme, concluding that without a protected right to free association voluntary codes without true independent monitoring have little to offer workers.

Non-governmental organizations and multi-stakeholder alliances have been very influential in developing voluntary codes and piloting their implementation. The Clean Clothes Campaign (CCC) is one of the major NGO players in the growth of codes, and in Chapter 14 Ascoly and Zeldenrust document the origins and development of their model code, up to its present-day pilot implementation. They also describe the CCC's solidarity work and critically assess the usefulness of codes. Another multi-stakeholder code with widespread support is the UK's Ethical Trading Initiative's (ETI) base code, and in Chapter 15 Blowfield presents an introduction to the ETI and what can be learnt from its pilots.

As leading corporations increasingly adopt codes of conduct, the issues of monitoring and verification have increasingly come to the fore. A whole new industry of social auditors has emerged, often made up of firms who in the past have provided other types of services to the corporate sector. In Chapter 16, O'Rourke analyses the use of third-party monitoring of codes, with an in-depth case study of PricewaterhouseCoopers (PwC), a major social auditing organization. He concludes that there are serious failings in the implementation of monitoring, and that the processes social auditors use are unlikely to uncover most workplace code violations. Oxfam has adopted a rather different approach in its role as a corporate buyer of fair trade goods. In Chapter 17 Wilshaw describes how Oxfam has developed fair trade principles for its purchasing from informal sector suppliers, along with techniques and indicators for measuring their effectiveness and social performance, and the lessons learnt.

Together these chapters present a variety of perspectives and cover a range of issues. As Richard Howitt points out in his Preface, there is little doubt that codes are here to stay. The key question now is how they will be used. We present this volume as a contribution to that debate.

ACKNOWLEDGEMENTS

We would like to acknowledge the support of the DFID Economic and Social Committee for Overseas Research (ESCOR) Social Policy Research Programme which supported our research on corporate codes of conduct.

NOTES

1   Although local production depended either on overseas markets (in the case of the extractive industries) or on imported inputs (in the case of manufacturing), it was not part of a complex integrated global production network.
2   A significant event in focusing attention on the activities of TNCs in developing countries was the ITT scandal in Chile in the early 1970s when it was revealed that

this US company had been involved in attempting to overthrow the democratically elected Popular Unity government led by Salvador Allende.
3   See Chapter 5 in this volume by Stephanie Barrientos for a discussion of value chain analysis and its significance in the context of corporate codes.
4   This is discussed in the next chapter.
5   For a discussion of the potential for raising labour standards based on competition between firms and bewteen verifying agencies, see Sabel et al (2000).
6   'Maquila' or 'maquiladora' is the term used to refer to export assembly plants in Mexico and Central America.

REFERENCES

Hepple, B (1999) A Race to the Top? International Investment Guidelines and Corporate Codes of Conduct, mimeo, Clare College, Cambridge

Jenkins, R (1999) 'The Changing Relationship between Emerging Markets and Multinational Enterprises' in P J Buckley and P N Ghauri (eds), *Multinational Enterprises and Emerging Markets: Managing Increasing Interdependence*, Pergamon, Oxford

Klein, N (2000) *No Logo*, Flamingo, London

Kline, J (1985) *International Codes and Multinational Business: Setting Guidelines for International Business Operations*, Quorum Books, Westport, CN

Kolk, A, R van Tulder and C Welters (1999) 'International Codes of Conduct and Corporate Social Responsibility: Can Transnational Corporations Regulate Themselves?' *Transnational Corporations*, Vol 8, No 1

NLC (2000) *Made in China: The Role of US Companies in Denying Human and Worker Rights,* National Labor Committee, http://www.nlcnet.org/report00, accessed 8 August 2000

Pearson, R and G Seyfang (2001) 'New Hope or False Dawn? Codes of Conduct and Social Policy in a Globalising World' *Global Social Policy*, Vol 1, No 1

Sabel, C, D O'Rourke and A Fung (2000) *Ratcheting Labor Standards: Regulation for Continuous Improvement in the Global Workplace*, Kennedy School of Government Working Paper, No 00-010, Harvard

Seyfang, G (1999) *Private Sector Self-Regulation for Social Responsibility: Mapping Codes of Conduct*, Social Policy Research Programme Working Paper No 1, Overseas Development Group, University of East Anglia, Norwich

Theobald, S (1999) Embodied Contradictions: Organisational Responses to Gender and Occupational Health Interest in the Electronics Industries of Northern Thailand, PhD thesis, School of Development Studies, University of East Anglia, Norwich

Wick, I (2001) *Workers' Tool or PR Ploy? A Guide to Codes of International Labour Practice*, Friedrich-Ebert-Stiftung, Bonn

Part One

Codes of Conduct and Global Deregulation

Chapter 2

The political economy of codes of conduct

Rhys Jenkins

STAKEHOLDERS AND VOLUNTARY CODES OF CONDUCT

The growth of voluntary codes of conduct since the 1990s has involved a wide range of stakeholders. These stakeholders have different interests, leading to contrasting views of the purpose of codes and to conflict over their scope, coverage, substance and implementation. In this chapter, the major stakeholders and their interests will be identified and the implications for codes of conduct analysed.[1]

Large corporations

Many of the companies which have adopted codes covering labour issues are large corporations with well-known brand names, which are either engaged in production overseas or are the nodal points of value chains which extend internationally.[2] These companies have a high public profile and tend to rely heavily on their corporate image, making them particularly vulnerable to negative publicity and the campaigns of non-governmental organizations (NGOs) (Klein, 2000, Chapter 15). Thus a major motive for the adoption of codes by such firms is to *protect their reputation*.[3] While some firms have adopted codes in the aftermath of a major public relations (PR) disaster, others do so to pre-empt external criticism or to forestall regulatory pressure. In some cases the adoption of ethical principles can *increase the commitment of company staff* although this is only mentioned explicitly as a factor in a few codes (OECD, 2000, Figure 6).

The fact that codes are seen as performing certain functions for companies has implications for the type of codes which they are likely to adopt. Adopting a very strong code which the company cannot meet would be totally counterproductive, leading to intensified external criticism, further calls for regulation and demoralized staff. Feasibility of compliance will involve an element of being able to meet conditions without entailing excessive cost. On the other hand, the code must also be externally credible if it is to protect the company's reputation and not be seen purely as a PR exercise.

Trade unions

The trade union movement has been involved in developing and negotiating codes at various levels.[4] Trade unions see codes as a way of preventing transnational corporations (TNCs) from undermining established labour standards by taking advantage of international differences in working conditions and levels of organization. However, they also envisage potential dangers were voluntary codes to be seen as a substitute for national labour legislation and international labour standards (Kearney, 1999, p208) or as an alternative to trade union representation and collective bargaining (Kearney and Justice, 2001, p78).

The unions emphasize the need for codes to incorporate the International Labour Organization's (ILO) core labour standards (particularly those which relate to freedom of association and collective bargaining), since the ILO is recognized by the international community as the organization established to set such standards (Kearney and Justice, 2001, p79).

There have been different views in the labour movement concerning the monitoring of codes, with some being prepared to countenance a role for the unions within the monitoring process, while others regard it as the role of the companies themselves to ensure that their suppliers are compliant (see Chapter 7 by Justice below). There is general agreement, however, that where companies are responsible for their own monitoring, there must be a proper system of verification to ensure the credibility of the monitoring system. With this in mind, the International Confederation of Free Trade Unions (ICFTU) is seeking a greater role for the ILO in developing standards for verification (Kearney and Justice, 2001, p86).

Non-governmental organizations

The 1990s saw a considerable increase in NGO activism around issues of corporate responsibility. A variety of different types of NGO have engaged with the labour aspects of corporate codes. These include: development NGOs (Oxfam, Christian Aid); NGOs with an interest in the welfare of children (Save the Children); human rights organizations (Amnesty International, Human Rights Watch) and those specifically concerned with labour rights (Clean Clothes Campaign, Coalition for Justice in Maquila). There are also corporate organizations which are sometimes regarded as NGOs, for example Business for Social Responsibility, the World Business Council for Sustainable Development (WBCSD) and the International Business Leaders Forum (IBLF).[5]

Many NGOs share a common perception that governments were not effective in controlling the activities of large corporations following the deregulation of the 1980s and that unregulated globalization would have negative social consequences in developing countries. In some cases there has been a tendency for NGOs to concentrate on issues which have an immediate appeal and can evoke a popular response such as child labour or indigenous rights.

Many Northern NGOs have rather similar views to the trade unions regarding the requirements for an adequate code of conduct. At a minimum, they should include the ILO's core labour standards, cover subcontractors and homeworkers and be independently verified. Transparency is also important, requiring that monitoring reports should be available to the public, a demand that many firms are reluctant to consider.

Shareholders and investors

Although they have grown rapidly in the UK in recent years, ethical funds have only just broken through to take more than 1 per cent of the market (Cowe, 2000). In the United States, which has a much longer history of ethical investment than the United Kingdom, investment in ethically screened portfolios doubled between 1997 and 1999, increasing their share of professionally managed investments from 9 to 13 per cent (Amnesty International, 2000, p69).

For the majority of shareholders, who are only interested in the value of their shares, the prime purpose of a code of conduct is to deflect criticism from NGOs and pressure groups which might otherwise have a negative impact on the company's share price. In the case of 'ethical' investors however, the existence of a corporate code might be an indicator of the acceptability of a particular company's share. Some ethical investors have developed their own code of conduct as in the case of the church-sponsored *Principles for Global Corporate Responsibility: Benchmarks for Corporate Responsibility* proposed by the Interfaith Centre for Global Corporate Responsibility (ICCR) in the United States, the Ecumenical Committee for Corporate Responsibility (ECCR) in the United Kingdom and the Task Force on the Churches and Corporate Responsibility (TCCR) in Canada.

Consumers

As in the case of investors, a minority of consumers are also concerned about the ethical dimension of the products which they purchase, as illustrated by the growth in demand for fair-traded coffee and other such products. However, these examples remain niche markets, supplying a predominantly middle class and relatively affluent and educated customer base.[6]

Consumer concerns are not solely expressed through individual purchases and there are examples where decisions about bulk buying have been informed by ethical concerns. There are cases where local governments have attempted to use their buying power in an ethical way, although this has been severely circumscribed in recent years by the actions of national governments. The most high-profile examples have involved the campaigns by students against the use of sweatshops in the manufacture of sportswear carrying university logos and names.

If a code is to perform the role of assuring consumers about the social conditions under which a product has been produced, it must be credible. In the early days of eco-labelling a great deal of cynicism was generated by exaggerated claims and self-certification by companies. It is vital, therefore, that there should be independent verification that companies are complying with their voluntary codes and that there should be some means of identifying those products which are produced in accordance with social norms. This can be done most readily through a labelling scheme which applies to those products which are produced ethically.

Southern exporters

Many of the new corporate codes have been developed to apply to suppliers or subcontractors. For example over 40 per cent of the codes covering labour issues in the Organisation for Economic Co-operation and Development (OECD) survey placed obligations on suppliers (see OECD, 2000, Table 4). This was particularly prevalent in the apparel industry where 26 out of 32 company codes surveyed were addressed to suppliers and contractors (OECD, 2000, p24).

Most of these suppliers operate in highly competitive markets where low prices and rapid delivery times are crucial to their success in gaining and retaining orders. Many are located in developing countries, where corporate social responsibility (CSR) is not generally seen as being very high on the business agenda (WBCSD, 2000, pp12–13). In most cases the demand for codes of conduct has been externally driven.

This results in an ambivalent attitude towards codes of conduct amongst Southern exporters. On the one hand, where their customers require them to meet certain labour standards, they need to comply in order to keep their markets. On the other hand, they are likely to perceive such measures as increasing their costs, either directly or indirectly. Where inspections reveal that suppliers are not complying with the code of conduct of their customers, then corrective action has to be paid for by the supplier. Restrictions in codes on hours worked and on overtime may make it more difficult for the supplier to meet the delivery schedules required by the buyer, and will certainly increase the cost of doing so. Subcontractors therefore favour relatively weak codes of conduct which will meet the requirements of their customers without imposing undue costs. They are opposed to any toughening of the regulatory regime or to measures that would strengthen the role of trade unions (Zadek, 2000, p16).

Workers in the South

Many of the industries in which codes of conduct are found are characterized by a non-unionized, predominantly female, labour force. As Pearson and Seyfang indicate in Chapter 4, women workers have specific demands which are often not covered by codes. Given the large pool of potential workers and the highly competitive nature of the industries in which they are employed, their status is often precarious, making stability of employment an important consideration.[7] Working conditions, particularly those relating to health and safety, are also an important factor for workers.

In this context, codes of conduct may be a double-edged sword. If a buyer threatens to terminate a contract with the workers' employer because an inspection reveals non-compliance with the buyer's corporate code, then the workers will fear that they will be laid off. This could result in a situation in which workers are prejudiced by measures whose ostensible purpose is to improve their situation. This may lead to a certain ambivalence towards codes on the part of some workers. If codes can threaten their employment and yet do not cover the issues which they feel have the highest priorities, then their scepticism towards corporate codes may well be justified.

Other stakeholders

Business associations at the international, national and sectoral level have been involved in the development of codes, or have adopted positions in relation to them. Since these associations tend to represent not only those large corporations who have taken the lead in adopting codes, but other less prominent firms who have not done so, they often take a minimalist position which is acceptable to the least progressive of their members.

Governments have also played a role in promoting corporate codes, often seeing them as an alternative to regulation. In the United States, the government instigated the White House Apparel Industry Partnership (AIP) which led to the formation of the Fair Labor Association, while in the United Kingdom the Department for International Development (DFID) set up and provided financial support for the Ethical Trade Initiative (ETI).

The growth of voluntary codes has led to the emergence of new stakeholders in the form of companies involved in monitoring and verification. Accountancy firms, such as Ernst and Young and PricewaterhouseCoopers (PwC), and verifiers involved in auditing quality standards, such as ISO 9000, have also moved into social auditing, and are playing a leading role in defining standards.[8]

Codes of conduct – a contested terrain

This review of the major stakeholders has revealed that because the goals of stakeholders differ, the roles which codes are expected to perform also differ.

This in turn implies that the key issues identified by stakeholders do not necessarily coincide and that the nature of the codes which they would like to see implemented also differ in terms of their scope, coverage and implementation. As a result, codes of different provenance, in terms of the parties which were involved in their formulation, are likely to display significant variation. In analysing specific codes, therefore, it is important to identify what interests were involved, and who was excluded from the process. In the next section systematic differences between codes are considered.

AN OVERVIEW OF CODE CONTENT AND IMPLEMENTATION

Most studies of voluntary codes of conduct distinguish between four broad types of codes (see for example OECD, 2000; Kolk et al, 1999). First, there are corporate codes which are adopted unilaterally by companies and which either relate to their own operations or are applied specifically to their suppliers. Second, business associations representing particular industries or broader groupings of employers have drawn up codes of conduct. A third type of code is developed through negotiations between several stakeholders, including firms or their industry representatives, NGOs and/or trade unions. Government may also be involved in the development of such codes. Finally, there are several inter-governmental codes which have been negotiated at an international level and are agreed to by national governments. The two most significant as far as labour rights are concerned are the ILO's Tripartite Declaration of Principles Concerning Multinational Enterprises and the OECD's Guidelines for Multinational Enterprise, both of which date back to the 1970s.

On the basis of the analysis in the preceding section, one would expect to find systematic differences between these various types of codes. Company codes will most clearly reflect the position of the large corporations which have taken the lead in adopting codes. Business association codes are likely to be weaker than those of individual companies, because they need to be acceptable to most companies within the organization concerned and therefore give more weight to the views of smaller companies, who are less exposed to pressures to adopt codes and have few resources with which to implement them. Multi-stakeholder codes and inter-governmental codes are likely to be more demanding than either business association or individual codes since they are the result of negotiations with other stakeholders such as trade unions or NGOs, which, as was seen above, are likely to make more stringent demands in terms of what they expect from codes.

The content of codes of conduct

One important indicator of the nature of different voluntary codes is the extent to which they incorporate the ILO's core labour standards, or even go beyond those standards. Core labour standards are those incorporated into the ILO Declaration on Fundamental Principles and Rights at Work adopted in 1998, which are binding on all ILO member countries. They are derived from the following ILO conventions:

- Freedom of Association (C87)
- Right to Collective Bargaining (C98)
- No Forced Labour (C29, C105)
- Minimum Age (C138)
- No Discrimination (C111)
- Equal Remuneration (C100).

The extent to which different types of codes refer to core labour standards can be illustrated using data from the OECD's inventory of codes of corporate conduct (OECD, 1999; OECD, 2000).[9] The inventory includes 153 codes which cover some aspect of labour relations. Of these, 101 are individual company codes, 30 are from business associations, 20 are classified as multi-stakeholder codes, and two are the work of inter-governmental organizations.

Table 2.1 indicates the proportion of codes of different kinds which refer to the main core labour standards. A number of patterns emerge from the table. First of all, as was expected, a far higher proportion of multi-stakeholder codes incorporate core labour standards than for either company or business association codes. Indeed three out of every five multi-stakeholder codes explicitly mention ILO codes, whereas these are very rarely mentioned in other types of codes. A second striking difference is the importance given to freedom of association and collective bargaining. This is the most frequently mentioned core labour standard in multi-stakeholder codes, being present in 95 per cent of cases, whereas it is the least frequently included standard in both company and business association codes. This is consistent with the importance which non-corporate stakeholders, particularly trade unions but also many NGOs, give to the need for codes to provide a basis for workers' self-organization.

Table 2.1 *Proportion of codes referring to core labour standards*

	Company codes (%)	Business associations (%)	Multi-stakeholder codes (%)	Total (%)*
No forced labour	41.6	20.0	65.0	39.9
No child labour	46.5	23.3	70.0	44.4
No discrimination or harassment	67.3	30.0	75.0	61.4
Freedom of association and collective bargaining	23.8	13.3	95.0	32.0
ILO codes mentioned	3.0	6.7	60.0	11.8
Total no of codes	101	30	20	153

* Includes two inter-governmental codes.
Source: Author's elaboration from OECD inventory of codes.

Table 2.1 also illustrates that there are important differences between individual company codes and those promoted by business associations. Consistent with our previous hypothesis, company codes are more likely to include a reference to each of the core labour standards, with the proportion of company codes mentioning each issue almost double the level amongst business association codes.

Given the relatively low proportion of business association codes and individual company codes that refer to the ILO core labour standards, what do these codes usually refer to? In both cases the most frequently mentioned commitment is to a 'reasonable working environment' found in 76 per cent of corporate codes and 80 per cent of business association codes (see Table 2.2). It is the only aspect which is more common in these codes than in multi-stakeholder codes. The second most frequently mentioned commitment is to comply with local laws. These can be regarded as minimal commitments for any code. A reasonable working environment is a very imprecise concept and, unless the statement is linked to specific health and safety standards, is impossible to monitor. Although compliance with local laws is a much more precise commitment, it is minimal in a different sense. Genuine corporate codes of conduct should go beyond meeting the legal obligations of a firm. A 'voluntary' commitment not to break the law is hardly a basis for claiming high ethical standards.

Some codes of conduct go beyond core labour standards and cover other issues such as working hours, wages, stability of employment and the use of casual labour. The contrast between multi-stakeholder codes and those drawn up by business associations is particularly stark. Seven out of ten multi-stakeholder codes refer to wages, whereas only one in six of the business association codes does so. Three out of five stakeholder codes refer to working hours, but fewer than one in seven of the business association codes do so. No business association code undertakes not to make excessive use of casual labour, and only 1 per cent of individual company codes give such an undertaking (see Table 2.2).

In addition, the fact that a particular aspect is mentioned in a code does not necessarily provide a full picture of the strength of a code. A code referring to compensation may state that the company must pay the legal minimum wage (which may be extremely low) or a 'living wage' but both would be listed as referring to compensation. Similarly, a statement about working hours is not very meaningful unless the number of hours permitted are specified. For example, 42 per cent of the multi-stakeholder codes which cover working hours set a maximum of 48 hours a week, while this is the case for only 11 per cent of company codes and none of the business association codes. Over 60 per cent of company codes and three-quarters of the association codes which refer to working hours merely commit to complying with the law. Thus the differences in coverage between codes of different provenance are reinforced when their substance is analysed in greater detail.

Table 2.2 *Aspects other than core labour standards covered in codes*

	Company codes (%)	Business associations (%)	Multi-stakeholder codes (%)	Total (%)*
Compliance with laws	69.3	53.3	70.0	66.7
Reasonable working environment	76.2	80.0	75.0	76.5
Compensation	51.5	16.7	70.0	47.1
Working hours	35.6	13.3	60.0	34.0
Right to information	9.9	20.0	15.0	13.7
Provision of training	29.7	30.0	40.0	32.0
Reasonable advance notice	2.0	0.0	5.0	3.3
No excessive casual labour	1.0	0.0	15.0	3.3
Flexible workplace relations	0.0	0.0	5.0	0.7
Human rights	22.8	26.7	30.0	24.8
Promotion	8.9	3.3	15.0	9.2
Total no of codes	101	30	20	153

* Includes two inter-governmental codes.
Source: Author's elaboration from OECD inventory of codes.

The implementation of codes

A code of conduct is, by definition, only a piece of paper unless it is implemented in practice. The adoption of a code involves a statement of principles concerning business behaviour, which is not necessarily the same as the application of those principles in the firm's operations. The International Organization of Employers, for instance, estimates that 80 per cent of codes are really statements about general business ethics which have no implementation methods (quoted in ILO, 1998, p7).

Thus it is important to ask what measures are in place to monitor compliance with labour standards. Unfortunately the OECD database does not provide information on what actually happens in terms of the implementation of the codes which are included, but only what the codes themselves have to say about implementation. However, both the existence of a statement about monitoring and the type of monitoring envisaged provide some indication of the seriousness of different codes.

Only a quarter of all codes in the database specifically mention monitoring in any form. However, as can be seen from Table 2.3, there are considerable differences between different types of code, with multi-stakeholder codes being far more likely to address monitoring issues, while they receive least attention in the case of business associations. The most common form of labour monitoring amongst the company codes involves the monitoring of suppliers, rather than the company's own activities. Monitoring by an external group and by the organization which has set up the code is most frequent with multi-stakeholder codes.

These findings are consistent with those of other studies. A survey of 132 codes by Kolk et al found that in 41 per cent of cases there was no specific

Table 2.3 *Labour monitoring in codes (per cent of total)*

	Company codes (%)	Business associations (%)	Multi-stakeholder codes (%)	Total (%)
By external group	7.9	6.7	15.0	9.2
By code owner	0.0	0.0	15.0	2.0
By company itself	2.0	0.0	30.0	5.2
By purchaser/contractor	12.9	3.3	5.0	9.8
Codes mentioning labour monitoring	24.8	10.0	55.0	26.1

Source: Author's elaboration from OECD inventory of codes.

mention of monitoring and in a further 44 per cent the firms themselves monitored compliance (Kolk et al, 1999, p168). Less than 10 per cent of company codes and 5 per cent of those set up by business groups had some form of external monitoring (ibid, Table 4b). In the United Kingdom, Ferguson's (1998) study of company codes found that none of them made a clear commitment to systematic monitoring and independent verification.

Conclusion

This review of the content of different types of codes covered by the OECD database confirms that different stakeholders have rather different expectations of codes. In particular those codes drawn up with the participation of trade unions and/or NGOs are likely to be the most demanding, both in terms of the issues covered and the inclusion of measures to ensure compliance. Conversely, the codes which are sponsored by business associations tend to be the least demanding because they need to be acceptable to the broad range of firms which make up the organization's membership, many of which are likely to resist the adoption of strong codes.

THE POLITICAL ECONOMY OF CODES: A CASE STUDY OF THE US APPAREL INDUSTRY

In order to put more flesh on the picture of conflicting views of codes presented in the chapter so far, this section will illustrate the struggles that are occurring with respect to corporate codes of conduct by examining what has been happening in the US apparel industry in recent years. Three different industry-wide codes have come into existence amid considerable acrimony. Different groups support these codes and the debates between them illustrate the conflicts which can arise around codes.

As was mentioned in Chapter 1, the origins of these codes of conduct can be traced back to the scandals of the early and mid-1990s concerning sweatshops producing garments for the top American brands and retailers, and the use of child labour. The Gap was subject to a high-profile campaign in 1995, and in 1996 chat show host Kathie Lee Gifford was reduced to tears on network television over accusations that the clothing line carrying her name was produced in sweatshops. The apparel industry feared that public concern might lead to Congress passing legislation to control such practices. At the same time, the Clinton administration was worried that exposés of this kind would derail its push for increasing free trade (Bissell, 1998).

It was in this context that President Clinton and Secretary of Labor Robert Reich brought together the White House Apparel Industry Partnership (AIP) in August 1996. The partnership included companies, trade unions, human rights groups, religious organizations and consumer advocates. The aim was to set workplace standards for the industry and a system to monitor compliance.

A preliminary agreement was reached in April 1997, but there continued to be differences between the partners. A particularly critical issue was the question of wages. The companies argued that they should only be required to pay the legal minimum wage in the countries where they operated. The unions and some NGOs argued that the minimum wage in many countries was insufficient to meet the basic needs of the population and that a code of conduct should involve a commitment to paying a 'living wage'. A second source of disagreement was the arrangements for monitoring compliance with the code, which unions and NGOs felt were inadequate and gave too much of a role to commercial auditing companies.

With the task force deadlocked, a sub-group consisting of four companies (Liz Clairborne, Nike, Reebok and Robert Van Heusen) and five NGOs (Business for Social Responsibility, the Lawyers Committee for Human Rights, the National Consumers League, the International Labor Rights Fund and the Robert F Kennedy Memorial Centre for Human Rights) met separately and in November 1998 proposed the setting up of the Fair Labor Association. Four other corporate members of the AIP task force accepted the proposal, but it was rejected by the trade unions (UNITE, the Retail, Wholesale and Department Store Union, and the AFL-CIO). It was also rejected by the ICCR (a coalition of religious investors).

There was, therefore, a clear division between what the companies wanted from a code of conduct, and what the trade unions sought to achieve. NGOs were split over the Fair Labor Association (FLA). The majority of those within the AIP supported it, on the grounds that it was a step in the right direction. However the ICCR and other organizations such as the Campaign for Labor Rights and Global Exchange were highly critical. This partly reflects the fact that NGOs cover a wide range of different types of organizations. It is not surprising that Business for Social Responsibility, as a group representing business, supported it. The Lawyers Committee for Human Rights also has close ties to the private sector, with many of its board coming from large corporate law firms. The National Consumer League's mission is 'to protect and promote the economic and social interests of American consumers' (http://www.nclnet.org/whoweare.htm), and receives corporate funding, although it has also been active around labour issues. As was suggested earlier, the interests of consumers in codes are somewhat ambiguous since they are interested in value for money as well as the conditions under which goods are produced.

Despite the refusal of the unions and ICCR to join, the FLA went ahead. The board of the FLA is made up of a chairman, six company representatives, six NGO representatives and one college/university representative.

The fact that the unions refused to endorse the FLA denied it the legitimacy which its proponents had hoped to achieve. The campaign within US universities and colleges, to ensure that clothing produced under license with college logos was not produced in sweatshops led to further developments. United Students Against Sweatshops (USAS) refused to accept FLA accreditation as a sign of good working conditions, and so an alternative organization, the Workers Rights Consortium (WRC) was set up. In contrast to the FLA, the board of the WRC has no industry representatives. It is made up of five university administration representatives, five representatives of USAS, and five independent labour rights experts. There is currently a struggle between the FLA and the WRC for support from universities with 155 affiliated to the FLA and 80 to WRC (34 are affiliated to both organizations) (Maquila Solidarity Network, 2001). This has become an extremely bitter dispute, with Nike in 1999 withdrawing sponsorship worth US$50 million from three US universities who had decided to work with the WRC rather than the FLA.

The third apparel industry initiative is the Worldwide Responsible Apparel Production (WRAP) Principles which were endorsed by the American Apparel Manufacturers Association in 1998. In contrast to the other two codes, this is therefore a business association code not a multi-stakeholder initiative. WRAP has a voluntary certification programme which is applied at the factory level. It started operation in June 2000 and since then over 225 factories from around the world have registered with WRAP. The board of WRAP is made up of a minority of top apparel industry executives and a majority of non-apparel industry related individuals.

Thus the US apparel industry has three competing codes of conduct – the WRAP Principles developed by the industry association; the FLA Workplace Code of Conduct agreed by some of the leading firms in the industry and some NGOs; and the WRC Model of Code of Conduct, which does not have any corporate involvement in its governance. As might be expected, there are substantial differences between the three codes in terms of content.

Content of the apparel industry codes

The weakest of the three codes is the WRAP Principles.[10] Although it covers some of the core labour standards such as child labour, forced labour and no discrimination, in other respects it is less than comprehensive. On freedom of association, it only recognizes the lawful right of free association including the right to join, *or not to join* (emphasis added), any organization. It does not, however, contain any mention of collective bargaining and is consistent with 'Right to Work' legislation which subverts collective bargaining. In terms of wages and hours, firms need only pay the legal minimum and not exceed the legal limits on hours worked. Even the provision for one day off in every seven-day period can be waived in order to meet urgent business needs. There is no mention of overtime pay.

The FLA Workplace Code of Conduct[11] goes significantly further than the WRAP Principles, reflecting the need to meet some of the concerns raised by NGOs. It mentions the rights of employees to collective bargaining as well as freedom of association. Employers are required to pay either the minimum wage or the prevailing industrial wage, whichever is the higher, and workers should not work more than 48 hours a week plus 12 hours overtime, or the maximum legally permitted, whichever is the lower. Overtime should be compensated at a rate at least equal to the normal rate of pay. In other areas such as harassment, abuse and discrimination, the Code is more explicit in specifying areas of concern than the Principles, which tend to be formulated in a very general way.

The WRC Model Code of Conduct[12] replicates the FLA Code in some areas, but also adds a number of other requirements. The treatment of forced labour, child labour, harassment and abuse and non-discrimination are very similar to the corresponding parts of the FLA Code. The clause on health and safety requires companies to abide by US or local health and safety standards, whichever is the more protective. On freedom of association and collective bargaining, licensees are required not to cooperate with government agencies or other bodies that prevent workers from organizing, and union organizers are to be allowed free access to employees. Some of the most significant differences between the FLA and the WRC codes are in the areas of wages and hours of work, reflecting the disputes between the different stakeholders which led to the split in the AIP discussed above. The WRC requires licensees to pay a 'living wage' and includes a definition of this. The maximum hours worked should be 48 hours a week or the local legal limit, whichever is the lower. In addition to one day off in seven, workers should also be allowed holidays and vacations. All overtime must be voluntary and paid at the legal premium rate, or where such a rate does not exist, at 1.5 times the normal hourly rate.

The WRC code is the only one of the three that has a specific section on 'Women's Rights'.[13] In addition to equal pay, treatment and opportunity, this clause mentions matters which are of specific concern to women workers, such as a ban on pregnancy testing, protection from dismissal following pregnancy, and protection from hazards especially those which endanger reproductive health.

Monitoring and verification

As well as differing in content, the three codes also differ in terms of monitoring and verification. The WRAP Certification Program is factory based. In the initial stage, factory management carries out a self-assessment to determine whether the facility complies with the WRAP Principles. It can then arrange an onsite evaluation by WRAP accredited independent monitors who will either recommend certification or identify areas where corrective action is required. Once certification has been achieved 'the facility may or may not receive an unannounced inspection to verify continued compliance'.

The extent to which WRAP provides for truly independent monitoring is open to question. The company to be inspected schedules the visit by the accredited monitors who will decide whether it is in compliance. Whether or not any unannounced visits are made subsequently to verify continued compliance is left open. Moreover, the independent monitors are paid a fee by the company that is being inspected. Monitors are not required to consult with local NGOs, religious organizations or human rights organizations, and there is no mention in the code of any need to interview workers. WRAP Certification can be attractive to suppliers if they can use it to satisfy their customers rather than having to comply with a number of individual company codes, and it has been endorsed by a number of apparel manufacturers' associations in Central America and the Caribbean, South Africa, the Philippines and Sri Lanka.

As was indicated earlier, the issue of monitoring was one of the factors which led to conflict within the AIP and it was a major reason why the trade unions and ICCR refused to participate in the FLA. Unlike the factory based WRAP, the FLA certifies particular companies or brands, based on monitoring of their own factories and those of their suppliers, contractors and licensees. Exceptions are granted where a factory is contracted for less than six months in any 24 month period, or where less than 10 per cent of its production is supplied to the company seeking certification. In order to obtain certification, a company must monitor 50 per cent of its suppliers in the first year and 100 per cent in the second year. Within two to three years, 30 per cent of suppliers must be externally monitored by FLA accredited independent monitors. Both the monitors and the facilities to be inspected are selected by the company, which also pays the monitors' fee.

Critics of the FLA argue that the monitoring system is neither sufficiently strong nor independent. The fact that a company can be certified when only 30 per cent of its facilities have been independently monitored, and that it has plenty of time to warn those which are to be inspected, limits the effectiveness of monitoring. There is also concern that companies will tend to select large audit companies, with whom they have links in other areas, to do the monitoring, thus compromising their independence (Light, 1998; Benjamin, 1998; Applebaum and Bonacich, 2000). There are also criticisms directed at the transparency of the process. The names of the factories used by the companies are not made public, and the monitors' reports are only made available to the FLA itself, with the public simply getting a summary of the findings in the FLA's annual report.

The WRC takes a rather different approach in that it does not plan to certify companies. It focuses specifically on production of apparel under license for US universities and colleges. It requires all licensees to abide by the terms of the code of conduct, but it does not have a systematic monitoring system. Rather it relies on spot-checks through unannounced visits by the WRC Agency. It puts particular emphasis on developing links with labour organizations and workers in the countries where licensed production is being undertaken. It will develop mechanisms for receiving and verifying workers' complaints regarding violations of the code of conduct. The WRC places considerable emphasis on transparency, requiring full disclosure of plant locations and labour conditions.

In terms of both content and monitoring and disclosure, therefore, there are significant differences between the three apparel industry codes. WRAP is clearly the weakest of the three and can be seen largely as a PR exercise by the industry to enable it to claim that it is doing something to eliminate sweatshop conditions. The FLA is a more comprehensive effort which includes some of the high-profile brand names which have been the target of campaigns, for example Nike, Reebok and Levi Strauss. It goes further than WRAP, both because the corporate side is dominated by these high-profile companies which are concerned to protect the reputation of their brands, but also because in order to acquire legitimacy it needed to be acceptable to at least some of the NGO members of the AIP. The WRC which, unlike the other two organizations, is totally independent of the apparel industry and has no corporate representatives on its board, has the most stringent requirements. Whereas WRAP and the FLA rely on an audit model applied to labour rights, the WRC's approach is more akin to the health and safety approach, with a system of unannounced visits by inspectors being utilized to verify compliance. It also seeks to involve workers and their organizations much more centrally in its activities.

SUMMARY AND CONCLUSION

A number of factors converged in the 1990s to give rise to the growth of voluntary corporate codes of conduct. These included the accelerated globalization of economic activity; the retreat of the state, especially from its role in regulating many aspects of business behaviour; the increased significance of brands and corporate reputation which made leading companies vulnerable to bad publicity; the growth of international communications which facilitated the dissemination of information about working conditions overseas; and the growth of NGOs campaigning around issues of human and labour rights.

A multiplicity of different interests can be regarded as stakeholders in relation to corporate codes of conduct. The goals of these stakeholders differ and consequently so do their objectives and expectations regarding codes. Codes of conduct should not therefore be seen as a manifestation of a newly responsible corporate sector balancing the interests of firms, workers, consumers and civil society. They are, rather, the outcome of the struggles of the different stakeholders to advance their own interests, subject to the constraints imposed by others. Codes therefore need to be analysed in terms of the groups which participate in them and those which are excluded from the process. They are the outcome of a struggle over who dominates the agenda.

One manifestation of this is the systematic differences which were observed between company codes, those adopted by business associations, and multi-stakeholder codes. Individual company codes tend to be quite limited, both in the extent to which they recognize the ILO's core labour standards, let alone incorporate other more exacting standards, and in the provisions which they make for independent external monitoring of their activities. Business association codes tend to be even weaker, operating on the 'least common denominator' principle, because they need to be acceptable to even the less progressive firms in the industry. Provided that they are sufficiently weak, they can prove attractive to Southern exporters as a guarantee of continued access to markets without incurring excessive costs. It seems likely that this is why apparel manufacturers' associations in a number of Central American and Caribbean countries, which rely heavily on exports to the United States, have endorsed the WRAP Principles.

When codes are the result of negotiations involving a number of different stakeholders, they are likely to be more comprehensive and to have stricter monitoring than those which are unilaterally adopted by companies. This reflects the pressure which other stakeholders are able to bring to bear on the companies. Even amongst multi-stakeholder codes there are substantial differences between codes depending on who is involved and who is excluded from them. Thus the WRC code which does not involve any direct corporate participation is more stringent than the FLA code which was rejected by the trade unions.

The debate over codes of conduct should not be couched in terms of whether or not they are a positive development or a corporate PR exercise. It is impossible to generalize about whose interests such codes serve. They should be seen as a contested terrain which can be used to advance the cause of workers in the South and to carve out space for them to organize and to struggle to improve their own wages and working conditions.

NOTES

1   See Jenkins (2001) for a fuller account of stakeholder interests.
2   See Chapter 5 by Stephanie Barrientos for a discussion of value chains.
3   An OECD survey found that the most common competitive advantage of codes

mentioned was to protect or enhance the company's reputation (OECD, 2000, Figure 6).

4   See Chapter 7 by Dwight Justice.
5   In addition there are Southern NGOs which often have a rather different perspective from the Northern-based NGOs. See Jenkins (2001).
6   See Tallontire et al (2001) for a review of studies on ethical consumers.
7   See Shaw and Hale, Chapter 8, who argue that workers who participated in workshops organized by Women Working Worldwide in Bangladesh and India identified measures which would give them greater job security as a key priority.
8   See Chapter 16 by Dara O'Rourke on the involvement of PricewaterhouseCooper in this area.
9   I am grateful to Kathryn Gordon of the OECD for making this database available to me.
10 The text of the WRAP Principles is available at http://www.wrapapparel.org/infosite2/principals.htm. For a detailed critique of WRAP see Maquila Solidarity Network (2000).
11 The text of the FLA Workplace Code of Conduct is available at http://www.fairlabor.org/html/CodeOfConduct/index.html
12 The WRC Model Code of Conduct is available at www.workersrights.org/
13 The FLA Code specifically mentions that there should be no sexual harassment or abuse, and no discrimination on grounds of gender, in the sections on harassment and discrimination, but does not have a separate section on women's rights. The WRAP Principles do not explicitly mention gender in any way and just have a general prohibition on any form of harassment or abuse, and discrimination.

REFERENCES

Amnesty International (2000) *Human Rights: Is it Any of your Business?*, London

Applebaum, R and E Bonacich (2000) 'The Key is Enhancing the Power of Workers', *The Chronicle of Higher Education*, 7 April, http://www.maquilasolidarity.org/resources/codes/applebona.htm, accessed 11 July 2001

Benjamin, M (1998) 'What's Fair about the Fair Labor Association (FLA)?', *Sweatshop Watch*, http://www.sweatshopwatch.org/swatch/headlines/1998/gex_fla.html, accessed 11 July 2001

Bissell, T (1998) 'Analysis of the Fair Labor Association', *Sweatshop Watch*, http://www.sweatshopwatch.org/swatch/headlines/1998/clr_fla.html, accessed 11 July 2001

Cowe, R (2000) 'Morality is a Spending Force', *Guardian*, 6 October 2000, p29

Ferguson, C (1998) *A Review of UK Company Codes of Conduct*, DFID, Social Development Division

ILO (1998) *Overview of Global Developments and Office Activities Concerning Codes of Conduct, Social Labelling and other Private Initiatives Addressing Labour Issues*, Working Party on the Social Dimensions of the Liberalization of International Trade, GB.273/WP/SDL/1(rev1), ILO, Geneva

Jenkins, R (2001) *Corporate Codes of Conduct: Self-regulation in a Global Economy*, UNRISD, Technology, Business and Society Programme Paper No 2, Geneva

Kearney, N (1999) 'Corporate Codes of Conduct: The Privatised Application of Labour Standards' in S Picciotto and R Mayne (eds) *Regulating International Business: Beyond Liberalisation*, Macmillan, Basingstoke, pp205-20

Kearney, N and D Justice (2001) 'The New Codes of Conduct: Some Questions and Answers for Trade Unionists' in I Wick, *Workers' Tool or PR Ploy? A Guide to Codes of International Labour Practice*, Friedrich-Ebert-Stiftung, Bonn

Klein, N (2000) *No Logo*, Flamingo, London

Kolk, A, R van Tulder and C Welters (1999) 'International Codes of Conduct and Corporate Social Responsibility: Can Transnational Corporations Regulate Themselves?', *Transnational Corporations*, Vol 8, No 1, pp143-80

Light, J (1998) 'Sweatwash: The Apparel Industry's Efforts to Co-opt Labor Rights', *Corporate Watch*, December 1998, http://www.corpwatch.org/trac/greenwash/sweatwash.html, accessed 18 May 1999

Maquila Solidarity Network (2000) *Critique of the Worldwide Responsible Apparel Production (WRAP) Programme*, April 2000, http://www.maquilasolidarity.org/resources.codes/wrap.htm accessed 01 August 2001

Maquila Solidarity Network (2001) *Codes Memo 7*, June 2001, http://www.maquilasolidarity.org/resources/codes/memo7.htm http://www.maquilasolidarity.org/resources/codes/memo7.htm, accessed 01 August 2001

OECD (1999) *Codes of Corporate Conduct: An Inventory*, OECD Working Party of the Trade Committee, TD/TC/WP(98)74/FINAL, Paris

OECD (2000) *Codes of Conduct – An Expanded Review of their Contents*, OECD Working Party of the Trade Committee, TD/TC/WP(99)56/FINAL, Paris

Tallontire, A, E Rentsendorj and M Blowfield (2001) *Ethical Consumers and Ethical Trade: A Review of Current Literature*, Natural Resources Institute, University of Greenwich, London

WBCSD (2000) *Corporate Social Responsibility: Making Good Business Sense*, World Business Council for Sustainable Development, Geneva

Zadek, S (2000) *Ethical Trade Futures*, NEF, London

Chapter 3

Labour rights/corporate responsibilities: the role of ILO labour standards

Jill Murray

INTRODUCTION

What should the content of corporate codes of conduct be? In recent times, there has been a trend towards defining corporate social responsibility in terms of the core labour standards of the International Labour Organization (ILO). This can be seen in the reference made to ILO core labour standards in various transnational instruments, including the United Nation's Global Compact (United Nations, 1999) and the European Community's Green Paper, *Promoting a European Framework for Corporate Social Responsibility* (Com (2001) 366 final, paragraph 56). Similar trends are occurring within national jurisdictions; see, for example, the Basic Code of the United Kingdom's Ethical Trading Initiative (ETI) (1998). A number of industry-wide agreements use the ILO standards, including the European Code of Conduct in the footwear sector (European Commission, nd) and the recent Banana Industry agreement signed in Costa Rica (IUF, 2001). An increasing number of individual firms ground their commitments on the terms of ILO standards, as seen for example in the agreement between the German multinational Freudenberg and the international trade union movement (Broughton, 2000), and in the retailer Sainsbury's code of conduct (discussed in Fridd and Sainsbury, 1999)

This chapter argues that we need to critically assess the use of ILO standards *by firms*. ILO conventions are *addressed to states*. Some of the important conventions call for a range of state action to guarantee the attainment of labour rights, raising questions about the capacity and appropriateness of assigning the role of implementing these standards to firms rather than states.

Clearly, it is appropriate that the ILO core labour standards form the heart of any business approach to the proper conduct of labour relations. The ILO has been recognized as the institution which must respond to questions of social justice in the global economy, and its 1998 Declaration of Fundamental Principles and Rights at Work has re-emphasized its, and its Member States', commitment to this role. (All relevant ILO material, including the texts of the core conventions and the 1998 Declaration can be easily accessed at the ILO website http://www.ilo.org.) It must also be stressed that it is important for firms to acknowledge the ILO as the source of self-adopted standards, so that use can be made by the firm and other interested parties of the ILO's supervisory and interpretive bodies when making sense of the terms of the conventions.

This chapter argues that for firms' ethical promises to work in the real world, the ILO core labour standards must be *elaborated upon* so that the actual role of the corporation is properly defined, and in some instances, *extended* to included other important 'non-core' matters.

We will see that the processes of elaboration and extension, necessary to apply ILO standards at the level of the firm, create a space for local, 'bottom-up' input into creation of corporate standards. Firms which adopt the approach advocated here therefore have the chance to involve local workers, non-governmental organizations, unions and other interested parties in determining the actual form of their commitment to ethical practice. Thus, the use of the ILO schema is far from the rigid, 'top-down' straightjacket which some authors portray it to be: its very nature calls for the democratic participation of the affected people and communities in the local application of ILO standards by firms.

The rest of this chapter is divided into four sections: the next section looks at the role and function of the ILO and the nature of its core labour standards. The subsequent section puts forward a theoretical argument in support of the idea of firms elaborating upon and extending the core labour standards in their codes of conduct, based upon the founding philosophies of the ILO. The following section discusses some examples where such elaboration and extension have occurred. The final section considers these issues about the content of codes of conduct in the broader context of the current debates about the use of such codes.

THE ILO AND CORE LABOUR STANDARDS

Background

The ILO was established in 1919, in part due to a recognition of the kinds of issues we would today associate with the concept of 'globalization'. As George Barnes – one of the group which negotiated the creation of the ILO – noted, it was feared that 'capital has no country' (Barnes, 1926, p36). The original ILO Constitution stated that 'the failure of any nation to adopt humane conditions of labour is an obstacle in the way of other nations which desire to improve conditions in their own countries' (ILO, 1944, preamble). To ensure that all nations would be able to adopt humane conditions of labour, the ILO set about creating a floor of labour conditions which would underpin international competition. To date, around 180 labour conventions have been created. These conventions are not in themselves legally binding, and the States which are members of the ILO are only under an obligation to bring each convention before the relevant national authority so that ratification can be considered. Ratified conventions may be denounced at set intervals, and the ILO's capacity to supervise and enforce even ratified conventions essentially relies upon state self-reporting and the public naming and humiliation of miscreant nations.

In 1998, in response to the 'new' globalization, the ILO issued a Declaration on Fundamental Rights and Principles at Work. This instrument commits all ILO member states to promote certain key conventions, whether they have ratified them or not. The International Labour Organization was itself re-organized to focus its attention on these core areas, and a broad programme aimed at encouraging ratification and enabling compliance through technical assistance (that is, practical help on the ground in the member countries) has been launched.

This re-focusing of the ILO's role has already had some success. Ratifications of the core conventions have increased, especially in relation to the 1999 Convention on the Worst Forms of Child Labour. And, as noted in the Introduction, the ILO has also succeeded in embedding its core conventions in a number of international instruments, including the Organisation for Economic Co-operation and Development's (OECD) Guidelines on Multinational Enterprises (substantially revised in 2000), the United Nation's Global Compact, and in the policies of the World Bank (Murray, 2001).

The core labour standards are the most important ILO conventions relating to freedom of association and the right to collective bargaining (Conventions 87 and 98), the elimination of all forms of forced or compulsory labour (Conventions 29 and 105), the effective abolition of child labour (Conventions 138 and 182) and the elimination of discrimination in employment and occupation (Conventions 100 and 111).

The nature of ILO core conventions

ILO conventions are designed to place obligations on states. This is so in a purely technical sense, because conventions are instruments which are 'addressed' to states. Each member state of the ILO must decide whether or not it ratifies an individual convention, and the form which implementation of a ratified convention will take. In addition to this technical meaning, it is clear from the content of the ILO conventions that the sphere they seek to influence is that of the national regulatory regime. There are a number of examples from the core labour conventions which demonstrate the kinds of obligations placed upon states by the ILO.

Example one: fundamental human rights

The ILO requires states to 'respect, promote and realize' the rights of workers and employers to create and join organizations which represent their interests. The conventions dealing with this fundamental labour right are expressed in classical human rights form: that is, the conventions seek to limit the power of the state in relation to certain individual actions, and any state action which might infringe or impede the fundamental right is prohibited in sweeping terms. (See the terms of Convention 87 on freedom of association.)

Example two: state policy

The core labour Convention on Discrimination (Convention 111) requires ratifying states to 'declare and pursue a national policy to promote, by methods appropriate to national conditions and practice, equality of opportunity and treatment in respect of employment and occupation ...'.

Example three: state choices

Some ILO conventions permit ratifying states to select from a range of possible rules or regulatory outcomes. A good example is the Convention on Child Labour (Convention 138), which contains a complex range of options from which states can select. With various provisos, the convention permits states to create rules excluding workers below the ages of 14, 15 and/or 18 from employment, depending on circumstances. Further, the convention states that a ratifying state 'whose economy and administrative facilities are insufficiently developed may ... initially limit the scope of application of this Convention', and states may permit 'light work' for children aged between 13 and 15 in certain circumstances.

These three examples show, in different ways, why it may be inappropriate and even nonsensical for firms to 'sign up to' or 'adopt' or 'reflect' the core labour conventions *in their original form.* The clearest and most common problem is that shown in Example three above: where the core conventions offer states regulatory choices, unless firms which 'adopt' the standard identify which of these choices *they* make, their adherence to the convention is meaningless. Without further elaboration in the case of the core convention on child labour, discussed above, we could not know whether the firm is committing itself not to employ those under 14, or under 15, or under 18. Further, it is clear that the ILO locates the site of decision-making about these exemptions from regulation in the realm of state action: firms do not have sufficient knowledge, nor the democratically accountable authority, to properly activate the blanket limitation provisions, for example those based on insufficient economic development.

Example two presents a different problem. Obviously an individual firm, or even all the firms operating in a single country, do not have the resources or power to institute a national policy in areas such as discrimination, poverty elimination and so on. It might be argued that this objection could be easily overcome: firms could simply adopt those elements of conventions it was possible for them to implement, and ignore those which needed the action of other institutions. But this concept of 'cherry-picking' terms from the ILO conventions presents important difficulties.

In an ideal world, as perceived by the ILO, all states would ratify and implement the body of international labour rules. Firms would thus be operating within national regulatory environments where, for example, national action plans aimed at abolishing child labour and sex discrimination and attacks on trade unionists were operating. These national regulatory environments, as we have seen, would not simply be a series of prescriptive rules: they would consist of policies, government expenditure, the participation of the social partners in determining techniques of implementation and so on. Furthermore, in relation to certain fundamental labour rights themselves, the ILO calls on states to limit their *own* powers in order to ensure that these rights are respected and upheld, a task which is clearly beyond the legal scope of any individual firm.

Much of the literature on corporate codes of conduct starts from the premise that firms are the chief actors in establishing labour standards. But, as we have seen, in terms of the ILO's schema, if we assume the state away, it is clear that individual firms or groupings of firms *cannot themselves fulfil* the conditions required to achieve proper implementation of the core labour standards. For an individual firm to abide by these conventions on the terms originally established by the ILO, it would have to *do more* than just mirror those clauses it was capable of adopting. This is clear from an examination of Example one above. If states are required to 'respect, promote and realize' the individual's right to freedom of association, in the absence of an effective state (or the presence of a state which actively violates labour rights), firms must take positive action to secure the rights of individuals. In the next section, a theoretical argument in support of this contention is made.

A THEORETICAL CASE FOR ELABORATION AND EXPANSION

In this section, it is argued that the underlying philosophy of the ILO itself provides a case which supports a call for firms to elaborate upon and, where necessary, expand their 'obligations' under the ILO core labour conventions.

The ILO can be seen as reflecting a political philosophy of pluralism, as this concept is understood in the field of industrial relations. That is, it reflects the view that there are two 'sides' engaged in economic activity – workers and employers – whose interests are different yet reconcilable. The process of reconciliation is best conducted by the two sides themselves, with the state ensuring that bargaining is conducted under conditions of equality, and that industrial peace and social justice are maintained. Thus the principle of freedom of association is central to the ILO. This is clear from the terms of the ILO Constitution of 1919, the tripartite structure of the ILO itself, the restatement of the ILO's mission in 1944 in the Declaration of Philadelphia, and in the 1998 Declaration on Fundamental Principles and Rights at Work, discussed above.

Central to an understanding of the underpinning philosophy of the ILO is an understanding of power. On one hand, the framers of the ILO Constitution perceived that the unalloyed power of the employer could create inhumane conditions: the forces of competition would drive down standards at the micro-level through the unilateral decisions of firms, and at the macro-level by the pressures placed by 'footloose' capital on the regulatory decisions of States. The founders of the ILO also recognized that the power of exploited labour could be a threat to public order and the security of the state, thus threatening the capitalist system of production if certain minimum requirements were not met.

Thus, the ILO was created to bolster the regulatory role of states by helping them to ensure that workers were not exploited through the unrestrained power of capital, and to protect society as a whole from the upheaval of worker revolution in response to such conditions. The key device which would secure equality of the bargaining parties was freedom of association (which I am taking to include the right to collectively bargain). Only by organizing collectively could individual workers hope to meet their employers on a 'level playing field' in terms of power. Hence the crucial role of the member states of the ILO was to do whatever was necessary to uphold and promote the principle of freedom of association within their sovereign territory.

The analysis of these power relations by Otto Kahn-Freund remains one of the most acute readings of these matters. (Kahn-Freund was a German academic who emigrated to England in the 1930s and became a respected commentator on the Anglo-Saxon traditions of labour law and relations.) His view of workplace relations closely mirrors the philosophy of the ILO as it was originally expressed, which is not surprising given the important role which American, British and other Western European participants played at the Conference which created the ILO in 1919.

Kahn-Freund writes:

> The individual employee ... has normally no social power, because it is only in the most exceptional cases that, as an individual, he has any bargaining power at all. ... Typically, the worker as an individual has to accept the conditions which the employer offers. *On the labour side, power is collective power.* The individual employer represents an accumulation of material and human resources, *socially speaking the enterprise is itself in this sense a 'collective power'.* (Emphasis added, Davies and Freedland, 1983, p17)

This quotation expresses very clearly one of the central ideas underlying the ILO's schema: *prior* to any action or intervention by the State, the capitalist firm is already a collective force, and it is only by diminishing this power that the collective force of labour can be given expression.

Kahn-Freund also argued that the reality of this power imbalance meant that passive measures to shore up freedom of association were not enough to secure the practical exercise of workers' influence at the workplace. Discussing a UK law which stated that workers should not be 'prevented or deterred' from union activity, he argued:

> [This law] means in the first place that no worker must suffer a disadvantage in the terms of his employment by reason of what he does in the interest of his union. ... But it means more; if an employee representing the union in the plant ... is denied the facilities which are indispensable for the exercise of this function, he is prevented from exercising it. Hence *the employer is under an obligation* to provide him with these facilities, such as the use of a notice board, a desk, a telephone, and, if the size of the plant justified this, an office. (Emphasis added, Davies and Freedland, 1983, p214)

In other words, the underlying philosophy of the ILO, and indeed the underlying philosophy of labour regulation in a number of developed countries for much of the twentieth century was that, 'absent the State', the status quo is an imbalance of power which favours the employer over the employee. If a particular state has not been willing or able to create a legal and social environment in which the right to freedom of association is realizable, then nothing exists to counter the power of the employer. To expect effective collective organization to emerge in the absence of the necessary facilitative and protective national regimes, especially if workers are particularly vulnerable and/or if the firm is itself 'statelike' in its power and size, is a pipedream.

Today, the views of Kahn-Freund must be updated to acknowledge the world of work as it really is. His emphasis on the factory or plant, and on the male manual worker organized into formal trade unions, must be built upon to include the many other forms of industrial organization. The telephone on the desk in the factory, proposed by Kahn-Freund above, may be an impractical solution to the challenges of organizing women who work at home, or sex workers on a city street. However, while we need to keep interrogating our ideas about the sites, gender and broader societal impact of 'work', the base concept of the imbalance of power remains real.

What corporate codes of conduct must do, therefore, is to *effectively self-limit the firm's power* to ensure that a more equalized balance can emerge from the collective representation of its workers and those affected by its operations. The likelihood of this occurring voluntarily is, of course, a matter of concern for many activists, and the reason why very few commentators are willing to consign all labour regulation to the sole responsibility of firms. It is clear, from the foregoing analysis, that *any firm which wishes to act consistently with the ILO schema has an active burden to secure the rights, freedoms, principles and standards enumerated by the ILO, and to set in place systems and procedures and internal guarantees which will overcome the power imbalance/s which exist in the status quo.* The firm must, therefore, elaborate upon the relevant terms of the ILO conventions to reflect the ways in which it is agreeing to self-limit its own power in order to respect the rights and uphold the obligations established by the ILO in its dialogue with states.

SOME USEFUL EXAMPLES

There a number of useful models of codes where firms are required to do more than simply 'adopt' the bare bones of core labour standards. One of the most interesting is to be seen in the original Sullivan Principles (Charnovitz, 1994). This charter was created for the use of American firms operating in South Africa during the period of apartheid (Murray, 1998.) The Sullivan Principles did not just set out principles: they established a framework of practical action which showed what steps firms would take in making these principles work at the local level. Another useful example is the OECD's Guidelines on Multinational Enterprises (OECD, 2000), which take the form of recommendations from OECD member states to firms operating from their territory. (Murray, 2001). The ILO itself has an instrument which today receives little attention, but which shows the breadth of demands which can be placed on firms: the 1977 Tripartite Declaration on Multinational Enterprises is a prime example of the extension of scope beyond the core labour standards themselves.

Making core standards work

Firms adopting the Sullivan Principles were not merely signing up to passively support a principle of freedom of association. Instead, firms were agreeing to 'proceed immediately to … *secure* rights of Black workers to the freedom of association and assure protection against victimization while pursuing and attaining these rights'. In addition to this positive obligation, firms were required to 'establish an appropriate and comprehensive procedure for handling discrimination and resolving individual employee complaints'. In relation to discrimination, firms were required to implement 'fair and equal' conditions, but also to 'design and implement a wage and salary administration plan which is applied equally to all employees, regardless of race, who are performing equal or comparable work', and to 'ensure an equitable system of job classifications', and to 'determine the extent upgrading … in the upper echelons is needed to accomplish (the objective) of the employment of Blacks and non-whites at all levels of company operations'.

Similarly, the OECD Guidelines on Multinational Enterprises elaborate on the principle of freedom of association. Firms should not just passively 'respect' the right of their employees to join unions, but also 'engage in constructive negotiations ... with such representatives with a view to reaching agreements on employment conditions.' Multinational enterprises (MNEs) should 'provide facilities to employee representatives as may be necessary to assist in the development of effective collective agreements', provide information 'which is needed for meaningful negotiations on conditions of employment', 'promote consultation and co-operation' on 'matters of mutual concern', and 'provide information to employees and their representatives which enables them to obtain a true and fair view of the performance of the entity or, where appropriate, the enterprise as a whole'.

Obligations beyond the firm

The Sullivan Principles also required firms to look outside the enterprise and take on certain responsibilities in terms of the local community, the firm's relations with the state government and with other businesses. The Principles required firms to *seek law reform* in areas where core labour and human rights standards were breached by the state. Thus, firms were to 'support the elimination of all industrial racial discriminatory laws which impede the implementation of equal and fair terms and conditions of employment, such as abolition of job reservations, job fragmentation and apprenticeship restrictions for Blacks and other non-whites'. Sullivan firms were also to 'support the elimination of discrimination against the rights of Blacks to form or belong to government registered and unregistered unions'.

The allocation of the firm's resources

As discussed above, the ILO labour standards place obligations on states to develop policies and to spend money to implement them. Firms which are seeking to replicate the obligations of states in relation to core labour standards should consider allocating funds to social goals which will bolster labour rights. Again, the Sullivan Principles provide a useful model. Firms were required to 'participate in the development of programmes that address the educational needs of employees, their dependants and the local community. Both individual and collective programmes should be considered, in addition to technical education, including such activities as literacy education, business training, direct assistance to local schools, contributions and scholarships'.

Obligations beyond the core labour standards

The core labour standards represent the ILO's view on the priority conventions which states should ratify and support, on the grounds that these standards are enabling procedural rules upon which a healthy industrial and civil society can be based. As has been argued already, various important issues are raised when it is firms, not states, considering the implementation of these (and other) standards.

In the absence of adequate state systems supporting core labour standards, firms must make an assessment of the status quo in which they are operating, and note all the risks to human dignity and decent work which are posed therein. It is more than likely that the attainment of the core labour rights and principles of the ILO will be dependent on the attainment of other conditions. (For example, it is unlikely that true equality of opportunity would exist for women at work without a satisfactory system of maternity and family leave.) It is also likely that in any given situation, issues of the timing of the attainment of certain rights must be assessed. Certain priorities may require immediate intervention. For example, if workers are being maimed or killed by unsafe working practices, the immediate priority must be for the firm to establish standards and systems in this area. Workers who are paid exploitative wages which condemn them to hunger and poverty may require a 'living wage' before they are able to exercise other rights recognized in the core labour standards.

As noted earlier, the concept of firms undertaking such surveys, and determining priorities for action in isolation from other groups – governments, civil society – is inappropriate. Yet this is the very kind of decision-making which is inherent in the concept of corporations self-regulating with the goal of attaining the core labour standards of the ILO. The fact that there are decisions to be taken, both in relation to how the core labour standards are elaborated upon and in which directions the core standards are extended to include other matters, means that there is a margin for discourse, debate and negotiation as to what form the responsible firm's self-regulation should take. This provides an opportunity (and indeed places an obligation on firms) for firms to consult with the relevant stakeholders as they carry out this survey and determine their joint priorities for action.

READING THE CODES DEBATE

This chapter highlights the gulf which is emerging between traditional regulatory forms, based on the use of state decision-making and resource allocation, and the explosion of interest in corporate self-regulation. Some proposals call for corporate self-regulation as an *alternative* to state rule, assuming away the traditional role of the state (see for example, Fung et al, 2001.) The idea that firms can and should single-handedly implement ILO standards has been shown to be based on a misconception of the nature of these standards.

However, this is a problem which can be addressed, at least up to a certain point. The fact that the broad obligations placed on states must be elaborated upon before they provide a meaningful basis for corporate self-regulation provides a 'space' in which local consultations can be undertaken and detailed consideration be given to local issues and preferences. This is important, because it shows that the use of the ILO core labour standards as the guiding principles for firms does not necessarily entail a loss of input and flexible application at the local level. The processes of elaboration and extension discussed in this chapter provide the practical means by which local workers and their communities can express their views on the priorities and actual conditions they require to attain the ILO ideal of 'decent work' (Somavia, 1999.)

It is true that codes of conduct based on the proposals made in this chapter would not be the brief, elegant statements of principles which increasingly appear in corporate Annual Reports and websites. But with added complexity comes the chance of real accountability, options for actual involvement at the local level, and the possibility of real changes in labour practices. It is clear from recent research into effective monitoring, that even complex regimes can be dealt with by sophisticated monitoring systems. Of course, the fact that such elaboration and extension must be based upon a self-limitation of the power of the corporation shows, if nothing else, how deeply problematic the use of such instruments can be.

Assigning important tasks from the sphere of government regulation to the private commercial arena has ramifications for the operation of democratic participation and accountability within states. We should remember that taking instruments designed to bind states and using them to attempt to bind firms is not a negligible step. It is worth recalling Mayne's conclusion:

> Perhaps the most important point to bear in mind is that governments have the basic responsibility for promoting and protecting human rights and the rule of law. However imperfectly they perform this role in practice, most of them are at least formally accountable to their citizens and as such are the body best suited in each country to mediate between the different interest groups in society when setting and enforcing standards. (Mayne, 1999, p246)

REFERENCES

Barnes, G N (1926) *History of the International Labour Office*, Williams and Norgate, London

Broughton, A (2000) *Global Labour Standards Agreement Signed at Freudenberg*, http://www.eiro.eurofound.ie/2000/08/feature/eu0008267f.html, accessed 2 July 2001, on file with author

Charnovitz, S (1994) 'The WTO and Social Issues', *Journal of World Trade Law*, Vol 28, No 5, pp1-25

Davies, P and Freedland, M (1983) *Kahn-Freund's Labour and the Law*, Stevens and Sons, London

Ethical Trading Initiative (1998) *Ethical Trading Initiative: Purpose, Principles, Programme and Membership Information*, http://www.eti.org.uk/_html/about/basecode_en/framesets/f_page.shtml, accessed 2 July 2001, on file with author

European Commission (no date) *A Charter for the Social Partners In The Footwear Sector: Code of Conduct* http://www.europa.eu.int/comm/employment_social/soc-dial/news/charterfootwear_en.htm, accessed 2 July 2001, on file with author

Fridd, P and Sainsbury, J (1999) 'The Role of Voluntary Codes of Conduct and Regulation – a Retailer's View' in S Picciotto and R Mayne (eds) *Regulating International Business: Beyond Liberalization*, Macmillan and Oxfam, Houndmills, Basingstoke, pp221–33.

Fung, A, C Sabel and D O'Rourke (2001) 'Realizing Labour Standards', *Boston Review*, Vol 26, pp1–45.

ILO (International Labour Organization) (1944) Constitution of the ILO, http://www.ilo.org/public/english/about/iloconst.htm, accessed 2 Jult 2001, on file with author

IUF (International Union of Food, Agricultural, Hotel, Restaurant, Catering, Tobacco and Allied Workers' Associations) (2001) *Towards Respect for Global Union Rights?*, http://www.iuf.org/iuf/editorials/banana01-00.htm, accessed 2 July 2001, on file with author

Mayne, R (1999) 'Regulating TNCs: the Role of Voluntary and Governmental Approaches', in S Picciotto and R Mayne (eds) *Regulating International Business: Beyond Liberalization*, Macmillan and Oxfam, Houndmills, Basingstoke, pp235–54.

Murray, J (2001) 'A New Phase in the Regulation of Multinational Enterprises: The Role of the OECD', *Industrial Law Journal*, Vol 30, No 3, pp255–270

Murray, J (1998) 'Corporate Codes of Conduct and Labour Standards', in R Kyloh (ed) *Mastering the Challenge of Globalization*, ILO, Geneva

OECD (Organisation for Economic Co-operation and Development) (2000) *The OECD Guidelines For Multinational Enterprises*, http://www.oecd.org//daf/investment/guidelines/mnetext.htm, accessed 2 July 2001, on file with author

Somavia, J (1999) *Decent Work*, Report of the ILO Director-General to the 1999 International Labour Conference

United Nations (1999) *The Nine Principles: A Compact for the New Century*, http://www.unglobalcompact.org/gc/unweb.nsf/content/thenine.htm, accessed 2 July 2001, on file with author

Chapter 4

'I'll tell you what I want ...': women workers and codes of conduct

Ruth Pearson and Gill Seyfang

INTRODUCTION

There has been much discussion in the last 30 years of the terms under which women workers have been incorporated into what is now known as the global value chain. Since the 1970s researchers and activists have produced a litany of evidence and complaints that working conditions are bad, wages are very low and non-wage benefits are often not paid, even when theoretically required by national labour laws (Elson and Pearson, 1981; Lim, 1990; Pearson, 1998; Razavi, 1999). Although part of the analysis of the subordinate position of women workers rests on their social construction as secondary and inferior workers, part also rests with the institutions of organized labour – the trade unions which have championed the rights and entitlements of male workers rather than their female counterparts (Humphries, 1977). This lack of representation has then been reflected in the marginalization of women from any form of collective bargaining, be it plant level negotiations, national industry standards or international tripartite agreements such as the International Labour Organization (ILO).

Not all analysts have condemned the employment of women workers out of hand. In spite of what can be seen as exploitative conditions from the point of view of best practice standards, some argue that it is wrong to compare women workers' wages and conditions with those in the global marketplace, and that we need to look at comparative work and alternatives within the locality of the particular group of workers (Lim, 1990). This claim has been strengthened by postmodernist critiques of development which accuse structural analyses of women's working situations of ignoring the agency and choices women exercise by (opting for) work in world market factories (Marchand and Parpart, 1995).

This position is backed up by case studies such as Diane Wolf's *Factory Daughters* (1992) which explores the ways in which young women exercise a (constrained) choice by opting to work in export factories in preference to unpaid family labour in agriculture, seeking the relative freedom and autonomy that life away from the family offers, as well as the opportunity to earn cash wages and accumulate financial savings for their futures.

However, as previous chapters in this volume elaborate, political developments have accompanied the recent intensification of the globalization of production. Not least of these has been the pressure from a number of sources in Northern consuming countries which have sought to insist that global labour standards apply to global production chains. Given the above, it would seem plausible that such pressures would provide opportunities for women workers to overcome their marginal positioning in two major ways: first they would claim a place at the negotiating table as key stakeholders in the outcome of partnership agreements on codes of conduct. And second, they would be in a position to raise issues which are specific to women involved in export production which tend to get overlooked when male-led unions or workers' committees are in charge of such negotiations. There are several logical outcomes of the inclusion of women workers as mainstream players in the new framework of codes of conduct aimed at regulating the working conditions of those involved in global production chains. These are the routine representation of women workers in the structures and negotiations of codes of conduct; the incorporation of issues central to the well-being of women workers; and ultimately an improvement in the general working conditions for women in global production chains. This chapter, therefore, sets out to explore the extent to which the experience of Voluntary Codes of Conduct (VCCs) reflects the assumptions in this argument.

WHAT WOMEN WORKERS WANT

In a comprehensive exercise in consultation with women workers in the export free zones in Nicaragua, a Central American Women's Network (CAWN) workshop in Managua with representatives of Central American women workers' groups, a report was produced on the issues concerning women maquila workers, drawing up a 'wish list' of items to include in a women's code of conduct (CAWN, 1999).

This list of desired working conditions reflects a central fact about women in world market factories – the desire to be able to continue working in export factories, together with the assurance that this employment will take place in a situation which defends their dignity, ensures appropriate remuneration, avoids arbitrary and inhumane treatment, guarantees freedom of association and collective bargaining and protects them from harm, in terms of both violence and harassment at work and unhealthy working conditions and processes. These demands also reflect the facts that women in such workplaces understand that not all production takes place within the factory – hence the demand to respect homeworkers – and that workers' entitlements extend beyond the factory floor to social security measures which include unemployment and sickness benefits, health services and pensions.

There are also a whole series of demands which reflect the ways in which women's productive and reproductive roles are intertwined – hence the call for protection and respect for pregnant women, and the banning of enforced overtime and a restriction of the working day to eight hours. These are demands which not only have a bearing on the rights of workers to equitable and non-arbitrary treatment at work, but also on the fact that outside of working hours women have responsibilities for household maintenance and reproduction which require 'liberation' from the workplace for defined and predictable time periods.

These issues are echoed by research with other women's organizations which have revealed the priorities given by women in their struggle for dignified work. A workshop held by Women Working Worldwide (WWW) with Bangladeshi workers recorded complaints about management harassment and intimidation, sexual harassment and abuse, lack of secure contracts, sub-survival wages, absence of contracts, prohibition of union activity, forced overtime and absence of maternity rights. Their draft code of conduct included a minimum wage for a minimum labour standard, maximum working hours (including overtime), statutory leave for holidays, maternity and social benefits, as well as rights to collective bargaining, health and safety, social security, no discrimination, and the provision of sanctions against violation of these aspects (Women Working Worldwide, 1998).

WHAT IS THE REALITY OF WOMEN'S WORKING CONDITIONS IN EXPORT FACTORIES?

The demands of women workers as listed above are a direct reflection of their experiences of working conditions in export-oriented production, which are summarized below.

Low wages

Wages in export production factories are often higher than those in alternative occupations, which is why many women are willing to work in them even when conditions are not optimal. Systematic information on wages, particularly from subcontracted suppliers in developing countries, is notoriously hard to obtain and much of the evidence cited comes from a range of 'grey literature' produced by campaigning groups, workers' organizations and journalists. The available data do suggest that many workers are unable to earn what might be considered a minimum subsistence or living wage. Very often workers' wage packets vary according to whether they reach management's – often impossible – productivity targets, so there is a large element of piece rate payment, forced overtime as well as deductions for a range of 'misdemeanours' including lack of punctuality, inaccurate working, absences for health, transport or family reasons. It is therefore very hard to quantify average wages against some notion of a living wage. A Nicaraguan study of maquila workers by the Maria Elena Cuadra (MEC) autonomous women's organization reported that a substantial number of factories in the Free Trade Zones paid below the legally established minimum wage. Their survey reported that 60 per cent of respondents were paid less than what MEC considered was a basic salary, with 67 per cent being dependent on fulfilling quotas. A minority complained that the companies failed to pay them for overtime worked (MEC, 1998). In Cambodia the starting wage reported by garment factories was £5 per week rising to £6.50 after training against an estimated 'poverty line' in Cambodia of £11 per week. In Saipan, a US territory in the Northern Mariana islands in the Philippines and home to 32 major garment factories, Chinese women were being paid a generous £2 per hour, although this worked out at less than £1.20 per hour after deductions, including a deduction for medical insurance which, legally, should be the responsibility of the factories (Abrams, 1999a). Most of the wages received by workers in Saipan had to be paid to the recruiters who had got them the jobs. Reports indicate that more than half of foreign-owned factories in Guangshou province in China paid their workers less than the minimum wage (WOW, 2001, p7).

Lack of protection and respect for pregnant women

Again there is no systematic information about the treatment of pregnant women in export factories but there are an alarming number of reports of abuses and lack of entitlements. The Nicaraguan study included a number of beatings of pregnant women amongst the list of physical abuses. In Saipan, there are reports of women being forced to have abortions to keep their jobs and suffering humiliation by management. Workers getting married or getting pregnant are in breach of their contracts and forfeit their £28 deposit and suffer further financial penalties (Abrams, 1999a, 1999b). In Nicaragua most factories conformed with the law, though MEC recorded a number of cases where women were prevented from attending prenatal, and post-natal medical care. Nearly half the women who had had babies were unable to return to their previous jobs, and half of those who did received lower wages. Most workers lost pay when they had to attend to sick children or relatives (MEC, 1998, p19).

Physical and psychological violence and sexual harassment

The Nicaraguan study reported 78 separate complaints concerning physical violence, many of which referred to 'Chinese' supervisors and management, as well as 313 complaints about verbal and psychological harassment. (MEC, 1998). In China, workers reported abuse from management, including shouting, physical abuse and fines, and beatings by guards for leaving the premises without permission. In El Salvador workers complained that supervisors both hit and screamed at them and that if they talked back they could be locked in an isolation room (UNITE, 2000). A 1999 survey of 35,000 workers in sub-contractor factories in Indonesia reported that 57 per cent of footwear and 59 per cent of clothing workers reported seeing abuse and cruel treatment by supervisors, including arbitrary fines, physical abuse, humiliation and punishment such as standing outside for hours or cleaning toilets. A worker from a Korean factory in Guatemala complained that '[t]hey treat us like machines. They shout at us. The supervisors hit us, threaten us. We are there to work only. If you complain, you are sacked and sacked without pay' (WWW, 2000a, p8).

Sexual harassment is less widely reported and notoriously difficult to research. A study of workers in a factory in Haiti producing items for Disney claimed that 17 per cent of female factory workers had been forced to have sex with their bosses under threat of being fired (Kernaghan and Verhoogen, 1996). According to research by the Korean Confederation of Trade Unions in 1997, 67.1 per cent of members admitted to experiencing sexual harassment at work (WWW, 2000b, p19). In Bangladesh, particularly, there have been extensive complaints about the physical and sexual intimidation of women on their journeys to work and in their dormitories, and several incidents of rape and murder have been reported against factory workers in Mexico and Thailand (Maquila Solidarity Network, 2000; Theobald, 1998). In Mexico, some 20 years after such abuses were first denounced, there are reports of forced pregnancy testing of job applicants and women workers were routinely 'patted down' and body searched by (sometimes armed) male guards on leaving for lunch and at the end of the day. In the Kathie Lee factory in El Salvador, pregnancy tests were mandatory, and paid for by workers themselves at a rate equivalent to 2 days wages. A positive pregnancy test led to dismissal. In Honduras there are reports of workers being injected with Depo Provera (a hormonal contraceptive) under threat of dismissal, though some workers apparently thought that the injection was a vaccination. There is also evidence of factory managers handing out contraceptive pills (NLC, 1998; nd)

Inadequate occupational health, safety and social security rights

Neglect of health and safety is rampant in export factories. One inspector reported blocked fire exits, sewing machines without safety guards, and workers held in padlocked rooms. Twelve workers died of suffocation in a factory fire at Globe Knitting Ltd, Dhaka, Bangladesh in September 2000, in premises which had no emergency exit, inadequate fire training and, according to surviving workers, the main doors on each floor were locked (National Garment Workers Federation, 2000). Grupo Factor X, which works with maquila workers in Mexico, have denounced the unsafe use of toxic chemicals, sometimes prohibited in the United States, and have linked this to reproductive hazards and birth defects in local communities (IRENE, 1998, p27), a link also raised in connection with electronics factories in the Northern industrial estate in Chaingmai province Thailand (Theobald, 1998). Cases of extreme neglect of workers' occupational health and safety include a report from China of one worker forced to carry on working after a sewing machine went through her finger; there was no safety guard on the machine. According to the Hong Kong Christian Industrial Committee who inspected factories producing for Adidas and Nike, some factories set a safety standard at losing no more than two fingers a month (Kwan, 2000). Other reports from China indicate that workers complained that they were given no protection from machines and reported several accidents involving loss of hands, problems with fumes and dust due to inadequate ventilation, and other occupation-related malaises including skin irritations and headaches (Corporate Watch and Sweatshop Watch, nd b). Similar problems were found in a Barbie/Disney factory in Thailand where workers were responsible for buying their own masks and protective gear (ibid), a common situation in other parts of the world.

The issue of women workers' access to toilets is a frequently raised grievance – though one that is rarely prioritized in union negotiations or in current experience with Voluntary Codes of Conduct. Nicaraguan workers complained about having to ask permission to use the toilet, in addition to restricted breaks and dirty facilities, with some firms putting a maximum of two to four toilet visits for the whole day (MEC, 1998, p16). In Cambodia, women had to seek permission and get a card stamped to go to the toilet (Abrams, 1999c). In Mexico, women cited inadequate toilet facilities and restricted access, with management in somes cases charging monthly fees for toilet paper and soap. In addition, the length of time workers were away from the line was recorded and/or supervisors would accompany workers. In a South Korean owned maquila producing for Kathie Lee (Walmart) in El Salvador, women complained that toilets were often locked and workers were limited to one visit per morning shift and one during the afternoon shift. In Kathie Lee's Mexican subcontractor, there were dirty bathrooms with no toilet paper, no seats, non-existent plumbing and no lighting. In a Guatemalan factory sewing Kathie Lee garments, toilet visits were strictly controlled and armed guards were on toilet duty to hurry up the workers (NLC, 1998).

Another issue which concerns women workers is the (non) availability of a safe and hygienic place for breaks. In Nicaragua, 44 per cent of factories had no designated eating place for workers to use and in 80 per cent no food was available; 49 per cent of firms only allowed half an hour for breaks with a further 15 per cent allowing less than 40 minutes (MEC, 1998).

The access of export workers to social security is another issue where actual empirical evidence is sketchy, though the fact that women workers prioritize this suggests that it is not universally provided. This is a particular issue for women workers because very often they are hired as temporary or contract workers or work in subcontracted workshops outside the formal sector – and thus are excluded from whatever statutory provision prevails.[1] The situation in China is widely seen as problematic, as the majority of export factory workers are rural migrants with no entitlement to social security safety nets or other provisions in the urban location of the factory (Davin, 2001). What workers in these factories report is arbitrary fines and deductions from their pay packets with little access to health care, education for children or housing (Cook, 2000). The fact that many workers do not receive formal contracts and are therefore constructed as outside the regulated labour force leaves many with no legal protection, as well as making problematic ccodes of conduct which depend on the enforcement of national standards.

Absence of freedom of association, the right to collective bargaining and human rights

Workers in many factories are aware that they are constrained from organizing to improve their condition. In January 2001, a group of workers in Puebla, Mexico at the Kuk Dong garments factory which produces Nike sweatshirts for at least 14 US universities began a protest over low wages (£22 for a 50 hour week). Following the arbitrary dismissal of the 20 workers involved, a further 800 workers protested through works stoppages, demanding the reinstatement of these workers and the right to organize an independent union (CAWN, 2001, p11). In Bangladesh workers' attempts at organization have been met with legal action and even jail. Many workers do not dare to try and join a union, not wanting to jeopardize their jobs (WOW, 2001, p5). In 1997, 18 workers were fired at NHI maquila, a Taiwanese plant in Managua's FTZ making denim jeans and dresses for high profile US labels. This was in contravention of the Nicaraguan labour law, but the company has resisted a ruling by the Nicaraguan Ministry of Labour to reinstate the workers (Corporate Watch and Sweatshop Watch, nd a).

Enforced overtime and over-long normal working day

In the Kimoy factory in Guangzhou, China, which produces clothes supplied to Disney, workers were required to work an eight-hour day plus three hours overtime, but are only paid for their overtime if their basic wage, calculated by piece rate, is insufficient to reach the minimum wage (WOW, 2001, p7). Nicaraguan workers reported not receiving payment for overtime and production bonuses and being forced to work irregular hours – that is being sent home early if there is not enough work and then being forced to 'make up' the hours at weekend peak production times. They also frequently worked nine hours without a break. The Wellco factory in Dongguan, China, a Korean factory which produced for Nike, was reported to have an 11-hour standard working day plus two to four hours of compulsory overtime (in contradiction of both Nike's Code of Conduct and Chinese law). Fines were imposed on women refusing overtime – amounting to up to a day's wages – and the quota system was often used to extract prolonged (unpaid) extra working time. Despite a law ensuring work-free weekends, the standard leave was two to four days per month with five days annual leave after working there for one year (Corporate Watch and Sweatshop Watch, nd c). In fact there are numerous reports from factories in China of excessively long working days (11-16 hours) with a six- or seven-day week, with fines being imposed on workers reporting in late or taking time off without permission (NLC, 2000).

Other issues: intensity of work, child labour and homeworking

Other issues raised by model codes, which include regulation of intensity of the workload, no docking of payment for work already carried out and respect for homeworkers, are much more difficult to scrutinize. But such demands, which form part of the conditions for a dignified working environment, also reflect women's perceptions and experiences of employment in export factories which is often characterized by arbitrariness rather than regulation. Where the system of piece rates gives rise to frequent forced overtime and oppressive management regimes, the inability of workers to resist the intensification of their workload is self-evident. With unclear or non-existent contracts and arbitrary rules about fines, deductions and overtime payments, it is too easy for factories to hold back payment for time already worked. The issue of child labour has been raised in other research and in a number of codes of conduct and allied initiatives. It is interesting that women workers should foreground this issue – partly in recognition of the fact that sometimes very young women are being employed and exploited in factories, particularly in Central America and East Asia. Women workers are also aware of the fact that child labour can be used to undercut even their low levels of pay so that regulation of the age of the workforce plays an important role in strategies to improve their own terms and conditions.

The two remaining issues are also significant. The inclusion of a demand to respect homeworkers acknowledges women workers' awareness of the complicated nature of international subcontracting chains and the fact that a lot of work in all countries is outsourced to sweatshops or homeworkers who have little opportunity to organize or press for improvement in their pay and conditions (see Chapter 9 for a detailed discussion of codes of conduct and homeworkers). It is significant that women workers and their organizations highlight this point which has been routinely neglected by mainstream labour unions and is becoming the focus of a great deal of international research and activity.[2] Finally the Nicaraguan model code makes a call for the display and dissemination of codes of conduct – where they exist – to make them accessible to all employees in the factory. Many researchers have reported that even where major importers have agreed a code of conduct, it is very rare for workers to have any knowledge of the existence and provision of such a code. Again, the inclusion of this demand by women workers points to an increasing self-awareness of their role in global production and the importance of organizing at different levels to clarify and extend their rights.

ARE WOMEN WORKERS INVOLVED IN ESTABLISHING THE CONTENT OF VCCs?

Women workers representation in codes of conduct negotiations

The evidence of the poor, and in some cases appalling, working conditions of women involved in export production in the fashion and footwear industries would indicate that women workers have a clear interest in being involved in the discussions about and construction of VCCs, as one avenue to address their grievances and contribute to a just and dignified working environment. It is interesting therefore to review the *process* by which most extant codes have been formulated and the role of women workers, their organizations and representatives within them.

In general, individual firms' codes are drawn up exclusively by the firms themselves with no input from workers' representatives. Usually they are monitored and verified by company appointed auditors. Therefore there has typically been no place for women workers or their interests to be represented in the process.

The design and implementation of multi-stakeholder codes involves a wide range of institutions and organizations including business associations, workers' groups, consumer campaign groups, NGOs, charities, international institutions, governments and churches. A review of 20 multi-stakeholder codes found that five were instigated by industry associations, seven by NGOs, five by workers' organizations and three by state bodies (this includes the ILO and OECD) (Seyfang 1999). However, the instigating body is only the first to sit down at the negotiating table where a code of conduct is to be drawn up – others are invited to join, in order to broaden representation and increase credibility and legitimacy. Of the same 20 codes, 14 have workers' representatives involved with drawing up the code; ten include NGOs, nine represent firms, and seven have some level of state involvement or representation. The workers' interests are exclusively represented by trades unions, and, where this is the case, some or all of the ILO Core Conventions of human rights at work are usually included. However, where NGOs are included, the issues covered tend to go beyond the ILO codes and cover more of the issues of concern to women workers. Non-governmental organizations tend to have been involved in drawing up 'model' codes such as those drawn up by the Clean Clothes Campaign or CAWN (which are described in detail later in this book), rather than those currently being operated by individual companies. The evidence would suggest that women workers' interests are best represented by women's work-based organizations, outside the traditional trade union movement. However there is little evidence of direct representation of women workers at the negotiating table. The exception is the 'Women's Code of Ethics' (the Nicaraguan code) developed by autonomous women's groups in Central America and supported by the Central American Women's Network in Solidarity with Maquila Workers (1999).

Monitoring and verifying codes

Although early initiatives in the field of self-regulation by firms relied mainly on internal assurances that standards were being met (and this is still the case with the toy industry codes), vigorous and effective NGO campaigns have pressed home the need for independent monitoring and verification of compliance. This increases the credibility and legitimacy of a code, as well as the transparency of the process and of the firm itself – factors which all boost public confidence. Of the 20 codes analysed in Seyfang (1999), 11 call for independent monitoring and verification, but it is the codes with NGO involvement which are most likely to insist on this (90 per cent of these do so). However, there are a range of interpretations of these terms, and some offer greater potential for transparency and accountability than others.

The Clean Clothes Campaign, along with its trade union and industry association partners in Europe, has developed a multi-stakeholder model of monitoring. This involves the formation of a Foundation (comprising representatives of the firms, workers' organizations and NGOs) who oversee the accreditation of monitors, certify firms who demonstrate compliance, and investigate complaints (see Chapter 14 for a detailed discussion of the Clean Clothes Campaign). There are a number of issues to deal with in such a model: is the prime purpose one of dealing with complaints, or making inspections? Should firms be allowed to choose the monitors? If they do choose, then the likelihood of accredited NGOs being permitted to undertake inspections is low, and so workers and unions may feel that the process is not at all honest and independent, and therefore be inhibited from raising issues or making complaints (Yanz et al, 1999; Clean Clothes Campaign, 1998).

The Central American code, drawn up by women workers groups, goes further and argues that monitoring should be conducted by workers themselves and by locally-endorsed organizations, so that 'the workers should feel able to completely trust monitors' (CAWN, 1999). These factors all require the education and empowerment of workers to ensure that codes are implemented, and in particular, since there are frequently no trade unions in the export factories, such capacity-building must be carried out without the traditional structure of workers' organizations (CAWN, 1999; Murray, 1998; Green, 1999; Bickham-Mendez and Köpke, 1999).

Are women's priority issues covered in codes of conduct?

Which issues are covered in codes of conduct, and whose interests do they represent? A checklist of issues (ILO conventions and further concerns) covered by the 20 codes surveyed in Table 4.1 reveals that while a majority refer to the ILO Core Conventions, few are comprehensive in their inclusion of those standards. A simple count of the number of codes which include each standard reveals, in common with other studies (Ferguson, 1998; Humphreys, 1999) that the most commonly cited labour standard is that relating to the minimum age of workers (19 of the 20 include this). The widespread inclusion of this standard above all others is possibly due to the high profile given to the controversial subject of child labour in Northern consumer markets, both by campaign groups and the media. Sixteen of the 20 codes included clauses on the rights to freedom of association and to bargain collectively; 15 codes include standards on health and safety, no forced labour, no discrimination, and the provision of minimum wages (though of these, only 11 stipulate the payment of a living wage); 14 codes refer to the hours of work, and in most cases the maximum normal weekly hours are to not exceed 48 plus 12 overtime, in two cases the local legal maximum or norm is to be mirrored instead.

Issues such as the payment of non-wage benefits, health and safety issues, reproductive rights, the provision of information on standards, and banning physical abuse, are more likely to have been included in codes with their origins in workers' organizations, than any of the other types of organization. This is a first indication of the issues which are considered more important by workers than by, for example, NGOs, firms or state representatives.

The issues which are included more often in codes with the input of workers' organization than that of any of the other parties, are: freedom of association and the right to collective bargaining, no discrimination, equal remuneration, health and safety, no physical abuse, information on standards, legally-due non-wage benefits, reproductive rights, and health service provision. Where NGOs are involved, the full set of ILO Core Conventions is usually included.

Moving on from the ILO standards, there are a wide range of other issues covered by codes, which go further and raise different sets of questions regarding whose interests are served, who is represented and what should be included in a code. One concern is that casualization of the workforce is a means of firms avoiding their responsibilities towards workers: security of employment contracts, and the requirement that workers be employed on proper contracts is a standard referred to in only eight of the 20 initiatives. Clauses about information on the standards being adopted being communicated to workers in a meaningful manner (in the local language, posted on notice boards and so on) were found in half of the 20 codes reviewed. The rights to freedom from physical abuse and sexual harassment were included in ten and six of the codes respectively.

Table 4.1 *Content of codes, showing number of multi-stakeholder codes including each issue*

Issue covered	Number
Total number of codes	20
* minimum age (C138)	18
* freedom of association (C87)	16
* right to collective bargaining (C98)	16
* no forced labour (C29, C105)	15
* no discrimination (C111)	15
* equal remuneration (C110)	15
Health and safety	15
Minimum wages	15
Hours of work	14
Living wages	11
No physical abuse	10
Information on standards	10
Security of employment/proper contracts	8
No sexual harassment	6
Non-wage benefits legally due	5
Reproductive rights	2
Other non-wage benefits	1
Health services	1

* ILO Core Convention.
Source: Seyfang (1999).

The remaining issues to be explored widen the scope of labour standards still further, and deal with non-wage benefits and reproductive rights, and as Table 4.1 shows, are far less commonly found in codes. The non-wage benefits in question are entitlements such as sickness, maternity and parental leave, the provision of health or other social services through the company, pension, national insurance and social security payments where applicable, and so on. Five of the 20 initiatives considered specify that the firm must ensure the provision of legally-due non-wage benefits, but did not go into detail about what these might be. Only the Interfaith Centre for Global Corporate Responsibility's (ICCR) model code for investment screening, and the Nicaraguan codes go further and state that additional provision of social and health services respectively must be made. The ICCR code, for example, includes the support and provision of 'essential social infrastructure of child care, elder care and community services' (clause 3.2, p4, in Sajhau, 1998, Part 4, Box 1).

The reproductive rights issue refers to protection of employment following pregnancy, and the prohibition of enforced contraception and pregnancy testing. Only two codes include this clause, the Nicaraguan code and the Labour Behind the Label model code – both of which were drawn up after considerable consultation with women's workers groups. It is notable that none of the codes make specific reference to the prohibition of many of the practices known to be a problem in export-processing factories and discussed earlier in this chapter, namely restriction of toilet breaks, provision of safe transport home for women workers, etc. These kinds of issues are primarily experienced by women workers, and an emerging picture from this analysis is that whereas traditional labour concerns such as union organization are becoming more commonplace in codes of conduct, the topics of particular relevance to women do not get a mention. In addition, many women workers organize themselves outside the traditional union framework, finding more favourable representation in, for example, dedicated women's organizations based around the workplace (Bickham-Mendez and Köpke, 1999).

CONCLUSIONS

The evidence represented here is, of course, not a systematic representation of all global production in all locations. However it does reveal that there is little evidence that the growing insistence of voluntary corporate codes of conduct are pushing working conditions standards and rewards upwards in the direction of a global acceptable norm. Rather, the hierarchy of wage levels in specific sectors are mirrored by a hierarchy in terms of working conditions and standards, in spite of the fact that contractors operating in different locations are in theory bound by the same corporate standards.

A common explanation of this discrepancy is in terms of the failure of adequate monitoring and verification procedures with much disquiet about international accountancy firms carrying out superficial audits which cannot reflect the reality of working conditions or give a voice to the experience of the workforce (see O'Rourke, Chapter 16 in this volume). Thus much effort has gone into discussion of alternative ways to monitor and enforce codes of conduct as well as widening participation and representation from shopfloor workers.

However, the evidence in this chapter points to more deep-seated issues which have as yet to be addressed in the discussion about VCCs. Given that the majority of the workforce in world market factories is female, it is important to consider the implications of the dynamics of gender relations as contractors, subcontractors, management and workers are all drawn together from very different gender regimes and conditions.

East Asian capital has entered export production, particularly in textiles and garments, in a number of South East Asian and Latin American countries because of opportunities to use these countries as export platforms and take advantages of access to European and North American markets. Such management regimes bring with them the labour relations prevailing in those sectors in their countries of origin and previous operation. In the case of East Asia, such labour relations include specific constructions of masculinity and femininity, which are perhaps more commonly enforced by violence and intimidation than is encountered in Western 'regulated' markets.

One of the issues which requires further airing arises from the fact that VCCs are often based on universal notions of minimum standards – but at the same time refer to compliance with national and local legislation. What they often fail to take into account is that complex chains of subcontracting leave women workers subject to the prevailing labour norms of different managements whose norms reflect particular gendered labour practices. Whilst women all over the world report dissatisfaction at the patterns of coercion, abuse and exploitation they face on the factory floors, it is not clear that the management and investors for whom they work have an equal stake in extending universal patterns of workers rights or of recognizing women's particular priorities and issues. Whilst trade union organizations would support women's demands for protection from physical and sexual harassment it remains the case that these are not the issues which are prioritized in most negotiations over the content of codes of conduct. And whilst much of the evidence amassed by observers and reporters focuses on the more extreme abuses of working conditions, it is also important to consider that not only do women workers lack a voice in the process of developing codes of conduct, but also they are frequently excluded from the establishment of national and local labour practices in their own countries to which many VCCs refer.

In these circumstances it is difficult to see the issue of uneven conditions and unenforced standards as purely a result of negligent or inadequate systems of supervision and monitoring or even as cynical public relations exercises by companies keen to promote their reputations with their customers without being serious about changing their practices. In subcontracting production from women workers in low wage countries throughout the world, global retailers simultaneously require two elements in order to maintain their position in a global marketplace. First they require a production system which is inherently flexible given that the kind of consumer-led markets they operate in necessitate rapid responses to nuanced changes in consumer preferences and demand. Hence they require a workforce which can deliver higher levels of production targets when required and that can also be dispensed with when demand is slack. As previous analyses have indicated, women workers have long been the targeted labour force in these circumstances, comprising, as Standing (1999) and others have argued, the quintessential flexible and docile labour force (Elson and Pearson, 1981; Pearson, 1998). What is meant by this is that women workers are likely to have least protection (from labour regulations and organizations) and be most susceptible to management techniques which rely on their compliance to escalating demands without becoming hostile and mounting effective resistance to the pressures to increase productivity. In earlier phases of globalization, this was achieved by American management being involved in direct foreign investment in countries such as Malaysia and Mexico. This management regime used patronizing and familial models and incentives to encourage young women workers to identify with the objectives of the enterprise and with the opportunities to aspire to a feminine global identity rather than a masculine workerist identity. However, the pace of flexible production has accelerated since the 1970s and 1980s and such gentle techniques are unlikely to achieve the high levels of productivity and flexibility required in today's flexible production. It might be time to recognize that international competitiveness currently depends on adopting labour practices which are at odds with the gender equity aspirations of Northern consumers, even when they are successful in getting a number of high profile players to support these. It may, therefore, be time to face up to the fact that achieving gender-equitable labour standards and meeting the aspirations of the women involved in export manufacturing might need to focus on gender relations of management and investment from different parts of the world – a strategy which might require quite different modes of gender politics than those currently being deployed by those pursuing a universalist codes of conduct as a route to the empowerment of women workers.

However the experience of multi-stakeholder codes and the involvement of women's organizations in articulating the priority for women workers provides an important starting point for a more broad-based political approach. The stronger, better organized and resourced these organizations are, the more access they have to research and information, the more able they are to participate in negotiating for (and monitoring) systems, the more likely it is that the particular priorities of women workers will be heard. As many of the case studies in Part 2 of this volume indicate, a vast amount of work on a global scale is being carried out by small networks such as the Clean Clothes Campaign or Homenet International. The support of development organizations and the labour movement in achieving growth and sustainability for these organizations in order that the voices of women workers are clearly heard in the next phase of development of company codes of conduct would be a useful step forward.

NOTES

1   For further discussion of the social policy implications of codes of conduct see Pearson and Seyfang (2001).
2   See Chapter 9 by Brill in this volume and McCormick and Schmitz (2002).

REFERENCES

Abrams, F (1999a) 'Shirts for the fashionable, at a price paid in human misery', *The Independent* 24 September 1999

Abrams, F (1999b) '£1.50 an hour wages in Britain's factories of fear', *The Independent* 27 September 1999

Abrams, F (1999c) 'Gap shorts cost £28, but the hard labour of women who made them costs just 20p', *The Independent* 25 September 1999

Bickham-Mendez, J and Köpke, R (1999) 'Opposing Globalisation: Women Workers' Movements and Hemispheric Competition and Cooperation in the Apparel Industry', mimeo, Central America Women's Network

CAWN (1999) *Central America Regional Workshop: Ethical Trade and Codes of Conduct*, 3-5 May 1999, Las Mercedes Hotel, Managua, Nicaragua, Summary of report, mimeo

CAWN (2001) *Newsletter* No 13, Central America Women's Network, London

Central American Network of Women in Solidarity with Maquila Workers (1999) *A Women's Alternative Code Of Ethics*, CANWSMW, http://www.enternet.de/maquila/maquila01.html, accessed 10 August 1999, copy on file

Clean Clothes Campaign (1998) *Keeping the Work Floor Clean: Monitoring models in the garment industry*, Clean Clothes Campaign, Brussels http://www.cleanclothes.org/1/cleaner.htm, downloaded on 9 April 1999, copy on file

Cook, S (2000) *After the Iron Rice Bowl: Extending the safety net in China*, IDS Discussion Paper 377, IDS, Brighton

Corporate Watch and Sweatshop Watch (nd a) *Blood, Sweat and Shears Feature: Nicaraguan Workers Fired for Union Activity at NHI Maquila*, http://www.corpwatch.org/trac/feature/sweatshops/countries/nica.html, accessed 25 November 1999, copy on file

Corporate Watch and Sweatshop Watch (nd b) *Sweatshop Barbie: Dynamics Factory* http://www.corpwatch.org/trac/feature/sweatshops/countries/thailand.html, accessed 25 November 1999, copy on file

Corporate Watch and Sweatshop Watch (nd c) *Blood, Sweat and Shears Feature: Wellco Factory, a Nike Subcontractor*, http://www.corpwatch.org/trac/feature/sweatshops/countries/clinal.html, accessed 25 November 1999, copy on file

Davin, D (2001) 'The Impact of Export-Oriented Manufacturing on Chinese Women Workers' Paper prepared for UNRISD workshop on 'Women's Employment, Export Manufacturing and Social Policy' September, mimeo, University of Leeds

Elson, D and Pearson, R (1981) 'Nimble Fingers Make Cheap Workers' in *Feminist Review*, No 7 pp87-107

Ferguson, C (1998) *A Review of UK Company Codes of Conduct*, Department for International Development, Social Development Division, London

Green, D (1999) *Views from the South: Conference Report on Ethical Trade*, NGO Labour Rights Network, London

Humphreys, R (1999) 'Exotic Embroiderers or Slaves to Fashion? Representation of Southern Women Textile and Garment Workers in Fair Trade and Ethical Trade Movements in the UK', unpublished MA thesis, Institute of Education, University of London

Humphries, J (1977) 'Class Struggle and the Persistence of the Working Class Family', *Cambridge Journal of Economics*, Vol 1 No 3 pp241-58

IRENE (1998) 'The Factor 'X' in Organizing Women Workers: Casa de la Mujer – Grupo Factor X: women's work in the Mexican maquilas' in *News From IRENE (International Restructuring Education Network Europe)* No 26, (Tilburg Netherlands), pp26-8

Kernaghan, C and Verhoogen, E (1996) *The US in Haiti*, National Labor Committee, http://www.nlcnet.org/Haiti11.htm, accessed 10 August 2000, copy on file

Kwan, A (2000) *Report from China: Producing for Adidas and Nike*, Hong Kong Christian Industrial Committee, http://www.cleanclothes.org/companies/nike00-05, accessed 11 September 2000, copy on file

Lim, L (1990) 'Women's Work in Export Factories: The Politics of a Cause' in I Tinker (ed) *Persistent Inequalities: Women and World Development*, New York and Oxford, Oxford University Press

Maquila Solidarity Network (2000) *Maquilas/EPZ: Mexico Vignette*, http://www.web.net/%7Emsn/5maqmex.htm, accessed 7 June 2000, copy on file

Marchand, M and Parpart, J (eds) (1995) *Feminism Postmodernism Development*, Routledge, London

McCormick, D and Schmitz, H (2002) 'Manual for Value Chain Research on Homeworkers in the Garment Industry' Draft, Institute of Development Studies, University of Sussex, Brighton

MEC (1998) *Diagnostico sobre condiciones socio laborales de las Empresas de las Zonas francas*, Moviminto de Mujeres Trabajadoras y Desempleadas María Elena Cuadra, Manuagua

Murray, J (1998) 'Corporate Codes of Conduct and Labour Standards', International Labour Organization Bureau for Workers Activities (ACTRAV) Working Paper, http://www.ilo.org/public/english/230actra/publ/codes.htm, downloaded 20 July 1999, copy on file

National Garment Workers Federation (2000) News item carried on the Clean Clothes Campaign mailing list 12 September 2000, copy on file.

NLC (1998) *Kathie Lee Sweatshop in El Salvador*, http://www.nlcnet.org/KATHLEE/elsalvinfo.html, accessed 10 August 2000, copy on file

NLC (2000) *Made in China: The Role of US Companies in Denying Human and Workers Rights*, http://www.nlcnet.org/report00/table_of_contents.htm, accessed 8 August 2000, copy on file

NLC (nd) *Young Women in Free Trade Zone Injected with Depro Provera: National Labor Committee Calls for an Investigation*, http://www.nlcnet.org/honduras/depopro.htm, accessed 10 August 2000, copy on file

Pearson, R (1998) 'Nimble Fingers, Revisited: Reflections on Women and Third World Industrialisation in the late Twentieth Century' in C Jackson and R Pearson (eds) *Feminist Visions of Development: Gender Analysis and Policy*, Routledge, London, pp171–89

Pearson, R and G Seyfang (2001), 'New Hope or False Dawn? Codes of Conduct and Social Policy in a Globalising World', *Global Social Policy*, Vol 1, No 1

Razavi, S (1999) 'Export-Oriented Employment, Poverty and Gender: Contested Accounts', *Development and Change* Vol 30 pp653–83

Sajhau, J-P (1998) 'Business Ethics in the Textile, Clothing and Footwear (TCF) Industries: Codes of Conduct', Sectoral Activities Programme Working Paper SAP 2.60/WP.110, ILO, Geneva, http://www.ilo.org/public/english/100secto/papers/bzethics/index.htm, downloaded on 12 April 1999, copy on file

Seyfang, G (1999) 'Private Sector Self-Regulation for Social Responsibility: Mapping Codes of Conduct', Social Policy Research Project Working Paper 1, Overseas Development Group, University of East Anglia, Norwich

Standing, G (1999) *Global Labour Flexibility: Seeking Redistributive Justice*, Macmillan, Basingstoke

Theobald, S (1998) 'Occupational Hazards in the Electronics Industry: Gendered Repercussions', *Gender, Technology and Development* Vol 2 No 1

UNITE (Union of Needletrades, Industrial and Textile Employees) (2000) *Sweatshops Behind The Swoosh*, http://www.uniteunion.org/pressbox/nike-report.html, accessed 30 August 2000, copy on file

Wolf, D (1992) *Factory Daughters: Gender, Household Dynamics and Rural Industrialization in Java, Los Angeles and London*, University of California Press

Women Working Worldwide (1998), *Women Workers and Codes of Conduct: Asia Workshop Report*, WWW, Manchester

Women Working Worldwide (2000a) *International Subcontracting: The New Face of the Garment Industry*, WWW, Manchester

Women Working Worldwide (2000b) *Organising along International Subcontracting Chains in the Garment Industry*, WWW, Manchester

Women Working Worldwide and Central American Women's Network (1999) *Central America Workshop Report on Ethical Trading and Codes of Conduct*, WWW and CAWN, Manchester

WOW (War On Want) (2001) *Sewing it Together: A Practical Guide to Globalisation in the Garment Sector*, WOW London

Yanz, L et al (1999) *Policy Option to Improve Standards for Women Garment Workers in Canada and Internationally*, Status of Women Canada, Ottawa, http://www.swc-cfc.gc.ca/publish/research/yanz-e.html, downloaded on 13 April 1999, copy on file

Chapter 5

Mapping codes through the value chain: from researcher to detective

Stephanie Barrientos

INTRODUCTION

Many codes adopted by Northern companies apply along their value chains in developing countries. The purpose of the code is to ensure that distant suppliers, over whom the buyer has only a certain amount of commercial leverage, meet minimum employment standards. In a globalized economy these value chains can be quite complex, with large numbers of suppliers at different points of the chain applying codes. Conversely, a single supplier could be producing for a number of global buyers, and be subject to a range of codes. The extent to which and how suppliers implement and comply with different codes will depend on a wide range of factors, including their location, size and employment conditions, but a crucial factor is also their position within the value chain.

If we wish to examine employment conditions and the effects of codes of conduct, it is important to understand how the value chain of a particular sector functions, and the position of any individual company within it. Yet in a globalized economy, where many commercial supply relations are fluid, this information is not necessarily easy to come by. Mapping the value chain through which codes operate can be quite a complex process, piecing together a wide range of information from diverse sources, much of it informal or anecdotal. At times it requires the skills of a detective as much as a researcher. Yet understanding the value chain can provide an important framework for evaluating codes, and can give non-governmental organizations (NGOs), unions and civil society organizations important global leverage in trying to influence those codes.

In this chapter I will explore how to approach value chain mapping, and how it can help to analyse the operation of employment codes of conduct. It draws on my own experience of researching gender and ethical trade, in which I have found value chain mapping an essential exercise. The paper does not provide a single 'blueprint' for mapping value chains. These are usually diverse and complex entities that vary between sectors and countries. Rather I aim to provide an overview of how this was done, drawn from my own experience of such mapping of horticulture in Chile and South Africa. From this experience, lessons can hopefully be drawn that are also useful to other studies and researchers in the field.

The next section of the chapter considers in more depth the reasons why a value chain approach can be helpful to analysing codes of conduct. The third section explains value chain analysis in more depth, and why it provides a useful framework for examining codes of conduct. The fourth section considers in practical detail how mapping of the horticulture value chain can be undertaken, and some of the complexities and difficulties involved. The concluding section considers the policy implications of this approach, and how it could help civil society organizations to use codes to improve the position of workers within the value chain.

EMPLOYMENT CODES IN A GLOBAL FRAMEWORK

Codes of conduct have come about in large part as a consequence of the process of globalization. Global sourcing means that a large part of what we consume has been partly or wholly produced in more than one country across the globe. Much labour intensive export production has been located in developing countries, where labour is relatively cheaper than in the North and regulation of employment conditions is often weaker. Global competition has led many developing country producers to promote themselves on the basis of ever lower labour costs, leading to a downward pressure on employment standards. Many workers in export sectors and export processing zones that produce expensive consumer goods themselves experience degrading working conditions, insecure employment and low pay.

Yet globalization has also played a part in the reaction against this situation. Global information flows and civil society organizations, particularly international NGOs and trade unions, have made Northern consumers increasingly aware of the origin of the goods they purchase and the adverse circumstances in which they are produced. Consumer-led campaigns have put pressure on large brand-name companies and retailers to address poor employment standards within their supply chains, or risk adverse exposure that could damage their reputation and market share. Company codes of conduct have thus arisen as a response to the adverse effects of global sourcing on working conditions in developing countries, and operate along many global supply chains (Barrientos, 2000). Examining global sourcing thus helps towards an understanding of both the nature of the employment conditions pertaining in many export sectors, and also helps to assess the operation of codes of conduct aimed at addressing those conditions.

Many case studies have documented the poor employment conditions that exist, especially for women and more vulnerable groups, in global export production in numerous developing countries (see for example Ward, 1990; Stichter and Parpart, 1990; Kabeer, 2000; Wichterich, 2000). Employment is often informalized, 'flexible', temporary, part-time or based on homeworking. Hours are long and overtime is often compulsory. Wages are variable, and can be based on piece rates and other bonus systems rewarding efficiency of output. Employment regulation designed for more permanent work is often avoided through the use of short-term employment, and in export-processing zones employment regulation is often void. Flexible workers rarely have access to social protection such as health and pension benefits. There are large numbers of women workers in this type of employment (Standing, 1989, 1999). This is partly because employers deem them to be more 'submissive' and accepting of poor employment practices. They are also deemed to have the 'nimble fingers' needed to produce high quality products, although this ignores the gender division of labour that steers girls into this type of work from an early age (Elson and Pearson, 1981; Pearson, 1998). Organization amongst flexible workers is often poor or non-existent, partly because the women drawn into this work have no tradition of unionization and unions are unable to relate to their specific needs. But it is also the insecurity of their work and a fear of losing employment that militates against any kind of 'militancy'.

In global sourcing chains, there are many complex factors that affect these forms of employment. Competition between producers for the patronage of global buyers is often intense, and they have to compete on a low cost/high quality basis. Producers themselves are therefore under immense pressure to reduce wages (or introduce systems that maximize wage efficiency) and lower labour costs. Otherwise, they risk losing orders to other firms within the sector, or to other countries altogether. Production orders are often given at very short notice, either because global buyers work on a flexible ordering basis to meet changing consumer demand or because there is no long-term supplier relationship (with the constant risk that buyers will go elsewhere). Firms use flexible work and compulsory overtime to adjust their levels of employment to meet changing orders, or risk making a loss as a result of the volatility of output. Within the complex subcontracting structures that are characteristic of many global sourcing networks, producers often receive only a small percentage of the final price, and pressure on their profitability leads them to offset the risks of production on a compliant and flexible workforce. These factors all contribute to an understanding of the conditions of employment many workers face. Working conditions result from the broader context within which global sourcing takes place.

At a local level, moves to address poor employment practices can be aided by an understanding of the value chain. The more information NGOs and trade unions have, the greater their ability to gain an improvement in working conditions. A mapping of the value chain will help to reveal which codes of conduct an employer is meant to be complying with, and the conditions they contain. It can reveal which agents in the chain are responsible for enforcement, and help to gain access to them as a means of pressurizing employers who fail to comply with the code. It can help to uncover the network of suppliers to a particular buyer, not only in that country but in others as well, and can be used as a basis for developing Southern solidarity movements aimed at addressing employment conditions across producers. It can identify the final destinations of the products, and potentially help to make global contacts with Northern groups in those markets who can put global pressure on companies to address bad employment practices within their supply networks. A value chain approach can therefore provide more comprehensive information about the operation of codes of conduct, and provide leverage to civil society and labour organizations involved in ensuring their compliance.

A VALUE CHAIN APPROACH TO MAPPING

Tracing the supply, or value chain allows us to situate employment within the context of global sourcing, and helps to understand the different factors affecting conditions of work (Barrientos, forthcoming). It facilitates an analysis of the firms operating in a sector locally and elsewhere, the intermediaries that are involved in the export process, the key buyers and markets that the firms supply, and the commercial relationships that exist between all parties in this complex global network of actors. Value chain analysis developed out of the work of Gary Gereffi on *commodity chains* (Gereffi and Korzeniewicz, 1994). He analysed the contemporary development of international trade and production in terms of global commodity chains. These involve the global integration of the dispersed activities linked to production, and linkages between economic agents from raw-material suppliers through to retailers 'in order to understand their sources of both stability and change' (Gereffi, 1994, p215).

The *value chain* approach is an extension of Gereffi's work. Rather than focus on the global production and retailing of commodities as physical entities, the concept of the value chain incorporates a clearer understanding of the analysis of all socio-economic aspects of the functioning of global sourcing. 'The value chain describes the full range of activities which are required to bring a product or service from conception, through the intermediary phases of production ...delivery to final consumers and final disposal after their use' (Kaplinsky, 1998, p13). In other words, trade is no longer through anonymous wholesale markets and intermediaries, but involves a globally integrated network of firms and agents. Whereas in an anonymous free market it would have been extremely difficult to trace the origin of a good or uncover the prevailing conditions of employment in production, the existence of an integrated network of firms in a global value chain facilitates the traceability of final consumer goods. The value chain approach analyses a global production and distribution system in which it has been possible to trace the employment conditions of more distant suppliers in the chain, creating an environment within which codes of conduct could be developed.

Gereffi divided global chains into two types. One was the more traditional 'producer-driven commodity chain' in which large transnational firms with high levels of capital investment play a central role in controlling the forward and backward linkages in the production system. The main types of industries characterized by this type of chain are automobiles, computers and electrical machinery. The other type of commodity chain he characterized as a 'buyer-driven commodity chain', in which large retailers, brand-name and trading companies play a central role in setting up decentralized production networks, often in developing countries. They do not own, but manage and control the outsourcing of the labour intensive production of final consumer goods (Gereffi, 1994, pp215–16). Company codes of conduct covering labour issues are more common in buyer-driven value chains, of the sort identified by Gereffi, than in producer-driven chains. Codes and standards also exist in producer-driven chains but they may be less concerned with labour and more with other aspects such as the environment and management systems. Buyer-driven chains tend to have more low-skilled labour-intensive production, involving a relatively high concentration of employment. Poor working conditions are often found amongst these workers, as employers seek to enhance profitability and competitiveness by reducing both wage and non-wage labour costs at the expense of employment standards. From a purely market perspective, the supply of low-skilled labour is likely to be high in many developing countries, putting a downward pressure on low-skilled wages. All these factors contribute to a downward pressure on employment standards within buyer-driven value chains.

The combination of an integrated production and distribution network, and poor employment conditions has contributed to the development of codes of conduct. Buyer-driven commodity or value chains are predominant in high-value brand-name goods such as Nike and Gap. The brand-name company does not manufacture the good, but attains a high economic rent through its marketing campaigns and creating a brand 'image' that consumers aspire to (Klein, 2000). The brand-name companies themselves do not undertake direct employment in production, but as a result of increased integration of the chain they may nevertheless face risks of exposure because of their links to suppliers operating unacceptable employment standards. Uncovering these links has allowed NGOs and trade unions to campaign more effectively in the North and South against exploitative working practices by many export producers. These campaigns have gained support from consumers with reasonable levels of disposable income, who pay high prices for brand-name goods and are easily shocked at the small percentage of the final price that goes to the workers producing the good. Important brand-name companies and retailers such as Nike, Gap and Levis, which depend on promoting a positive marketing image as a means of competing for market share, have been keen to avoid any adverse publicity they could attract as a result of bad employment practices in their value chains. These campaigns have thus led to the introduction of codes of conduct, in a move by global buyers to ensure their suppliers meet minimum conditions of employment. Codes of conduct are a means of offsetting the potential risks of bad publicity, and of promoting themselves as ethical companies to their final consumers.

Mapping global value chains helps to trace these links but can be a complex process, involving a number of different levels of investigation.[1] Value chains comprise both vertical integration, with forward and backward linkages, as well as horizontal integration across networks of suppliers and agents feeding into global buyers. Some value chains are horizontally integrated, with one company undertaking a number of functions along the chain and a more hierarchical structure. Other value chains are more disaggregated involving arms-length relations between a larger number of firms (McCormick and Schmitz, 2002). Value chains can cross regions and countries and can cross sectors where different inputs are required.

An idealised value chain is depicted in Figure 5.1, reflecting some of these features. Working from the bottom up, employment in global value chains can be very diverse and fluid. It can comprise full-time permanent workers, part-time or casual and temporary workers, homeworkers or contract workers (working via an agent). Fluidity of employment also means that one person could regularly be working for more than one employer within the sector. Moving up the chain, much employment within global value chains is at the level of suppliers or subcontractors that feed the producers making the final good. The supply or subcontract network, which can also change over time, then feeds into a number of producers able to complete the final good. At a horizontal level, the supply and producer network can be spread out regionally and internationally. Producers distribute their products through exporters, importers and other agents, as depicted on the right of Figure 5.1. However, some producer/exporters could be horizontally integrated, undertaking all these functions themselves, as depicted on the left of Figure 5.1. The final goods then go to the main retailers or brand-name companies, where there is usually a higher degree of concentration, with buyer companies able to exert backward controls through the chain. Consumers provide the final point of sale and link within the chain.

An important aspect of value chain analysis is the study of governance within chains. This involves examining the power that different players or companies have over others at different points of production and distribution, and how this can affect the functioning of chains (Kaplinsky, 2000). Within buyer-driven value chains, the large global buyers in the North clearly have

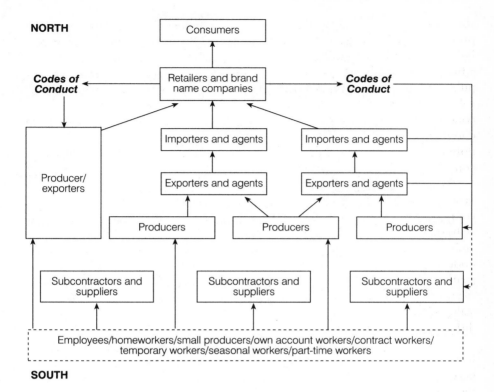

Figure 5.1 *Mapping of a value chain*

enormous power, as they are able to place or remove orders from any firm within their chains. But power relations between firms can be complex as we move along value chains, with some firms more dependent than others or exposed to higher levels of risk.

Most, though not all, codes are applied by companies that are global buyers within value chains. They are usually implemented to meet the conditions of supply to many large global buyers. It is their dominant position as buyers that allows them to implement codes, along with a series of standards relating to production and product specification. The ultimate sanction against non-compliance is the threat of being de-listed as a supplier. Codes are thus only 'voluntary' to the suppliers in that the alternative is to find new outlets.

Monitoring and auditing procedures for codes of conduct are often applied through the use of intermediary agents within the value chain, and their position can affect the stringency with which compliance is enforced.[2] Codes of conduct are monitored and audited either by the buying company, or more often their agents within the value chain (exporters or importers) or by external professional auditors. The costs of compliance, monitoring and auditing of codes are nearly always met by the suppliers themselves (which can be costly in the case of multiple audits), or by other agents within the value chain, rarely by the global buyers themselves. Reflecting the buyers' codes, many exporters and importers also now have their own employment codes, which they make a condition of supply, as a means of assuring large buyers that all the products they handle come up to standard. With the exception of codes implemented by local trade associations and professional bodies, most codes of conduct therefore operate through the value chain, as depicted in Figure 5.1 by the downward arrows.

Many producers supply multiple buyers in different markets, and have to comply with multiple codes that apply varying standards.[3] A more detailed mapping of the value chain should help to reveal the different codes affecting a producer, though in complex supply networks this is not always an easy task. Whilst codes of conduct apply to direct producers of final goods, they do not necessarily apply to subcontractors or homeworkers. Sometimes this layer within the value chain is overlooked, or it is left to the producers themselves to ensure backward compliance. Hence the downward direction of codes to subcontractors in Figure 5.1 is depicted by dotted lines. Understanding the value chain helps to unpack the more complex operation of codes of conduct, and assess more concretely how they might translate in terms of their effect on actual employment conditions.

A value chain approach thus allows us to move beyond the more technical aspects of supply, and to examine the network of actors and activities that facilitate the functioning of global production and distribution. It also allows us to consider the socio-economic context within which value chains operate at different 'nodes' or locations, and the different pressures that can affect the functioning of value chains (Barrientos, 2001). This can help to contextualize company codes operating along value chains. In between a formal Northern company code, and a woman worker producing electrical circuits in Asia, or a seasonal fruit picker in Latin America, lies the complex web of intermediary companies, including distribution agents, producers, input suppliers and subcontractors, all functioning as part of the global value chain. How a company code of conduct is translated in terms of its effect on employment conditions will depend in part on the form this value chain takes. How committed a producer is to any particular buyer will affect the stringency with which their code is implemented. The greater the number of intermediary companies, especially in the case of subcontracting and homeworking, the less likely it is that a producer will have to comply with the code that operates further along the value chain. Translation of a code will also depend on the existence and activity of civil society and labour organizations at different nodes of the chain, and how active they are in pressing for improvements in labour standards. This could be both at the Northern and/or Southern ends of the chain, creating the potential for new forms of global action between campaigning groups.

FROM RESEARCH TO DETECTIVE – HOW TO TRACE INFORMATION ON VALUE CHAINS[4]

From a more practical standpoint, mapping value chains is not necessarily an easy operation, often requiring the skills of a detective as much as a researcher.[5] This section highlights some of the main ways to go about it, and some of the practical problems it is possible to encounter, drawn from my experience of mapping horticultural value chains in South Africa and Kenya (see Barrientos et al, 1999a, 1999b, 2000). One of the main problems in mapping value chains is that there is little central data that can be drawn on. Governments keep statistics on the movement of goods for the purposes of taxation and balance of payments accounts. But there is little central information on the networks of firms that produce these goods, especially when they cross international boundaries. This has to be pieced together by the researcher through multiple sources of information. Much of this information can be commercially sensitive, as firms wish to guard company secrets from their competitors. Firms may also wish to keep information from labour organizations or NGOs in case it is used in a campaign against them. However, by piecing together information from multiple sources, it is possible to trace the connections until, finally, the map of the value chain falls into place, a bit like a detective solving a crime.

When starting out, it is always best to begin by finding any existing articles or publications on the sector by looking for background publications on codes (such as Barrientos et al, 2000; Blowfield, 2000; Diller, 1999; Van Liemt, 1998; Pearson and Seyfang, 2001and Seyfang, 1999). A literature search in a local library, or through a search engine on the internet can help to uncover publications relevant to a particular sector. Having found one or two articles, the references can provide important leads to further publications or material. If it is not possible to gain access to an academic library, references can be traced through the internet, followed by an email or letter to authors, who may have offprints they can send. Another source of written information are NGOs, trade unions and civil society organizations. They often produce so-called 'grey' material that has limited circulation, or old newsletters or reports, which may be of interest. A key source of information on any sector is its trade literature. In most sectors there are trade magazines and publications that inform those working in the trade. These are rarely obtainable in public or academic libraries, but it may be possible to find relevant trade associations (some of which sometimes have small libraries) or business libraries where they can be accessed. Again the internet can be a powerful access to trade publications. Old press articles can also be helpful; they are often short, but can provide important leads.

Another important step is to check all open statistical sources that exist. Government departments usually hold relevant statistics on employment, output, trade and consumer trends. Statistics can also be obtained from international sources such as Eurostat, United Nations organizations (for example the International Labour Organization (ILO) for employment data, UN Food and Agricultural Organization for agricultural data, the World Bank or UN Human Development Report for more general country data). Much of this data can now be acquired via the internet if it is possible to gain access, greatly reducing the time and cost involved in acquiring it. The main problem with this type of data for value chain mapping is that it tends to be fairly aggregate. It can provide a useful overview (for example the quantity of exports of a particular good from a country), but it does not provide any detail of who produced what or how.

The next level of information is from people with knowledge of the sector being mapped such as academics, professional organizations, NGOs or trade unions that are linked to the sector. Contact can be made by email, letter or phone, requesting further information, or via contacts who may help to map the value chain within which these codes are now operating. 'Key informant' interviews with the main individuals within organizations with knowledge of the sector[6] is an important source of data and information. This is where the 'detective trail' really starts. Keeping good notes (or sometimes using a tape recorder) provides an important record of the information given, but also of any leads to other sources of information or individuals 'in the know'. It is often easier to contact someone with the name of an intermediary they know, if the key informant is willing to allow his or her name to be used. Often mapping a value chain can lead to interviewing a pyramid of key informants – it is time-consuming but can give access to invaluable information.

Key players in a value chain are the companies themselves. Initially a wide variety of companies need to be mapped, from the large global buyers through all the intermediary companies they use (importers, exporters and other agents in the chain). The trade literature will have supplied background information on this, and most larger companies now have websites that can provide important information. But this type of global research is not easily undertaken alone. An individual researcher in the South may need to make contact with researchers in the North with similar interests to get a full global picture of the value chain being mapped. Conversely, an individual researcher in the North may need to contact similar minded researchers in the South. Resources and capacity can be a significant constraint to this type of research, but through global networks of researchers (including email lists), and good use of the internet, it can be possible to acquire the relevant information.

Once an overview of the value chain has been acquired, it is necessary to identify the codes that operate within them. Who are the key global buyers, and which are the main trade associations internationally, that are applying codes of conduct? What codes are being used? This information can often be acquired through company websites, or through writing directly to the equivalent ethical sourcing managers within the companies. It can also be acquired through the websites of the main organizations involved in ethical trade such as the Ethical Trading Initiative or Social Accountability International, or through NGOs that campaign around ethical trade (see the Appendix to this volume for a listing of useful websites). It is important to know which agents within the value chain are involved in implementing codes, including importers and exporters. There are also a number of professional companies offering auditing and training services in relation to ethical trade (such as Bureau Veritas Quality International (BVQI), Verité and Société Général de Surveillance (SGS)) that may also have general information about codes. They are unlikely to give commercially sensitive information, but background material from their websites and publications can help in the mapping of codes along the value chain. Regional trade associations may also have codes of conduct of their own, which can be accessed through the web or through trade information sources. Getting to know the codes in operation in the sector is important – what they include, how they are monitored, and how stringent their application is. These provide the standards that companies further down the value chain are being required to observe.

Once a good overview of the chain has been obtained, the ground level research begins. It is important to know both the number and structure of the firms within the value chain, and establish their connections to global buyers or trade associations to know whether or which codes different companies are implementing. This information can be acquired through more formal research methods, such as questionnaire surveys, or it can be done through more informal or participatory methods. For a more detailed examination of alternative research methods see for example Mikkelsen (1995), Nichols (2000) or Casley and Kumar (1988). Which research methods are used will partly depend on the specific type of mapping being undertaken, and the information needed. Ideally it may be best to obtain a list of all companies in the sector (such as from a trade association or Chamber of Commerce), interview or survey a sample of them, and, through the companies, interview or survey a sample of their employees. Realistically, however, many companies may be unwilling to participate, or give access to their workers. In this case, more informal research methods may be required, and the skills of a detective come into play again.

If there are problems gaining access to companies for information, it is necessary to think laterally. Not all companies are the same. Some smaller companies may be willing to give information on their larger competitors or vice versa. Seeking out individual companies that are more progressive on codes and open to giving information can provide a helpful first step. Companies at one point in the supply chain may be unhappy divulging information about themselves, but more willing to give information about companies at another level of the value chain. Companies are made up of people, often with an immense knowledge of their sector, who move around within the commercial world. How the researcher presents him or herself, and the contacts developed can be an important factor in accessing the right person, but persistence can often pay off. Keeping sources of information confidential is often important in the commercial sector, and it is important not to make future research impossible for others. Public information from company reports and registers of companies plus trade literature can provide supplementary information that can be more openly used, allowing the jigsaw to be pieced together. The resulting data and information may not be fully rigorous, but it could provide informative case study material for a mapping of codes within a value chain.

Worker interviews are key when mapping codes of conduct through the value chain. The point of the code is to address employment standards, usually upstream within the chain. The dilemma here is that where conditions of employment are good and meet the code, an employer is more likely to give access to their workforce. It is where the employment conditions are poor that access is more likely to be denied, yet these may be the workers it is most important to interview. However, many workers may be wary of talking, especially if they fear any repercussions from their employer. Alternatively, where interviews have to take place in the evening workers may be exhausted, or busy with childcare and domestic responsibilities – this is especially true for women after work. Sensitivity is very important in worker interviews, both to the personal requirements of the interviewee, and to ensuring confidentiality. The worst possible outcome of researching codes is that a worker interviewed loses their job as a result. This raises important issues regarding the ethics of research, which need to be carefully considered before entering a potentially sensitive situation (see Mikkelson (1995) for a more detailed discussion of these issues).

Accessing workers outside their work location can also be difficult. They are dispersed, many flexible workers change employment regularly and they may live at a distance from their workplace. It may be possible to approach the workers of a company through their trade union, local advice centre or a local NGO using contacts made when carrying out the broader mapping of a chain. Sometimes it is possible to find other places where workers congregate such as churches, community centres, social clubs or even bars. Once contact has been made with a few workers, it may be possible to trace others through snowballing techniques, tracing connections through workers' friends and social groups in the same company producing a network of contacts. There are risks of bias in this approach, for example if the first contact was a trade union representative, she or he may only provide contact with other trade union members. Triangulation may be important, using as many different contact sources as possible, and checking back with key informants regarding the data and information acquired. Workers can provide information about the nature and conditions of employment, which can be essential for assessing codes of conduct. They can also sometimes provide important information about the value chain. They do not usually have access to hard figures, but they may know who their company supplies simply because they put the logo on the product or prepare goods for dispatch or transport.

Once information has been acquired from all these sources, it is possible to construct a fuller mapping of the value chain, and the implementation of codes of conduct along it. This should be able to show which companies are implementing codes, what the standards of these codes are, which suppliers different codes apply to, what the mechanisms of monitoring and verification are, and the extent to which codes are being complied with. Obtaining all this information in a comprehensive way for a complex value chain may be beyond the ability and resources of an individual researcher. Research teams are more likely to get more comprehensive results, especially when working across international boundaries, but that usually requires funding. Even providing a small case study of codes operating in a section of a value chain can provide important insights, and will gradually add to a wider picture of the operation of codes of conduct as future research is compiled.

CONCLUSION – POLICY IMPLICATIONS OF MAPPING CODES THROUGH VALUE CHAINS

This chapter has focused primarily on the nature of value chains, and provided some indications of how to map codes of conduct through a value chain approach. I have examined some of the reasons why there has tended to be a downward pressure on employment conditions within buyer-driven value chains, which are labour intensive and where there is tight competition between suppliers. A consequence of globalization has been increased consumer pressure on brand-name companies and retailers to address this problem. Codes of conduct have tended to be introduced within buyer-led value chains, both to reduce the risk of exposure of bad practice within their value chains, and to promote an ethical image in a competitive consumer market. Mapping buyer-driven value chains can be a complex process, depending in part on how they are structured. I have given some fairly practical advice on how to go about mapping codes within a value chain based on my own experience in horticulture, but different countries and sectors are bound to vary, especially at a local level where there is often diversity. A key point coming out of this chapter, though, is that a value chain approach can help to provide important information about which codes are applying within a particular chain, and what levels of compliance on employment standards particular suppliers are being expected to meet.

I have focused primarily on the research side of mapping codes through value chains. But there are also direct policy implications that can be underpinned by this type of research. First, codes of conduct in themselves are only statements of the standards suppliers are expected to meet. The actual effect of codes on employment conditions will depend on their implementation in diverse local contexts. Given that this usually takes place through the value chain, the more information that exists, the more likely it is that codes will have a positive effect on the workers they are intended to benefit. Companies are not always keen to publicize information on codes, but investigative research can help to provide it. This can enhance the work of professionals and civil society organizations involved in the implementation of codes. Whether they be company representatives, social auditors, NGO and trade union officials, or workers themselves, research helps to enhance transparency in the process of code implementation, and especially in local monitoring and verification, and that can only enhance the process.

Ethical trade came about originally through NGO and trade union campaigns in the South and North. Mapping codes through value chains can enhance global advocacy and campaigns around codes. If done comprehensively, it can reveal the global connections that exist both horizontally across the different networks of suppliers in various countries, and vertically in terms of the particular global buyer they supply. Once these connections are made, it is possible for civil society organizations involved in code implementation in different places to link together. The Clean Clothes Campaign, for example, provides connections between a large number of local organizations in different countries linked to garment production (see Chapter 14 by Ascoly and Zeldenrust). Links between Southern labour organizations can help to strengthen global advocacy aimed at improving labour conditions, especially when linked to Northern NGOs and consumer groups able to exert pressure at the other end of the chain.

Accessing global buyers (directly, or indirectly through a Northern NGO) could give local labour organizations a point of leverage over local employers. It is because of the integrated connections between suppliers and global buyers, as revealed by the value chain approach, that these organizations have been able to apply pressure. This is linked to governance, which is an important aspect of codes operating along value chains. Whilst brand-name companies and retailers rarely own any of their supplying companies, they still exert a high degree of control over them in order to meet all their requirements and specifications.[7] Introducing codes of conduct along their value chains is another form of control that extends beyond the technicalities of production to the conditions of production. Their ability to control suppliers results from their power as large global buyers, and puts them in a strong position to enforce codes. A supplying company is likely to be less worried by the prospect of a strike by its workers (whom it may deem easily replaced), than by the potential withdrawal of a large order by a well-known brand-name company because it is not meeting its employment standards. Mapping the value chain can thus help to provide leverage, and advance the implementation of codes of conduct, with the ultimate aim of improving the employment conditions of large numbers of often vulnerable workers who produce high-value products for global consumer markets.

NOTES

1   More detailed discussion of the issues and methodology is given in McCormick and Schmitz (2002) and HomeNet (2001); here we give an overview, and discuss some of the practical experiences drawn from horticulture.

2   Some companies use professional auditing companies to carry out audits of their suppliers, but often these functions are undertaken by technologists or buyers from importing or exporting companies within the value chain.

3   One firm in China had to undergo 40 audits for codes within three/six months – see Blowfield in Insights 2001.

4   This section provides a very practical overview of how to go about mapping a value chain. Some readers only interested in the broader issues but not wishing to undertake a mapping themselves may wish to skip the section.

5   There are different types of mapping that can take place. Mapping can involve analysing the structure and number of firms involved in a value chain; it can trace prices or value added along the chain; or examine the number and gender of employees at different nodes of the chain. See McCormick and Schmitz (2002) and Kaplinsky (2000) for further information on this. In this paper, we assume a fairly simple mapping of the companies and structure of the chain.

6   Sometimes the main person in an organization may have more knowledge but less time to talk, whereas an assistant or deputy has less information but more time to help.

7   Many suppliers in global value chains already have to meet conditions regarding production specification, the technicalities of production, management systems and the environmental effects of production.

REFERENCES

Barrientos, S (2000) 'Globalisation and Ethical Trade: Assessing the Implications for Development', *Journal of International Development*, Vol 12 pp559–70

Barrientos, S (2001) 'Gender, Flexibility and Global Value Chains', *IDS Bulletin*, Institute of Development Studies, Sussex, Vol 32, No 3, pp83–93

Barrientos, S, S McClenaghan, and L Orton, (2000) 'Ethical Trade and South African Deciduous Fruit Exports – Addressing Gender Sensitivity', *European Journal of Development Research*, Vol 12, No 1

Barrientos, S, A Bee, A Matear and I Vogel (1999a) *Women and Agribusiness Working Miracles in the Chilean Fruit Export Sector*, Macmillan, Basingstoke and St Martin's Press, New York

Barrientos, S, S McClenaghan and L Orton (1999b) *Gender and Codes of Conduct: A case study from horticulture in South Africa*, Christian Aid, London

Blowfield, M (2000) 'Ethical Sourcing: A Contribution to Sustainability or a Diversion?', *Sustainable Development* Vol 9, pp191–200

Casley, D and K Kumar (1988) *The Collection, Analysis, and Use of Monitoring and Evaluation Data*, World Bank Publications, Washington DC

Dicken, P (1999) *Global Shift*, 3rd edn, Paul Chapman Publishing, London

Diller, J (1999) 'A Social Conscience in the Global Marketplace? Labour Dimensions of Codes of Conduct, Social Labelling and Investor Initiatives', *International Labour Review*, Vol 132, No 2, pp99–129.

Elson, D and R Pearson (1981) 'Nimble Fingers Make Cheap Workers, An Analysis of Women's Employment in Third World Export Manufacturing, *Feminist Review*, Spring

Gereffi, G (1994) 'Capitalism, Development and Global Commodity Chains' in L Sklair (ed) *Capitalism and Development*, Routledge, London

Gereffi, G and M Korzeniewicz (eds) (1994*) Commodity Chains and Global Capitalism*, Greenwood Press, Westport

HomeNet (2001) *HomeNet Mapping Pack – A Guide to Action Research with Homebased Workers*, HomeNet, Leeds

Insights (2001) *Richer or Poorer? Achievements and Challenges of Ethical Trade*, March, No 36, http://www.id21.org

Kabeer, N (2000) *The Power to Choose*, Verso, London

Kaplinsky, R (1998) 'Globalisation, Industrialisation and Sustainable Growth: The Pursuit of the Nth Rent', *IDS Discussion Paper* 365, Sussex

Kaplinsky, R (2000) 'Spreading the Gains from Globalisation: What can be learned from value chain analysis', *IDS Working Paper* No 110 May, Institute of Development Studies

Klein, N (2000) *No Logo*, Flamingo, London

Van Liemt, G (1998) 'The Social Policy Implications of Codes of Conduct, with Particular Reference to the Relations between Companies Adopting such Codes and their Suppliers and Subcontractors', Paper presented at the International Workshop on Global Production and Local Jobs: New Perspectives on Enterprise Networks, Employment and Local Development Policy, Geneva, International Institute of Labour Studies, 9–10 March

McCormick, D and H Schmitz, (2002) *Manual for Value Chain Research on Homeworkers in the Garment Industry*, Institute of Development Studies, Brighton, prepared for Women in the Informal Economy: Globalizing and Organizing (WIEGO)

Mikkelsen, B (1995) *Methods for Development Work and Research, A Guide for Practitioners*, Sage, London

Nichols, P (2000) *Social Survey Methods, A Fieldguide for Development Workers*, Oxfam, Oxford

Pearson, R (1998) 'Nimble Fingers Revisited: Reflections on Women and Third World Industrialisation in the Late Twentieth Century' in C Jackson and R Pearson (eds) *Feminist Visions of Development Thought*, Routledge, London

Pearson, R and G Seyfang (2001) 'New Hope or False Dawn? Voluntary Codes of Conduct, Labour Regulation and Social Policy in a Globalizing World', *Global Social Policy*, Vol 1, No 1, pp49–78.

Seyfang, G (1999) 'Private Sector Self-Regulation for Social Responsibility: Mapping Codes of Conduct', Working Paper No. 1, Overseas Development Group, University of East Anglia

Standing, G (1989) 'Global Feminization Through Flexible Labour', *World Development*, Vol 17, No 7, pp1077–95

Standing, G (1999) 'Global Feminization Through Flexible Labour: A Theme Revisited', *World Development*, Vol 27, No 3, pp583–602

Stichter, S and J Parpart (eds) (1990) *Women, Employment and the Family in the International Division of Labour*, Macmillan, London

Ward, K (ed) (1990) *Women Workers and Global Restructuring*, Cornell University, ILR Press

Wichterich, C (2000) *The Globalized Women, Reports from a Future of Inequality*, Zed Press, London

Part Two

Codes of Conduct – Perspectives from Stakeholders in Global Production Chains

Chapter 6

Beyond codes: lessons from the Pentland experience

Lesley Roberts

Pentland – starting out

Pentland is a group of footwear, clothing and sports businesses, owning a number of international sports and leisure brands and licences. Some brands are internationally traded, such as Speedo International, Ellesse, Kickers, Berghaus, Mitre and La Chaussure Lacoste. Pentland also supplies own-label footwear and clothing to well known high street retailers, mostly in the UK.

The profile of Pentland's supply chain has changed a great deal over the last decade, with the major part of its product now being made outside Europe, mainly in South and East Asia. Many of the products are labour intensive and cost pressures within very competitive markets have driven production to low-cost countries.

When, in 1995, Pentland's Chairman, Stephen Rubin, was elected President of the World Federation of the Sporting Goods Industry (WFSGI), he became aware of the criticism being directed at the sports goods industry in relation to conditions in supply chains. His response was to set up a WFSGI Committee on Ethics and Fair Trade (CEFT), which convened a conference in Switzerland and invited relevant governmental, United Nations and welfare organization representatives, among others, to consider the issues with industry representatives and advise on how best to address them. The conference resulted in a number of CEFT initiatives, including the adoption of a WFSGI Code of Conduct – Guiding Principles.

Parallel to these developments, Pentland's policies (otherwise known as Code of Conduct)[1] concerning human rights and the environment were developed and agreed by the Board in 1995 and 1996. At this time, the WFSGI was taking a very active role in developing an industry response to the issue of child labour in the football stitching industry in Pakistan. Pentland as the owner of Mitre, which provided the official ball for the English Premier League and the FA Cup, was directly involved in these discussions.

Pentland is now an active member of the Ethical Trading Initiative (ETI) and the WFSGI and, through its holding company Roberts Stephen Holdings plc, it is a corporate member of the International Business Leaders Forum (IBLF).[2] It plays an active part in the development of policies and programmes within all these organizations. Its corporate policies have recently been revised in the light of the experience of the last five years.

CHILD LABOUR IN THE FOOTBALL INDUSTRY IN PAKISTAN

In 1995 there were a number of media reports in the United States concerning abusive child labour in the soccer ball industry in Sialkot, Pakistan. Later that year the Human Rights Commission of Pakistan (HRCP) documented child labour in a number of sectors, including footballs produced in and around Sialkot, Punjab. The HRCP acknowledged that the worst problems were in the tanning, surgical instruments and carpet sectors, since the work in these sectors was intrinsically hazardous to young workers. (Human Rights Commission of Pakistan, 1995). An international campaign directed at the international sporting goods industry was initiated by the trade union movement with the support of some US-based non-governmental organizations (NGOs).

Pivotal to later events was a meeting hosted by the WFSGI in Verbier in Switzerland in November 1995 of the industry, United Nations (UN) bodies and a number of NGOs on hazardous and exploitative child labour (WFSGI, 1996).

It was soon clear that unilateral action by some of the larger companies would in no way respond to the root causes of child labour in the Pakistan industry. The main root cause was identified as poverty (SCF, 1997), poor schooling provision and low parental awareness of the value of education, especially to girl children. Just removing the children from stitching footballs would not necessarily reduce overall levels of child labour and in the worst case might result in children taking more hazardous work. A more coordinated response was required, and partnerships developed with social groups to ensure that change would ultimately benefit the communities affected and consequently the children. The WFSGI brought together an international partnership of UN agencies and the non-governmental sector with local industry to eliminate child labour from the industry, taking into account economic and social factors.[3]

From 1997, the Sialkot Chamber of Commerce and Industry, the International Labour Organization (ILO), Save the Children Fund (UK) and UNICEF, with local organizations, have initiated a number of programmes, for example workplace monitoring, micro-credit, women's training, teacher training, improving school infrastructure and governance. Funding has come from the industry (local and foreign) and the US and UK governments. These programmes have largely removed children from football stitching (SCF, 2000). More importantly, however, the programme has positively affected other sectors, such as surgical instruments, where children have been found performing hazardous work.[4]

LESSONS LEARNT

The Pakistan programme, however, has raised a number of issues and hopefully some lessons have been learnt:

- Problems are often complex and require a range of initiatives for impact and sustainability, often provided by a number of different agencies (government, non-governmental, industry).
- Programmes involving different partners need time to develop so that the different agendas can be appreciated and roles tailored.
- Programmes requiring social change need to be implemented over years rather than months.
- Good social research is an absolute necessity, especially in the area of child labour and homeworkers, many of whom are women. These groups of workers are almost by definition vulnerable and the impact of any programmes on their well-being has to be part of any ethical purchasing strategy (HomeNet, 2000). In the case of Sialkot, the initial strategy to bring homeworkers into large units, which could be inspected, marginalized many women workers. Many women were not able to work in the units because of domestic responsibilities and for cultural reasons. The programme was subsequently amended to allow small home units to be inspected under the programme, but the damage had been done.
- The media pressure to deliver on 'no child labour' meant in reality that young workers were deprived of relatively well-paid work, to avoid any possibility of photos being taken of young people stitching balls.
- Research must be culturally and gender sensitive for effective programme design (SCF, 1997; Saeed, 1998).
- Programmes must take place within the context of the market. The cost of improvements, if implemented over a short time period, can affect prices adversely, possibly encouraging business to move elsewhere (Cummins, 2000).
- The monitoring programmes are often private and not public initiatives and, as such, costs are born by the manufacturers; these costs can be quite onerous if added to the costs of improvement programmes. At the moment there is little discussion as to whether this is an ethical issue or not.

Several lessons were learnt by Pentland:

- Pentland had to be pro-active and identify for itself areas of poor labour conditions and conduct research in partnership with local agencies. Public campaigns demand an instant response which is often not in the best interests of workers, communities and the industry itself;
- Pentland had to prioritize for maximum impact;
- Pentland, being a relatively small player in the market and a minority purchaser in many factories, needed to develop programmes/projects with a range of partners which would begin to impact on the sector or community in a sustainable way – factories were much more likely to improve conditions if they thought that others were also doing so; using peer pressure to encourage change was likely to be more effective in the long run;
- improvements would have to be 'step by step' to keep costs down and engage the factories, which have their own priorities to take into account, not least to keep their business going;
- although the public relations aspect of 'business standards' was important, the importance of doing the 'right thing' was more important – in the long run Pentland would enhance its reputation by the success of the partnerships and programmes rather than any 'quick fixes'.

FACTORY MONITORING

Identifying the supply base

Identifying a company's own supply base might seem to be a straightforward procedure, but, in fact, for most companies it is an ongoing problem. Pentland has 14 operating companies, operating relatively independently, sourcing a wide variety of products, at a range of price points in many countries around the world. Pentland is the sole or major customer from very few factories. A large number of agents are involved. The base unit for Pentland is a factory unit, defined as subject to a single personnel department, having unified production procedures and so on. In existing databases within the Group this 'unit' was usually not identified, instead there were data on a company, on an agent, maybe a factory complex. For one supplier there might well be different factories, possibly in different countries.

The database of suppliers will always be a little out of date because of changes in the supply base. Some operating companies have a fairly static supply base, others, for example in the fashion industry, change suppliers more often.

The other problematic area was the extent to which subcontractors would be audited, especially in the case of processes such as printing, embroidery, dyeing, which might only be carried out for certain items and not all the time.

Of particular concern were those processes which would be deemed hazardous, like printing (chemicals) and embroidery (noise) and where work is subcontracted to small workshops and homeworkers.

China presents unique problems concerning the name of the factory. It may have two English names; the Pinyin (romanized Mandarin) version of the Chinese name or the English translation. The versions may be different depending on the writer's/translator's preference. One factory site might have two registered factories because of local rules or international quota regulations. A further issue is identifying the owner(s) of factories; the legal owner might be different from the actual owner, again because of local laws governing factory ownership. This has implications for assigning legal responsibilities for health and safety in the factory.

The nature of the business relationship

It was established early on that the business relationship was a critical factor. If the business relationship was weak (business very small, business falling, no regular orders) then the factory had very little incentive to make the improvements that were suggested. Other factors which need to be taken into account, and which will govern implementation of the policy, are:

- *Product* – high technology and skilled workforce or low technology and unskilled workforce. High technology will mean a limited choice of supplier; the workforce is likely to be relatively stable, have a better level of education and be better paid.
- *Size of factory unit* – a larger unit will have dedicated human resource people, better management systems, medical facilities and so on. Labour laws and health and safety regulations often are less rigorous for smaller production units.
- *Country* – it would not be fair to expect factories in countries that are at an early stage of industrial development to exhibit the same levels of management and systems as countries which have reached a high level of industrial development. The standards are the same, factories and countries are just at different stages of implementation.
- *Ownership of factory* – a state owned factory cannot instantly make a decision to invest in new machinery, similarly in joint ventures the partners need to agree on investment and management decisions. Management that has its roots in the local community is more likely to be responsive than if they are foreign.
- *Worker profile* – worker representation is likely to be weak if the majority of the workforce is young, female and migrant, than if it is more mature, male and with roots in the local community. Some countries have well-developed worker representative organizations, in others independent trade unions are not allowed.

- *Membership of employer bodies* – many employer organizations have taken up the issues of corporate social responsibility and factories are much more responsive if they feel that they are all subject to similar scrutiny.

Starting to apply standards

Pentland has designed a modular system made up of six modules:

1 Fire Safety
2 Hazardous Substances
3 Machine Safety
4 Worker Health
5 Pay and Hours
6 Young Workers

The application of this system is the responsibility of the operating companies. The modules encourage the factories to create systems and records. Therefore great importance is placed on such things as fire certificates, fire drill documentation, accident book, machine maintenance records, personnel records and so on.

A wide variety of Pentland employees and associates visit the factories – designers, technicians, quality controllers, agents, contract negotiators, as well as senior executives – and everyone is expected to be aware of the programme and report any major problems they observe. In practice, however, there is usually one person who has the main responsibility for implementing the modules in their most important factories, in a progressive way, beginning with Module 1.

Reviews are carried out by the Group Business Standards Department (BS) in coordination with the operating company and covering the whole of the Ethical Trading Initiative Code,[5] within the constraints of all audits, time, complexity of the issues, legal, infrastructure and context. Most reviews include an independent element by using independent organizations for the worker interviews and/or for health and safety.

PERSISTENT PROBLEMS

There are a number of external factors which tend to impact on working conditions in clothing, footwear and sports good production around the world (see Box 6.1). As a result, a number of problems occur among developing country suppliers. Persistent problems are most common where the general standard is non-compliant, that is that the problems are across the board and not just in one factory. There is no advantage for the factory to improve since it will not give it any significant advantage over its competitors and might, indeed, price the factory out of the market. This is particularly the case if most of its

BOX 6.1 EXTERNAL FACTORS INFLUENCING WORKING CONDITIONS

Global economics – We buy from suppliers that can deliver a quality product, on time and at a competitive price. Increasingly, production of goods with a high labour content is located in the developing world, especially in the Far East. Factories are located in countries where labour is cheap. Suppliers are under pressure to keep prices down as well as having to deliver on quality and with short lead times.

Management – The management of many factories, especially in the developing world, is already struggling to keep up with customer demand in terms of lead times, delivery and quality. Investment in people (training) and people management are low priority. Productivity levels are often low.

Worker representation – Many workers are young and from rural areas. They are new to factory working. They have little or no experience of trade unions or ideas of how to negotiate for better conditions. In some countries trade union activity is poorly developed; in some countries trade unions are highly politicized; in some countries it is illegal to organize independent trade unions.

Some factories do have unions but their effectiveness is limited in a number of ways:

* selection of representatives is not open;
* representatives are not clear about their role and function;
* there is poor reporting back to workers;
* they are co-opted by management or managers are members.

Workers do have views on improving conditions in the factory but they lack the means to communicate these ideas to management. Too often they are left out of discussions on improving conditions.

Government infrastructure – Whilst most countries have the legal framework to protect workers' rights, few countries have adequate inspectorates to monitor the implementation of this legislation and prevent abuse. In some countries the local authorities fear that foreign investment will just move elsewhere if they enforce the law too rigorously.
    Companies can play a role here by working together with international organizations, trades unions and governments to improve awareness and performance of inspectorates so that the local law is effective.

Consumer demand – Competition is fierce in clothing and footwear manufacturing and consumers are very demanding on price and quality. In certain markets fashion trends are changing, not just from season to season, but within the season. Lead times, especially with merchandise from the Far East, can be very short; it is estimated that lead times at the factory for unbranded shoes might only be 45–60 days, for branded shoes this can be extended to 90 days.

other customers are not at that time requesting such standards. The type of issue where this is a problem includes forced and excessive overtime, homeworking and the use of certain chemicals.

Most issues are complex and require action by many different organizations for an effective and sustainable improvement. Excessive working hours, for instance, is a particularly difficult problem to tackle, especially if Pentland is not a major customer and where changes could only go ahead with the agreement of other customers. Insisting on an immediate reduction in excessive overtime hours can leave workers unable to earn enough money to meet their needs. Workers may leave en masse to work in another factory which is not even attempting to improve working conditions and where they can continue to work long hours and receive higher wages.

In the case of chemicals in the workplace, Pentland has identified a number of external issues which inhibit progress (see the later section on a project in Vietnam). All of these issues require action by many different actors – industry, unions, governmental and non-governmental institutions – working together to provide a coordinated response with scarce resources. Footwear and apparel are, after all, not the most hazardous industries in most countries; in the UK, the construction, transport and agricultural sectors top the league tables for death and serious injury (HSE, 1998/9).

PARTNERSHIPS IN ACTION

Vietnam

Pentland companies source footwear and apparel from Vietnam. As a result of quotas placed on China, Vietnam has now become the third largest exporter of shoes to Europe, behind China and Indonesia. Exports, at only 750,000 pairs in 1990, rose to roughly 140 million pairs by 1998, from about 170 enterprises, employing around 500,000 workers, mainly women.[6]

Pentland identified a number of external factors which were inhibiting improvements in working conditions in the area of chemical safety, such as:

- poor knowledge of the substances used;
- little or no information from suppliers on hazards associated with the chemicals;
- poor management of the hazards presented;
- little or no training for workers on safe handling techniques;
- inappropriate fire training for dealing with chemical fires;
- lack of local supplies of protective equipment or appropriate containers;
- factory medical staff ignorant of potential occupational health effects of particular jobs;
- low awareness of occupational safety limits for the chemicals used.

Although Pentland could offer training to factories to improve matters, this would need to be backed up by the appropriate institutions in order to be sustainable.

Nike and adidas-Salomon had already begun working in this area and, with Pentland, a programme of action was started in 2000 in cooperation with the Vietnamese government and others[7] under the management of the Prince of Wales Business Leaders Forum and the Vietnam Chamber of Commerce and Industry. Funding comes from the brands and the UK Government.

The programme's aims are:

• improving conditions in the workplace – in particular with regard to the choice, storage, handling, use and disposal of chemicals used in the manufacturing process;
• reduction of noise, fumes and dust, thereby providing a healthier and safer environment for workers in the footwear industry.

India

In 1997, Christian Aid published a report on child labour in the sporting goods industry in Jalandhar (State of Punjab) and Meerut (State of Uttar Pradesh) in India. They estimated that about 10 per cent of the total labour force was made up of children - about 25,000. Although the sporting goods industry covers a number of sports and different items (cricket bats, shuttle cocks and so on) the ensuing campaigning and research focused on the stitching of footballs. Mitre, a Pentland company, was again implicated, and has taken a lead role in promoting a programme of action.

The ILO, together with the Federation of Indian Chambers of Commerce and Industry sponsored a study by the VV Giri National Labour Institute of child labour in the football industry in Jalandhar, which was published in September 1998 (VV Giri National Labour Institute, 1998). The report indicated that children (under 14) involved in the industry and who were *not* attending school numbered under 1500. The Sporting Goods Foundation of India was established by the major exporters in Jalandhar to address this and similar social issues, with 0.25 per cent of export revenues as their financial contribution.

The ILO proposed a similar initiative in February 1999 to the one undertaken in Sialkot. This was rejected by the Government of India, supposedly because the size of the problem was small compared to other situations and the work was not considered particularly hazardous. The Indian Government was also reported as being unhappy with the funding for the monitoring programme through the International Programme for the Elimination of Child Labour (IPEC) of the ILO.

In July 1999, a meeting was held in Jalandhar of the major exporters in cooperation with the World Federation of the Sporting Goods Industry,

Pentland Group, Mitre, adidas-Salomon, UNICEF, SGS, Save the Children Fund and CRY (an Indian NGO) to agree a programme of action. A two-year agreement between the SGFI and Société Général de Surveillance (SGS) on monitoring was signed in July 1999. The Federation Internationale de Football Association (FIFA) is supporting the project.

The Sporting Goods Foundation of India (SGFI) established a Steering Committee with the participation of UNICEF and Save the Children, UK. SGS was contracted to undertake monitoring. The SGFI has been collecting 0.25 per cent of export values from the participating manufacturers and FIFA has committed funding for three years.

The monitoring programme of stitching units and centres began at the beginning of 2000. Very few children have been identified as 'stitching and not going to school'. The programme needs to clarify the criteria for children who are stitching as to when this affects their education. However, it is clear that there are many children in and around Jalandhar who have either never started school or who dropped out very early and who are possibly working in other sectors.

The Punjab Government is participating in the National Child Labour Project and has approved that SGFI take responsibility for three of the 25 schools to be established for the re-integration of children into the school system. The SGFI has contracted the Centre for Research in Rural and Industrial Development (CRRID) to conduct an awareness-raising programme in and around Jalandhar, using posters, magicians, meetings and other means of reaching those involved. SCF is also assisting in teacher training (Sports Goods Foundation of India, 2001).

GOING FORWARD

The application of codes of conduct to supply chains is a relatively new phenomenon and methodologies are still being worked through. It is unclear the extent to which the factory workers, the business, the industry and the wider community will benefit in sustainable ways. It will be some time before any impact can be properly assessed and the relative merits of certain approaches evaluated. What is clear is that it is a very complex undertaking for most companies, requiring resources and commitment at all levels of the company to push improvements through.

NOTES

1   There are a number of terms that are used to denote a 'code of conduct', such as 'terms of engagement', 'global sourcing principles', 'human rights policy'.
2   The Prince of Wales Business Leaders (PWBLF) recently changed its name to International Business Leaders Forum (IBLF).

3   Partners' Agreement to Eliminate Child Labour in the Soccer Ball Industry, Atlanta February 1997.
4   WFSGI newsletters August 1997–January 2000, IPEC–ILO programme documents.
5   The Ethical Trading Initiative (ETI) brings together companies, trade unions and NGOs to identify and promote good practice in the implementation of corporate codes of labour practice. For more details on the ETI, see Chapter 15 by Blowfield. For the complete ETI Code see http://www.ethicaltrade.org
6   Dan Owen and Ken Kaplan, Footwear Industry Toxic Chemical Health and Safety Project – Vietnam, DFID, April 1999.
7   The members of the Steering Committee are: International Business Leaders Forum, Vietnam Chamber of Commerce and Industry, Action Aid, adidas-Salomon, Pentland Group, Environmental Resources Management, Friedrich Ebert Stiftung, HUNEXCO, International Federation of Red Cross and Red Crescent Societies, Mekong Development Facility, Ministry of Health, Ministry of Labour Invalids and Social Affairs, Ministry of Science Technology and Environment, Ministry (Directorate for Standards and Quality and Vietnam Standards Institute), National Institute of Labour Protection, National Institute for Occupational and Environmental Health, Nike, Société Général de Surveillance (SGS), Vietnam General Confederation of Labour, Vietnam Leather and Footwear Association.

REFERENCES

Cummins, E (2000) *The Pakistan Football Industry: Trends and Prospects*, UK Department for International Development, London
HomeNet (2000) 'The Position of Homeworkers', paper given at a workshop organized by the Natural Resources Institute and the University of Hertfordshire Business School, Emerging Issues in Ethical Trade – The position of Marginalised Groups, March
HSE (1998/9) *Labour Force Survey 1998/99*, Health and Safety Executive
Human Rights Commission of Pakistan (1995) *Child Labour in Pakistan – Sialkot/Kasur*, Rights of the Child series: No 9, Lahore
Saeed, A T (1998) *Women's Stitching Centres – Exploring Avenues*, Sialkot Implementation Team/Sialkot Child Labour Project
SCF (1997) *Stitching Footballs: Voices of Children in Sialkot, Pakistan*, Save the Children, May
SCF (2000) *Children Labour Project Sialkot, Social Monitoring Report, Project Progress Report April–June 2000*, Save the Children, Sialkot/Islamabad
Sports Goods Foundation of India (2001) *Newsletter April 2001*, Jalandhar
VV Giri National Labour Institute (1998) *Child Labour in the Sports Goods Industry, Jalandhar – A Case Study*, Noida, India
WFSGI (1996) *The Way Forward*, Conference on Human Rights, World Federation of the Sporting Goods Industry

Chapter 7

The international trade union movement and the new codes of conduct

Dwight W Justice

OLD CODES AND NEW CODES

International trade union organizations have long been concerned about the power of multinational corporations (MNCs) and were among the first to demand codes of conduct addressing the behaviour of international business. In the 1970s trade unions joined the calls for a United Nations Code of Conduct for Transnational Corporations. The International Confederation of Free Trade Unions (ICFTU) closely followed the United Nations (UN) Commission on Transnational Corporations and provided it with expert advisors as well as detailed comments on its draft code.

Although negotiations for the UN code stalled and the effort was shelved in 1992, the 1970s produced two codes. Trade unions were involved in both. Through the International Labour Organization (ILO), trade unions participated in the formulation of the Tripartite Declaration of Principles concerning Multinational Enterprises and Social Policy, which was adopted in 1976. Through the Trade Union Advisory Committee (TUAC) to the Organisation for Economic Co-operation and Development (OECD), trade unions influenced the development of the OECD Guidelines for Multinational Enterprises, adopted in 1977. For well over 20 years international trade union organizations sought to make the ILO Declaration and the OECD Guidelines work by promoting them and by using their follow-up procedures.

Thus, when the issue of codes of conduct emerged again in the first half of the 1990s, the international trade union organizations viewed them in the light of their extensive experience with the UN, ILO and OECD codes and in the

BOX 7.1 THE INTERNATIONAL CONFEDERATION OF FREE TRADE UNIONS

The International Confederation of Free Trade Unions (ICFTU) is the world association of national trade union centres. The ICFTU has 221 affiliated organizations in 148 countries and territories representing 156 million workers. Membership is open to free trade union organizations, that is to bona fide trade unions independent of outside dominating influence such as by employers, governments or political parties. Free trade unions derive their authority and legitimacy from their members and have a freely and democratically elected leadership. ICFTU affiliates agree to accept the aims and constitution of the ICFTU. The ICFTU is governed by representative and democratic structures and is not dependent on outside financing. Central functions of the ICFTU include the defence of trade union rights, the representation of the workers' interests with international organizations, and the building and exercise of global trade union solidarity.

International Confederation of Free Trade Unions
Boulevard du Roi Albert II 5, B-1
B-1210 Brussels
Belgium
Tel: (main switchboard): (32 2) 224 0211
Fax: (32 2) 201 5815
Email: internetpo@icftu.org
www.icftu.org

context of subsequent developments. These developments included the emergence of a serious international debate over trade and labour standards and the emergence of new ways in which trade union organizations were beginning to engage multinational companies.

The codes issue re-emerged when companies began to adopt them. These companies were involved in the marketing or manufacture of brand-name goods produced internationally through outsourcing. Their codes of conduct concerned the labour practices of their suppliers and subcontractors. These unilaterally-adopted company codes of international labour practice were fundamentally different from the codes of the 1970s. Although the ILO and OECD codes were voluntary, they are part of an international framework of principles agreed to by governments, employers and trade unions and recommended to companies. Indeed, when formulating the earliest of these new codes, most companies ignored established standards in favour of creating their own.

In the 1970s, the views of the international trade union movement were often close to those of the governments of many developing countries which were concerned over what they perceived as a threat to their sovereignty by the growing power of MNCs. Indeed, one purpose of the international instruments during this period was to protect the sovereignty of host countries by defining the responsibilities, including the social responsibilities, of international business.

By the 1990s, it was evident that the challenges to workers' rights presented by subcontracting, licensing, joint ventures, the use of Export Processing Zones and other changes in the organisation of business and international production were at least exacerbated by the international competition among developing country governments to attract foreign direct investment (FDI). The companies adopting codes were responding to negative publicity generated by reports of dangerous working conditions, inhumane working hours, starvation wages, brutality and the widespread use of child labour involved in the production of clothing, footwear, toys and other labour-intensive manufacturing, as well as in the production of agricultural products. Their purpose in adopting these codes did not include protecting the sovereignty of governments but was to address situations created by the failure of national governments and of the international community to enforce acceptable labour standards.

The new codes of conduct were considered at international trade union meetings including the ICFTU/ITS Working Party on Multinational Companies and the ICFTU Economic and Social Policy Committee. In November 1998, a joint ICFTU-ITS-TUAC technical meeting on codes was held in Brussels. In the early debates over the new codes, the views of trade unionists varied considerably but many trade unionists had no opinion. Some trade unions, together with non-governmental organizations (NGOs), supported campaigns demanding that companies adopt codes. Some of the earliest codes had been adopted by companies which had consulted trade unions. Other trade unions dismissed the codes as empty public relations exercises. Many trade unionists, including many in developing countries, were unaware of their existence. As codes became better known, there continued to be differences among trade unionists in their perceptions of their likely effect. Some trade unionists saw the new codes as the privatization of labour law and a means of avoiding regulation. Others saw in the new codes potential for assisting governments in developing or applying law. Some trade unionists saw the new codes as a dangerous substitute for collective bargaining and believed that they would be used by business to avoid trade unions. Others saw in the new codes potential to create space for workers to exercise their rights. In the end, all of these seemingly contradictory perceptions proved true to one degree or another.

The first challenge for trade unionists was whether to involve themselves at all. Although the company pledges were rarely credible, the case for taking the new codes seriously was strong. The new codes were about labour practices and therefore of fundamental interest for trade unions. More importantly, the new codes were addressing two of the long-held trade union concerns arising out of the conduct of international business. The first was that MNCs seemed to have international policies on almost every aspect of their business except for labour practices, an aspect they insisted must be dealt with at the national or local level where law and practice could be taken into account. The new codes, then, had a radical element. They represented the formation and promulgation of international labour policies by MNCs and, as such, addressed a long-time trade union goal.

The second way in which trade union concerns were being addressed involved the scope of application of the codes. The trade union concern was that employers were using subcontractors to avoid the obligations of the employer while, through their economic power, they controlled the conditions of work. Where workers were permitted to bargain collectively this meant that the workers did not have access to the real decision-makers. In addition, the organization of labour-intensive manufacturing had evolved into lengthy production chains and increasingly elaborate systems of subcontracting that were removing workers from any legal protection. The new codes were meant to apply to the labour practices of the company's suppliers and subcontractors. They were an acknowledgement by the companies adopting them of at least some responsibility for the working conditions of the people who do their work whether they were employees or not. That many companies had this moral responsibility is what trade unions had been saying all along.

Not all trade unionists appreciated the positive aspects in these two characteristics of the new codes. These aspects, their international dimension and their scope of application beyond the employment relationship, were what made the new codes truly new. Questions over how to implement or monitor the new codes as well as the need for verification arise because of these two characteristics. For instance, the international characteristic raises questions about the application of codes in countries governed by repressive regimes. It also raises the question about whether there are appropriate partners that could negotiate codes with companies. How one enterprise can compel, oversee or prove code compliance of another enterprise raises lots of new, interesting and controversial questions. There are, however, few real questions concerning the responsibility of any enterprise towards its own employees or the ability of any enterprise to fulfil this responsibility.

The trade union experience is that workers are protected only by the application of good labour laws and through their self-organization and collective bargaining. Trade unionists have no reason to believe that philanthropy or business ethics alone would do any good unless they related to this fact. It was clear early on that many businesses wanted the new codes to become substitutes for regulation and use them to avoid trade unions. For trade unionists, the overriding consideration was how the new codes could promote the application of good laws and how they could be used to help workers join or form trade unions.

It was clear that, in order to avoid the new codes becoming substitutes, business must not be permitted to invent its own standards. The next section shows how international labour standards were introduced into the code debate. This chapter will subsequently consider two of the more controversial issues in the debate over the new codes. These issues are whether codes should be negotiated and who should monitor them. Here the focus will be on how the two characteristics of the new codes pose challenges in developing a trade union response. The chapter concludes by noting that the new codes, noted above, have become part of a larger debate over corporate social responsibility (CSR) and how this debate has renewed interest in one of the 'old codes' of the 1970s.

INTERNATIONAL STANDARDS

One now widely-accepted contribution of the international trade unions was that code provisions should be based on minimum internationally recognized standards, explicitly cited, and should reflect all of the fundamental human rights standards of the ILO. Initially, the international trade union movement became directly involved with codes of conduct as a result of ongoing activities in the area of health and safety and then through its long-standing campaign against child labour.

The first instance concerned a campaign directed at the international toy industry that had its origins in the May 1993 factory fire at the Kader toy factory in Thailand. In November 1993, the ICFTU coordinated an international trade union mission of inquiry to Thailand that released a report of its findings. The findings implicated the company but also the government of Thailand and the major toy companies that were using this company as a supplier. In December 1993, the ICFTU Executive Board called for 'education campaigns to raise public awareness about working conditions associated with producing toys and to direct pressure … on the toy industry.' ICFTU affiliates were encouraged to promote a 'Charter on the Safe Production of Toys' that had been developed by the Hong Kong Toy Coalition, a group that included the ICFTU-affiliated Hong Kong Confederation of Trade Unions.

ICFTU affiliates joined this campaign and, together with the ICFTU, worked with NGOs, some of which were also involved in other campaigns over labour practices including those directed at companies marketing athletic footwear. In 1995, the ICFTU met with the Toy Manufactures of America (TMA) and also joined the Trades Union Congress, the World Development Movement and the Catholic Institute for International Relations in discussions of a code of conduct with the British Toy and Hobby Association (BTHA). The BTHA formally published its code in January 1996 and in May 1996 the International Council of Toy Industries adopted a similar code. The TMA had adopted a code in June 1995. Neither the trade unions nor the NGOs found any of these toy codes satisfactory. However these association codes were only 'models' and were misleading where they had the effect of suggesting that all member companies of the association announcing a code had also adopted or applied this code, when, in fact, many of these companies did neither.

The trade union experience in the international toy campaign was formative. This experience included cooperation with various NGOs that were campaigning for codes and it also included the discussions with the representatives of toy companies and toy associations. Neither the companies nor their associations wanted to address the issue of trade union rights and preferred engaging NGOs rather than trade union organizations. On several occasions it was suggested that some of the US-based member companies were opposed to trade unions in principle. The business representatives were not familiar with universal ILO standards and indicated that they had been very concerned not to appear to be imposing 'western values' on other cultures. The BTHA brought a public relations (PR) agency to the discussions. Among other things, the trade unions concluded that it was essential that the link between the exploitation and abuse of workers on one hand with the repression of their rights on the other was understood.

Trade unions also concluded that codes should be based on ILO standards. They rejected the argument that because ILO conventions are meant to be adopted and implemented by governments, they were inappropriate to apply to business. The ILO Tripartite Declaration, supported by employers as well as workers and governments, was, among other things, about applying ILO standards to the behaviour of business. Among the many advantages of referencing ILO standards in codes of labour practice is that a body of jurisprudence accompanies ILO conventions. The meaning of a code, and hence its credibility, is clear. Codes that are composed of vague 'feel good' language are not really transparent or credible because their meaning is not clear.

The second instance of involvement with the new codes issue concerned the use of child labour in the manufacture of leather soccer balls (see also Chapter 6). The ICFTU had in the course of its child labour campaign obtained video documentary evidence showing children stitching footballs bearing the label of the Federation Internationale de Football Association (FIFA). The evidence came from Sialkot, Pakistan where 80 per cent of the world's soccer balls are made involving what, at that time, was estimated to be 7000 child workers. FIFA agreed to meet with the international trade union organizations during the time of its EURO 96 event.

The international trade union organizations prepared the text of a code of conduct that incorporated lessons learned during the discussions with the toy industry. Host country formulations were abandoned in favour of international norms, and the draft code was not limited to child labour but reflected all of the fundamental human rights standards of the ILO, which were explicitly referenced. On 3 September 1996, FIFA and the international trade union organizations announced that they had 'agreed on the text of a Code of Labour Practice for the production of footballs carrying the FIFA authorised marks, in a continuing effort to eliminate the use of child labour and other exploitative practices.'

The major sporting goods companies that would be affected by the FIFA code included all of the major producers of athletic footwear subject to campaigns over labour exploitation – among the largest and most influential members of the World Federation of Sporting Goods Industries (WFSGI). As with the toy industry, some companies appeared to be opposed to trade unions in principal, and the WFSGI reacted strongly against the FIFA Code and developed its own 'model code of ethical conduct for the production of all sporting goods', which contained many deficiencies, some of which were dealt with later in response to pressure and developments.

On 14 February 1997, 56 soccer ball manufacturers, including companies such as Adidas, Mitre, Nike and Reebok, announced an agreement on a voluntary programme committing the companies and their subcontractors to end the use of child labour in Sialkot. The ILO, the Sialkot Chamber of Commerce and Industry and UNICEF were also parties to this agreement. Although this agreement was clearly meant to sidestep the FIFA code, the international trade unions welcomed the involvement of the ILO in this kind of work, believing it would result in more and better monitoring linked to a more serious programme resulting in the transition of children from work to school than would otherwise have been possible.

UNILATERAL CODES, NEGOTIATED CODES AND FRAMEWORK AGREEMENTS

The FIFA code, and others which have been developed from it, explicitly reference ILO Convention 98 on the Right to Organise and Collective Bargaining and explicitly state that their provisions are minimum standards only and must not be used as a ceiling or to discourage collective bargaining. Indeed the formulators of these codes had deliberately avoided provisions that were more appropriate for collective bargaining. The content of these codes did not resolve the problem of companies engaging NGOs in relationships that suggested that trade unions were not needed. This could be illustrated by how various parties saw the term 'continuous improvement.' Companies found the familiar term a way of reconciling what was possible with what they felt was only aspirational in codes. Some NGOs found the term useful in seeking ongoing relationships with companies. For trade unionists, the term was a management term appropriate for use in manufacturing and in quality control but completely inappropriate when applied to human rights.

One trade union response was to demand that companies negotiate their codes of conduct with trade unions. Another response was to treat the new codes as management policy and to advise companies as to code content and implementation but to avoid becoming a party to either. This second view questioned whether there was an appropriate trade union organization to negotiate these codes. The problem was that almost all of the companies adopting the new codes are operating in sectors where most workers do not belong to trade unions and in countries where trade union rights are not respected. Indeed, the exploitation and abuse of workers, which led to the need for a code in the first place, occurs because the rights of workers to join or form independent trade unions and to bargain collectively are not respected.

In several countries national trade union organizations have jointly agreed to codes with home-based MNCs meant to apply to their international operations or to their suppliers in other countries. Some of these national organizations recalled how, during the 1980s, trade unions in the home countries of MNCs operating in South Africa during apartheid were able to negotiate codes on behalf of black workers in South Africa. Other trade unionists believe that the home country trade union role in South Africa was justifiable only because the workers concerned had already established genuine, albeit illegal, trade unions and the trade unions negotiating the codes closely cooperated with these trade unions.

The trade unionists that preferred to view codes as management policy felt that it was important to distinguish between speaking out on behalf of workers who are not represented and seeking to negotiate on their behalf. To say that it is possible to negotiate for unorganized workers is to say that workers can be represented without their own trade unions. In their view, the moral obligation of all trade unions toward unorganized workers is to assist them in joining or forming their own trade unions and to prevent or discourage others – whether they be governments, political parties, employers or NGOs – from claiming to speak for them.

Although this controversy is not entirely resolved, it may be by the growing appreciation among trade unionists that codes of conduct are not the only way to engage MNCs over labour practices and that there is always at least one appropriate trade union organization to engage any multinational company. These organizations are the International Trade Secretariats (ITSs). Because ITSs have affiliates throughout all regions of the world, often in both home and host countries, they are the legitimate international voice of workers in their respective industries or economic sectors. Every multinational company has an appropriate social partner in an ITS, which is the legitimate representative of the workers' side of its industry.

A framework agreement is an agreement negotiated between an MNC and an ITS concerning the international activities of that company. Although an international code of conduct can be part of a framework agreement, the main purpose of a framework agreement is to establish an ongoing relationship between the MNC and the ITS which can solve problems and work in the interest of both parties.

The first, and the most comprehensive framework agreement to date, established a formal relationship between the International Union of Food, Agricultural, Hotel, Restaurant, Catering, Tobacco and Allied Workers' Associations (IUF) and the French food multinational Danone (formerly BSN.) The IUF had been meeting with the company regularly since 1986 and, in 1988, they signed a 'Common Viewpoint' with the company which pledged the parties to work jointly in five areas: training; access to information; gender equality, respect for trade union rights and employment. Subsequently, the IUF and the company negotiated agreements in each of these five areas. In June 1995, the IUF signed an agreement with Accor, the French hotel and catering chain, and, in June 2001, they signed an agreement with Chiquita, the US-based banana multinational.

Other ITSs have also entered into framework agreements. The International Federation of Building and Wood Workers (IFBWW) has entered into four framework agreements: with Swedish furniture marketer IKEA (May 1988); with German pencil maker Faber-Castell (March 2000); with German construction group Hochtief (March 2000); and with Swedish building related services and project development company Skanska (February 2001). The International Chemical Energy and Mining (ICEM) reached agreements with the Norwegian oil company Statoil (July 1998 and March 2001) and with Freudenberg, a leading multinational in non-woven and allied products from Germany (July 2000). Union Network International (UNI) has an agreement with Spanish telecom giant Telefonica (April 2000) and with the French multinational retailer Carrefour (May 2001).

Some codes were neither unilaterally adopted nor the result of an agreement between two parties. The Ethical Trading Initiative (ETI) and the SA 8000 codes are sometimes referred to as 'multi-stakeholder codes' because they were adopted following negotiations involving representative of companies, NGOs and trade unions. The codes required negotiating because the stakeholders were part of a follow-up programme which could involve certification of code compliance or monitoring.

The ETI deserves special note because it is the only multi-stakeholder organization concerned with codes of conduct that incorporates international trade union organizations formally in its structure (see also Chapter 15). The ICFTU and two ITS, the IUF and the ITGLWF, are involved, in addition to the Trades Union Congress (TUC), the national workers' organization of the UK. The ETI is a partnership of companies, NGOs and trade union organizations meant to serve as a forum whereby information relating to code implementation, monitoring and verification can be exchanged and as a means of conducting pilot studies to test various ways of monitoring and verifying codes. International trade union support is possible because the ETI takes an experimental approach and is not a certification programme.

SOCIAL RESPONSIBILITY AND THE SOCIAL PARTNERS

By the late 1990s, it had become clear that the new codes of conduct had become part of a larger debate over corporate social responsibility (CSR). The concept of CSR was that a responsible company must take into account the impact of its activities on society. The idea was that business should recognize and engage all of its stakeholders. The term 'stakeholders' meant any individual or group affected by the operations of the company. This stakeholder concept fits well with the idea of supplier codes and not just because the workers concerned were stakeholders – in the CSR concept, suppliers were 'stakeholders' too.

Trade unions appreciated the stakeholder concept to a point. This point was where the idea of 'business and stakeholders' began to replace the notion of social partners and social dialogue. More and more home country governments came to view CSR as a kind of 'third pillar' where business goes beyond what is required by the law or the results of social dialogue and the collective bargaining framework. Governments were using CSR as a substitute for their own failure to address the social consequences of globalization. Trade unionists often found themselves the only ones in the room to notice that business was using CSR not to go beyond, but to go around regulation and trade unions. They were not entirely alone. CSR was an insider concept. The public continued to understand the social responsibility of business to include good industrial relations and respect for the law.

So did the Secretary General of the United Nations. In January 2000, Kofi Annan announced the Global Compact and invited companies to support nine principles in the area of human rights, workers rights and the environment that were based on already agreed international principles. International trade union organizations were also invited to join, as were international NGOs. Some NGOs criticized the Compact for failing to include implementation and monitoring procedures. The trade unions did not see the Global Compact as a code. They did not want the Global Compact with its very general principles to replace better codes that had been adopted. Nor did they want to suggest that the controversies over monitoring and verification had been resolved. The Global Compact was a form of international social dialogue and an opportunity to engage companies internationally and to influence the CSR debate. Trade unions are the human side of industry as well as an important part of civil society. Kofi Annan understood this dual nature of trade unions when, at a high level meeting on the Global Compact in July 2000, he said 'Labour unions can mobilise the workforce – for after all, companies are not composed only of their executives'.

CSR moved from a concept to become an industry as consultants and enterprises emerged, offering CSR services to business. Among these services were social auditing and reporting as well as 'risk assessment' services. The trade union concern with this industry is that it is assisting business in redefining the expectations of society instead of responding to them.

Codes of conduct covering labour practice continue to be useful for this purpose because as private voluntary initiatives they always require a positive commitment by a company before they apply. This is in contrast to instruments such the OECD Guidelines which apply to all multinational enterprises based within the OECD or adhering countries whether the enterprises have accepted them or not. The Guidelines reflect the consensus of the member governments of the OECD as to what constitutes responsible behaviour of international business. The OECD Guidelines were revised in 2000. Among the changes has been a strengthening in the follow-up mechanism and the extension of their application to companies doing business in non-OECD countries. For trade unions, the revision of the OECD Guidelines was particularly timely. What was needed at this point in the debate over CSR and codes was a reaffirmation and reassertion of the expectations of society by legitimate governments. And that is what happened.

Chapter 8

The emperor's new clothes: what codes mean for workers in the garment industry

Linda Shaw and Angela Hale

BACKGROUND

During the past twenty years, the nature and context of international labour has changed dramatically. When Women Working Worldwide (WWW) was launched in 1985 little attention was paid to the labour conditions in international supply chains and there was a clear need for support mechanisms for women workers in globalized industries such as garments and footwear. WWW began a programme of awareness raising to draw attention to the ways in which global restructuring was bringing many young women into the labour force for the first time but in ways which undermined their rights as workers and subjected them to harsh and exploitative conditions, especially in the textiles and garments sector. WWW also looked to undertake specific solidarity campaigns when particular abuses came to their attention.

The role of WWW in drawing attention to the plight of a new global female workforce was not without its critics who saw these issues as primarily the province of the international trade union movement. However there were reasons why WWW developed this work. In the first place, the Cold War reality of a divided movement internationally which limited the effectiveness of and scope of much solidarity actions – graphically portrayed in the publication *Where were you brother?* (Thompson and Larsen, 1978). In addition, it was also apparent by the late 1980s that many of these young women workers, including those employed in Export Processing Zones, remained beyond the reach of union organization – either because unions were repressed, or in some cases through

---

BOX 8.1 WOMEN WORKING WORLDWIDE

WWW was established in 1985 following the organization of a conference on 'Women on the global assembly line'. It is a small organization based in Manchester which works with an international network of groups and activists supporting women workers. Most are in Asia but there are also links with groups in Central America, Africa and Eastern Europe.

WWW's particular concern is with the way in which changes in the global economy have a direct impact on the working lives of women. The aim is to increase awareness of these changes and to support the development of appropriate organizing strategies. The focus is on industries supplying the world market, particularly those producing consumer goods such as garments and footwear. The aim is to build international links between workers in these industries and between workers' representatives and those acting on their behalf in Europe.

Women Working Worldwide
Rm 412 Manton Building
Manchester Metropolitan University
Rosamond St West
Manchester M15 6LL
Tel: 0161 247 1760
Fax: 0161 247 6321
Email: Women-ww@mcr1.poptel.org.uk
www.poptel.org.uk/women-ww

---

lack of interest in organizing them by a male-dominated union leadership (Romero, 1995). In addition as more evidence emerged of the growing importance of informal sector employment in the garments sector in both the North and the South, the absence of a union presence here also became clear (with one or two notable exceptions) (Boris and Prugl, 1996). Finally, and this was a problem specific to the garments sector, the continued trade protection afforded to production in Europe and the United States by the Multi-Fibre Arrangement and the related protectionist stance of many Northern garment unions also limited international connections and solidarity actions (Kabeer, 2000).

Building support through the trade union movement for garment workers seemed fraught with difficulties as we approached the 1990s – yet at the same time changes were taking place which highlighted the potential power of consumers. The garment industry was restructuring in a way which increased the power of retailers and newly emerging brand names and at the same time exposed them more to public scrutiny. This was illustrated in 1989/90 when a small Philippine workers union, whose members were locked out by a UK garments multinational, appealed for support (Shaw, 1997). Joint solidarity actions and related publicity campaigns by WWW and the nascent Clean Clothes Campaign (CCC) in the Netherlands provoked a range of escalating responses from the companies targeted, including libel actions in both countries (CCC,

1993). These responses served to confirm both the power and vulnerability of brand name reputations in the face of committed campaigns. Support in the United Kingdom was forthcoming from women unionists in the Transport and General Workers Union, more concerned with solidarity than whether the Philippine union was too closely connected to a national union federation allied to the communist party.

This and other campaigns indicated that sensitivity to negative publicity was high, but most retailers initially maintained that they had no responsibility for working conditions in the countries in which they operated. As campaigners, the challenge was therefore to hold both retailers and manufacturers publicly responsible for conditions throughout their international supply chains. One of the first to respond was Levi Strauss following the publication of an article in 1992 in the *Washington Post* on the production of Levi jeans by Chinese prison labour in the US Pacific colony of Saipan. Levi Strauss drew up a comprehensive code of labour standards for all its overseas suppliers. The speed with which other companies followed suit, particularly in the United States, meant that the ground shifted for campaigners (Ross, 1997). The seeming success of getting labour standards onto the corporate agenda was offset by the enormous challenge of ensuring that this was more than a public relations exercise.

In the United Kingdom, the movement developed in two directions. WWW and other campaigning organizations joined together to form the Labour Behind the Label network which became the UK arm of the European Clean Clothes Campaign. At the same time the issue of company codes became part of the agenda of the UK Trade Network, of which WWW was also a member. The UK Trade Network is a forum for non-governmental organizations (NGOs) to meet and discuss trade issues, particularly those relating to the World Trade Organization (WTO) and other intergovernmental meetings. It includes NGOs who are also campaigning and in dialogue with companies in sectors other than garments, such as food and toys. A UK Trade Network subgroup was set up called the 'Monitoring and Verification Working Group', whose remit it was to discuss how to ensure the proper implementation of codes by UK-based companies. This was the beginning of the UK Ethical Trading Initiative (ETI) which was to become a multi-stakeholder organization representing companies, NGOs and trade unions.[1]

Meanwhile a further critical element in these developments has been a significant increase in the number and scope of Southern-based organizations working to improve labour conditions in export industries. Different forms of women worker organizations have continued to develop throughout Asia and in other regions and it is through networking with these organizations that WWW decides on its priorities and carries out programmes of collaborative work. Organizations of home-based workers (see the next chapter) have also developed both at a local, regional and international level with the success of gaining the ILO convention on home-based work in 1996. The vast majority of homeworkers are, of course, women. Many of these women worker organizations have enabled the testimonies and experiences of women garment workers to be heard internationally – an essential counterbalance to the bland reassurances by many corporations that working conditions were acceptable. They also, of course, fuelled much of the media coverage and hence sensitivity of retailers to negative publicity.

Labour-based codes were, in large part, a response by the corporate sector to the presence of these sustained campaigns and actions across many countries. Although WWW does not see codes as the solution to the exploitation of workers, it is seen as important to continue to engage with attempts to follow through these developments. Since codes have been adopted as a response to public pressure, campaigners have a certain responsibility to try to ensure that they mean something in practice. For WWW this means participating in the ETI whilst still maintaining a strong campaigning focus. It does not necessarily mean accepting the manner in which codes of conduct and 'ethical trading' are currently being promoted but rather adopting a strategy of 'critical engagement' with what has largely become a company driven agenda.

INVOLVING WORKERS

It is our engagement with grassroots women worker organizations especially that has informed our view that one of the key problems with the way in which the ethical trade movement has developed is the top-down manner in which codes have been adopted. In our view most codes have been produced by companies without any negotiation with workers or even any attempt to seek their views. In the case of the ETI and other multi-stakeholder initiatives, there has been consultation with NGOs and trade union officials, but these are in the country where the companies are based, far removed from the workplace itself. Codes of conduct are typically introduced on behalf of workers, without their knowledge or consent. It is simply assumed that workers will see these initiatives as being in their interests.

Given this reality it would seem that one of the priorities for workers' rights organizations, whether trade unions or NGOs, should be to ensure the future involvement of workers. Where codes already exist, the immediate priority should be to make sure that workers understand them and also that they accept that codes are a useful mechanism for protecting their rights. Only then will workers be able to use codes as a negotiating tool and be in a position to monitor their implementation. This is important not just as a matter of principle, it is also essential for the success of any monitoring initiative. Workers are the only people who can really know the everyday realities of the workplace so without their genuine involvement any system of monitoring has limited value.

It was within this context that in 1998 WWW decided to carry out a small research and consultation exercise on codes with some of our partners in Asia (WWW 1998). This involved working with a workers' organization in each of six Asian countries: Indonesia, the Philippines, Sri Lanka, Bangladesh, Pakistan and India. All work at the grassroots level and engage directly with women workers in garment factories. They undertake organizing, support and education work with workers, though none of them is constituted in the form of a traditional trade union. Typically most operate from a centre close by, but outside, the workplace. Also typical is the lack of any independent union presence in the women's places of employment. The programme was held in two stages, firstly a small research project to map the extent of workers' knowledge about codes. This was followed by an education programme.

The findings from the initial research programme clearly demonstrated that workers knew nothing about codes even when they were working in factories supplying well-known companies that had codes, such as Nike and the Gap. When the concept was explained to them they showed a high level of scepticism, based on a distrust of anything introduced by management and on widespread experience of corruption. Many felt that even attempting to find out whether their companies had codes could lead to victimization or dismissal. Nevertheless, they wanted to know more and welcomed WWW's suggestion of an educational programme on the issue of codes. WWW therefore raised funds for a programme with the same six Asian organizations and also for a similar programme in Central America through the Central America Women's Network (CAWN).

For the second stage of the project, all our partners held workshops and consultations with workers based in factories producing for export. In Asia over 80 workers participated in this programme. Participants were predominantly, but not exclusively, women. These educational workshops proved to be vital – workers could not even begin to respond to codes without first knowing what they were and how their factory/work fitted into a wider international context. Willingness to explore the potential of codes was demonstrated by their involvement in the education exercises, which used materials assembled by WWW and then translated into local languages by our partners. The engagement of so many in the process is a real achievement given the overlong working hours endured by garment workers. Not only did participants give up their few hours of leisure time but many also feared victimization so that the sessions were sometimes held in secret. Yet groups in all six Asian countries reported that the programme had been positive and productive, in a meeting held in Sri Lanka in December 1998 (WWW 1999).

At this meeting, reports from our partners on their education programmes demonstrated that participants were able to take a sophisticated perspective on codes, viewing them with caution and well-founded scepticism but also recognizing the potential for new forms of action and international solidarity. Few workers had previously questioned where their products went after leaving the factory, and many became enthusiastic about using brand labels as a way of tracing supply chains and developing links with other workers. They began to see that codes of conduct could be a useful tool in confronting some of the problems of organizing in the context of globalization. However the general feeling was that the implementation of national legislation remained more important since this applied to all workers, not just those producing for export.

For many, learning that garment workers in other countries faced similar problems was a revelation, as the report from Sri Lanka emphasized:

> It came as a revelation to them that women workers in distant countries suffered similar problems to theirs, such as restrictions on using the toilet, forced overtime and victimisation for attempting to unionise (WWW, 1999).

Workers' own assessment of what should be included in any code on labour standards was explored. Participants in three workshops – in Sri Lanka, Bangladesh and India – drew up their own list. For workers in Bangladesh and India, a key priority was that there should be a proper legal relationship between workers and employers, especially to designate them as regular not casual workers. This would provide more job security under their labour legislation. Other key issues related to hours of work, notably the right to refuse overtime and to take regular holidays. Particularly significant was the priority given to demands specific to women workers, notably the rights of pregnant women, freedom from sexual harassment and the rights to use toilet facilities whenever they wanted to. Although it can be argued that the best company codes do cover most of these concerns, they tend to be obscured by more generalized language and the overall emphasis is different.

On the freedom of association and rights to collective bargaining there was strong support from participants in all countries for the position of trade unions and campaigning organizations. All participant organizations reported that workers felt the impact of codes would be minimal unless they had the right to organize. Most were working in situations where trade unions had little presence. Those workers who did have experience of unions mainly saw them as remote, as well as sometimes corrupt and right wing. A key question this raises is under what circumstances codes could promote trade unionism which is independent and genuine in representing the interests of women workers. In spite of their experiences, for workers no code could be acceptable unless it included freedom of association and collective bargaining. However, even when this was included in company codes, there was little confidence that these rights would be implemented unless workers were already in a position to act collectively.

In discussing the relationship between codes and national legislation, it was felt that codes should not become a substitute for struggles to improve labour legislation and its implementation. It was also pointed out that codes might have a negative impact on homeworkers who might lose work if the production chain became more formalized in response to codes. It was suggested that legislation could be designed to protect the rights and interests of these sectors.

Overall the findings of this initial research and education exercise reinforces WWW's position that it is unrealistic to expect codes to be effective unless more support is given to workers' own educational and organizing strategies. How much more could have been learnt if such consultation had taken place before codes were drawn up. Workers need to understand where codes are coming from and also have the confidence and collective support to report company violations. This means more resources for workers' own organizations so that they can act from a position of strength. In view of this, the debate taking place in multi-stakeholder initiatives about which mechanisms to use to involve workers in monitoring or verification procedures is premature. The reality is that most workers are not in a strong enough position to be involved and would therefore be constantly vulnerable to retaliation by companies. In such a context even the best intentioned initiatives could become another mechanism for undermining workers' ability to protect their rights.

UNDERSTANDING THE DYNAMICS OF THE INDUSTRY

The Asian research and education also reinforced the importance of looking at codes and the industry in general from the workers' perspective. We have, therefore, developed a second strand of research on codes which relates them more generally to the dynamics of the garments sector and specifically whether the nature of the industry itself undermines the effective implementation of codes. In the case of garments and footwear it is clearly retailers and brand-name companies that are driving the industry. Competition between these companies is intense. The strategy adopted in the face of this competition is to concentrate on design and marketing whilst reducing production costs through outsourcing to low wage economies (Gereffi and Korzeniewicz, 1994). Pressure is constantly put on contractors, agents and trading companies to provide lower cost goods. Meanwhile, with the increasing number of countries involved in export production, local manufacturers are locked into fierce competition for orders. Middlemen who have to meet the cost demands of the buying company maximize their own profits by squeezing manufacturers. Rather than turn down an order, local manufacturers often accept unprofitable deals and make them work by increasing pressure on their own workforce, for example through forced or unpaid overtime and by subcontracting to small workshops and to homeworkers, the lowest paid workers at the end of the chain (ILO, 2000).

There has been a massive increase in subcontracting in the garment industry. This is not only a response to intense competition but also to the rapid changes and fluctuations in fashion. By reducing the regular factory workforce and using subcontractors, employers can react to changes and at the same time keep costs to a minimum. The complexity of many subcontracting chains is daunting. Yet it has to be confronted if appropriate strategies are to be developed to really protect the rights of workers in these industries. It was with this in mind that

WWW organized a conference 'Organising along International Subcontracting Chains in the Garment Industry' in September 2000 (WWW, 2001a). The aim was to develop a fuller understanding of how international subcontracting operates, to exchange information on the implications for workers and to discuss possible organizing strategies. Included were not only representatives of garment workers but also other players such as designers, shop workers, academics and consumers. Presentations from workers' organizations from the United Kingdom, Thailand, the Philippines, China, Bangladesh, Pakistan, Sri Lanka, Mexico, Brazil, Guatemala, Eastern Europe and Palestine all confirmed that the increase in international subcontracting is undermining wages and conditions in the industry.

Participants argued that corporate strategy was undermining the rights of all workers in the industry, even those in main production sites. Speaker after speaker reported that intense global competition in the garment sector was resulting in lengthening production chains where the work was subcontracted out, often eventually to workers in the informal sector. The whole industry works on the basis of flexibility, intensity, short termism, competition and insecurity. It is therefore no surprise that workers themselves are faced with these problems. Redundancy is an everyday reality for workers in higher-wage economies of Europe, North America and also Asia. Even in low-wage economies there is the constant threat of further relocation. Flexibilization also means that garment workers face insecurity on a daily basis. They are typically employed on a casual, part-time, temporary basis and periods of intense work can be followed by periods of complete loss of earnings. Intensification of work is also a direct result of retailing strategy. Local manufacturers are under constant pressure from buyers to reduce costs and to meet production deadlines. They respond to the pressure by increasing working hours and reducing numbers on production lines. So-called 'voluntary overtime' is not only associated with low wages but also with the threat of job losses if orders are lost through unmet deadlines. The same pressure is exerted on home-based workers, who may work day and night in an effort to meet impossible deadlines.

The irony of this situation then is that whilst companies at the top of international subcontracting chains are adopting codes of conduct they themselves are creating the conditions that operate against their implementation. If the demand for flexibility translates into insecurity and periods of intense overtime, it is unrealistic to expect standards on working hours and proper working contracts to be adequately implemented. If competitive pressure is such that costs have to be cut, it may be impossible for local contractors to increase wage levels and bring health and safety measures up to international standards without going out of business. In any case, if they have no long-term stake in the business their aim will be short-term profits rather than investment in improved working conditions. All these issues need to be addressed by any initiative genuinely committed to improving workers' rights.

Any companies who are seeking to overcome these dilemmas are also faced with the practical problems associated with increasingly complex subcontracting chains. Although retailers drive the industry, many do not actually know where their goods are produced. Most companies operate through agents, trading companies or local contractors. These middlemen increase their power by providing as little information as possible. Often overseas companies do not know the names or locations of factories they are buying from and these can change rapidly from one week to the next. Even if the factory itself is known it is highly unlikely that local contractors will reveal the extent of outsourcing to smaller production units and homeworkers (White and Munger, 1999). Furthermore, most companies buy from a range of local suppliers, so that, even if they know where they are, it may be impossible to monitor them all.

PUTTING CODES IN A BROADER CONTEXT

Given the dynamics of the industry, the prospects that codes offer for improving working conditions in the garments industry might seem fairly remote. Indeed there are many activists and organizations working on the garment sector that take this view. Yet there are others who are more optimistic, seeing codes as offering a potential tool in efforts to promote worker organization and education. However, this will only be possible if workers have a sense of ownership, if they feel that codes are actually there to support them. A core feature of the codes process has to be a strategy of genuine consultation and participation with workers in the industry. Ironically there is a danger that activists and policy makers in Europe and North America will be so absorbed into codes debates that any consultation with workers themselves seems merely to complicate the process. However such consultation is absolutely essential.

It is also important to see codes work as only one of a series of strategies to support women worker rights and conditions adopted by campaigners and organizations working on the garment sector. Any evaluation of codes work needs also to discuss their effectiveness in the context of alternative approaches. Given the global nature of the garments sector, coupled with minimal traditional union presence among the majority of workers, there has been a tendency to develop strategies which also take as their starting point international regulation and actions, as codes have done. These include social clause proposals, the promotion of 'core labour standards' and the negotiation of international framework agreements. It also includes the use of legal action against companies as a way of holding them to account for their international operations.

The situating of core labour standards within a broader human rights agenda has much to recommend it – not least if it contributes to a revitalized ILO with a stronger international role. However, WWW's work on codes and workers' rights, especially the consultation process with women workers, also points to some critical limitations of this rights-based strategy as expressed through a social clauses approach, for example. Our research and consultation has suggested that the existing core labour rights – specifically the right to organize and collective bargaining – may be inadequate in meeting the needs of women workers in key ways.

Recent research undertaken in India and in the Philippines (WWW, 2001b), exploring how they themselves define their rights, found that women workers were unable to access these rights, not simply because there was no union, but crucially because they were often not recognized as workers. This could occur in several ways. The informal nature of much garment employment in India means that the women had no official record of their employment. They were legally 'invisible' workers. In the Philippines, women's access to 'worker' status, and hence worker rights, was limited by their being kept on casual contracts. What women workers defined as their rights varied according to their situation but consistently included and prioritized a wider range of rights than those covered in the core labour standards. These were felt necessary to deal with problems such as compulsory overtime, low pay, casualization, lack of employment stability, sexual harassment and childcare. Interestingly, whereas codes may clearly lack credibility in their implementation, they do, however, attempt to address many of these problems raised by workers. By contrast the all-inclusive anti-discrimination clause receives little attention in the social clause debates and international attention on violations of core labour rights focuses largely on the union related clauses. Although this is very much in its early stages, the development of a broader agenda, put forward by women workers themselves, indicates the need for a critical reappraisal of the contents of core labour standards.

International framework agreements are another strategy being developed by several international union organizations.[2] They represent a form of international collective bargaining with multinational companies in different sectors, including garments. In some ways this can be seen as a strategy to situate the gains of code initiatives within the familiar union territory of collective bargaining. The agreements are made between the International Trade Secretariat responsible for the sector, such as the International Union of Foodworkers, and a specific company, for example Danone.

Although not much research has yet been undertaken, Framework Agreements are likely to suffer from similar problems of monitoring and verification as codes. Also the key issue of how far down the subcontracting chain the agreements apply has yet to be clearly defined. They may prove to be effective only when the company directly employs the workers covered by the agreement.

It is clear that neither codes of conduct, nor these alternative strategies, sufficiently address the issue of gender. Industries such as garments operate on the basis of gender specific exploitation. It is therefore no accident that it is women workers whose rights are most systematically denied. We have yet to see, at the international level, the emergence of a strategy that reflects this reality.

Codes themselves are not especially limited in this respect. In fact it could be argued that, with their wider agenda, they have the potential to reflect the expressed concerns of women workers in a way that the core labour standards do not. This has yet to be demonstrated but could be an area for further research.

Perhaps the most significant question that needs to be asked about all these strategies is the extent to which they are grounded in the demands and organizing strategies of the workers themselves. In this respect, although codes themselves are a top-down strategy, the campaigning networks that are developing around code implementation are contributing to the development of a new organizing model. This takes as its starting point not a single site of production but the international subcontracting chains that increasingly link workers and consumers in the North as well those in the South. However, for such networks to be effective, more support is needed for women workers organizing at the grass roots level. There also needs to be a stronger alliance between new forms of organizing and the more traditional labour movement.

Putting codes into the context of diverse strategies adopted by the growing network of groups, organizations and campaigns over labour conditions in the international garments industry is important. It reminds us that ten years ago companies routinely refused to accept responsibility for labour conditions in their production chains. Codes, whatever their failings, at the very least represent a corporate admittance of liability for working conditions. This is clearly the result of the development of global campaign networks bringing together older and newer forms of labour and consumer activism. These are the real drivers of change not the codes themselves.

NOTES

1   For more details on the ETI, see Chapter 15 by Blowfield below.
2   See Chapter 7 by Dwight Justice for a discussion of International Framework Agreements.

REFERENCES

Boris, E and E Prugl (1996) *Homeworkers in Global Perspective*, Routledge, London
Clean Clothes Campaign (1993) 'Continuous Global Relocation', *Clean Clothes* No 1, November
Gereffi, G and M Korzeniewcz (eds) (1994) *Commodity Chains and Global Capitalism*, Prager, Westport CT
ILO (2000) *Labour Practices in the Footwear, Leather, Textiles and Clothing Industries*, ILO, Geneva
Kabeer, N (2000) *The Power to Choose*, Verso, London
Romero, A (1995) 'Labour Standards and Export Processing Zones: Situation and Pressures for Change', *Development Policy Review*, Vol 13, pp247–76

Ross, A (1997) *No Sweat*, Verso, New York

Shaw, L (1997) 'European Clean Clothes Campaigns' in A Ross *No Sweat*, Verso, New York, pp215–20.

Thompson, D and R Larsen (1978) *Where were you brother?*, War on Want, London

White, H and F Munger (1999) *Dynamics of the Global Assembly Line* available online at www.verite.org/dynamic_verite.html, downloaded 26 June 2001.

Women Working Worldwide (1998) *Report of a Preliminary Research and Consultation Exercise*, Women Working Worldwide, Manchester

WWW (1999) *Women Workers and Codes of Conduct: Asia Workshop Report*, Women Working Worldwide, Manchester

WWW (2001a) *Workshop Report: Organising along International Subcontracting Chains in the Garment Industry*, Women Working Worldwide, Manchester

WWW (2001b) *Women Garment Workers Define Their Rights: Reports from the Philippines, Sri Lanka and India*, Women Working Worldwide, Manchester

WWW and the Central America Women's Network (1999) *Women Workers and Codes of Conduct: Central America Workshop Report*, Women Working Worldwide, Manchester

Chapter 9

Can codes of conduct help home-based workers?

Lucy Brill

Homeworkers' organizations identify two major areas of concern about codes of conduct. First, the problems with 'codes on paper' – the fact that up until very recently, the vast majority of codes make no mention of home-based workers or other informal sector workers, despite the accumulating evidence that they are producing goods which are marketed by transnational companies (TNCs), and are thus participating within global subcontracting chains. Second, there are difficulties with 'codes in practice'. Here the situation is complex, there are some signs that companies can respond to concerns about labour rights by shortening supply chains and bringing work into factories where working conditions are easier to monitor, thus adversely affecting home-based workers who may lose their livelihoods.

There are, however, a few positive examples. Some companies take a gradual approach towards implementation to protect workers' livelihoods. While most model codes do not make explicit reference to homeworkers, the United Kingdom's Ethical Trading Initiative (ETI) drew attention to this issue and called upon partner organizations to 'promote the immediate adoption of more limited provisions for homeworkers' (Ferguson, 1998, p29). Here I examine two contrasting cases where codes of conduct have been introduced specifically with the aim of improving the situation of home-based workers, and discuss whether, and how, codes of conduct might be used by a homeworkers' organzsation.

DEFINITIONS OF HOME-BASED WORK

HomeNet adopts a broad definition of homeworking, which includes all those who work inside, or in the environs of their home, in urban or rural settings and

---

BOX 9.1 HOMENET INTERNATIONAL

HomeNet International is an international solidarity network, set up in 1994, for organizations of home-based workers, with the following objectives:

- To support grass roots organizing of home-based workers throughout the world, in order to improve their living and working conditions.
- To extend the network and to encourage the development of new homeworkers' organizations, through its current mapping programme and through information, exchanges and visits.
- To ensure that the voice of home-based workers is heard at national, regional and international levels through advocacy, representation and campaigning work and publications.

HomeNet members seek to reach out to the great numbers of home-based workers who are still unorganized and without any rights, to ensure that through their collective organizing, they will be able to voice their demands and bring about change in their lives. HomeNet campaigned for the adoption of the Convention on Home Work by the International Labour Organization (ILO), which was adopted in 1996. HomeNet members work with home-based workers in urban and rural areas, in developed and developing countries, in a range of industries and sectors. They include trade unions, non-governmental organizations (NGOs), people's organizations and collectives active with home-based workers; the network also builds broad alliances with supporters in many different fields, including research, policy, statistical and advocacy work.

HomeNet
Office 20,
30–38 Dock St.,
Leeds, LS10 1JF,
Tel: 44 113 217 4037,
Fax: 44 113 277 3269,
Email: homenet@gn.apc.org

---

in both the North and the South. This definition includes not only dependent 'piece rate' homeworkers, whose work is provided by an identifiable employer (and who are covered by the 1996 ILO Convention on Home Working), but also home-based 'own account' workers, who market their goods themselves. This breadth of focus reflects not only HomeNet's primary objective which is to organize rather than to research[1] home-based workers but also the reality of many homeworkers' experience. The fact that most home-based workers are women, who are seeking to combine their domestic responsibilities with the need to earn an income, reflects the continuing power of traditional gender roles, in both developing and developed countries.

The majority of home-based workers are situated on the margins (but most definitely form an integral part) of the global economy, and operate in employment situations where the relations of production are often difficult to determine and subject to change. Most homeworkers within the garment industry, for example, are paid on a piece-work basis and are usually described as 'self-employed' or 'independent' workers. However, closer study reveals that their working conditions are often very similar to those working in the factories – they are dependent on a single supplier, who provides them with unsewn pieces of clothing and specifies exactly what needs to be done.

This group is frequently contrasted with 'own account' homeworkers who may be independent artisans or craft workers. Such workers have greater control over the design and marketing of their work: they decide for themselves what goods they will produce, then assemble the necessary raw materials and finally sell their work directly to the final customer. HomeNet uses the term 'own account' for this group, rather than 'micro-entrepreneur', because these workers often do not 'choose' to set up their own business, particularly when they live in areas where there are simply no alternative source of livelihood – in India for example rural own account homeworkers are often poorer than the urban piece rate home-based workers.

Whilst it is clear that there are differences between the two groups it is also important to recognize that not all homeworkers can be categorically assigned to one group or the other – there is a continuum of employment relations and many homeworkers are best situated somewhere in between disguised waged employment and truly independent own account producers. Some, for example, switch between piece work and own account – a weaver may produce goods for a subcontractor when work is available but make items to sell to local customers when it is not (HomeNet, 2000a, p7). In addition, there are also own account homeworkers who share many features with genuine independent workers but are economically dependent on traders, money-lenders and so on. Although these workers cannot be defined as dependent in legal or statistical terms, because there is no identifiable employer providing the work, in organizational and economic terms, and in their ability to make a decent living and make provision for illness and other contingencies, they are still dependent on more powerful economic actors, and may be just as vulnerable as the piece rate worker (HomeNet, 1995, p6).

HOMEWORKERS AND GLOBAL CHAINS

There is now a substantial body of evidence which shows that homeworkers participate in subcontracting chains which can span the globe or stretch no further than the nearest council estate. Furthermore, homeworking may even be increasing as companies seek to reduce overheads and introduce 'flexible' working practices, and in some areas, to respond to the challenge posed by workers' organizations within the Export Processing Zones. Home-based workers are arguably one of the most flexible forms of labour – they are paid only for the work that they do, very rarely have a contract of employment or any social protection, and even pay their own heating and lighting bills.

Research on the UK garment industry demonstrates that many major retailers use local homeworkers within supply chains (Phizacklea and Wolkowitz, 1995), and a more recent study of homeworking has confirmed this (Brill, 2000). During the 1960s and 1970s, many garment manufacturers closed their UK factories and shifted production to Asia, attracted by the promise of both a plentiful supply of low-cost labour and also by expanding new markets in these countries. In the 1980s, the pendulum swung back in the other direction as the introduction of 'just-in-time' production methods brought new incentives for the more volatile product lines (for example women's fashions) to be sourced closer to markets. Many suppliers began to subcontract these orders to UK-based workshops and homeworkers, whilst they continued to source basic lines (for example school uniforms) from Asia (Mitter, 1986).

HomeNet members also report that these same global economic trends are eroding the differences between piece rate and own account homeworkers as, on the one hand, the casualization of waged labour weakens the position of dependent piece rate home-based workers and, on the other, the commercialization of traditional craft or agricultural production is threatening the independence of small own account producers. The image of many craft industries in developing countries – as a traditional production process which is an integral part of a subsistence way of life – often masks these developments, as does the lack of research in many of these sectors. Documented examples of the commercialization of traditional home-based industries include gem cutting in Rajasthan and Gujarat (Smith, 2000) and kilim weavers in Turkey (HomeNet, 2000a). Both these industries were once traditional activities where the work was done within family units but as commercial interests become involved, artisans lose their independence and the relations of production become closer to those of waged labour rather than of an independent family enterprise.

DANGERS OF CODES FOR HOMEWORKERS

In spite of this evidence, the vast majority of codes make no mention of informal sector workers of any kind and so it is realistic to assume that the concerns of any homeworkers who might be involved in a particular subcontracting chain are likely also to be ignored when a code is implemented on the ground. Although in fact relatively few attempts have been made to put codes into practice, there is already some evidence that if the interests of home-based workers are not taken into account, they can be adversely affected.

A critical issue here is the often substantial gap between the reality of homeworkers' working conditions and the requirements of the codes; this means that their livelihoods may be jeopardized if a code is implemented without careful preparation. Most homeworkers operate in the informal sector where pay rates are typically a third to a half of minimum wage levels; their working hours are largely unregulated and often highly irregular – they can go weeks or months with no work, then be offered last minute orders which they have to work through the night to complete on time.

There is some evidence that companies may respond to bad publicity by shortening supply chains and bringing all the work into factories, leaving the most vulnerable groups of workers in an even worse position. The case of the restructuring of the football stitching industry in Sialkot in Pakistan illustrates this point, and also highlights the invisibility of home-based workers. During the mid 1990s a series of high profile child labour campaigns focused on the use of child workers within the football stitching industry but largely ignored the unsatisfactory working conditions of the rural home-based women workers who were often working alongside the children. Although these marginalized women living in outlying villages were not highly paid, research conducted by AURAT, a HomeNet member organization in Pakistan, found that the rates paid for football stitching were higher than any other in the 34 different trades in leather and textiles studied (Dayal, 1997, p7).

In response to consumer concern about the use of child labour, some companies insisted that in future all their footballs were to be produced in new factories set up in the towns. In so doing these companies failed to recognize either the importance of the work for the village women – or the factors that made it impossible for them to move to the towns and find work in the new factories (such as domestic responsibilities and cultural constraints). Although several other TNCs adopted a more flexible strategy to minimize the use of child labour in football production by moving the work into village 'stitching centres', even here there is still evidence that many women lost out as a result of the changes. Thus, for example, a Save the Children Fund evaluation of 18 villages with stitching centres concludes that:

> The community perceives that women's involvement in football stitching has decreased to 25–50 per cent, thus adversely affecting the economic condition of the households. Moreover once the stitching centres were established women were being exploited in terms of reduced wages; now they are paid lower wages for stitching at home (SCF, 1999, p22).

In presenting this case study it is important to note that it is a particularly extreme example of top-down implementation of codes, fuelled by the panic surrounding the child labour issue at the time – and also that in reacting as they did, the companies broke their own recommendations on the child labour issue (which state where breaches in the ban on child labour are identified changes in the production process should be implemented in such a way as to ensure that former child workers are integrated into education and are not driven into even more exploitative forms of employment). However there is also anecdotal evidence from other HomeNet members to suggest that even in the developed countries there are examples of homeworkers losing out when codes or legal regulations are implemented without first consulting the homeworkers and making a careful assessment of their situation.

POSITIVE EXAMPLES

If codes of conduct are to help homeworkers then these workers must be involved in their production, implementation and monitoring. For this to take place effectively, the homeworkers must first be organized so that they can articulate their concerns and ensure that these are addressed within the codes. It is important that this process includes all homeworkers involved in a particular chain of production – whether they are disguised wage workers or own account producers – although it is also important to recognize that the concerns of different groups may vary considerably. A further difficulty here is that trade unions have often been reluctant to organize home-based workers so that up until recently they have been largely unrepresented, not only in the debates surrounding ethical trade and codes but also in broader issues such as labour rights and social protection issues. Racist and sexist attitudes contribute to this problem, as does the traditional image of homework as an outdated practice that should be phased out, and which may threaten the jobs of other union members. However, there are some positive examples where homeworkers have organized and have achieved positive improvements in their employment situation as a result. For example SEWA, the Self Employed Womens' Association in Gujarat, India has over 300,000 members, one-third of which are homeworkers (Jhabvala, 1994; Rose, 1992). This organization, which is now recognized as a trade union in its own right, has organized many different campaigns and strategies to improve home-based workers' working conditions and also developed social protection and credit schemes to assist them further.

Australia: homeworkers produce their own code

There are also a few traditional trade unions which have taken a different approach to home-based workers; one such is the Textile, Clothing and Footwear Union of Australia (TCFUA) in Australia, which also provides a good example of how codes can be used constructively to advance the interests of home-based workers. During the early 1990s, redundancies in the Australian garment industry, accompanied by a dramatic increase in homeworking, left the TCFUA with little alternative but to seek ways of organizing home-based workers. One element of their strategy involved the use of a code of conduct, which was drawn up following research which not only revealed the appalling working conditions of many of the homeworkers but also demonstrated that they were producing clothes which were ultimately sold by all the major retailers.

Although Australian labour law theoretically already guaranteed homeworkers equal treatment with factory workers, the majority of the women, many of whom were drawn from refugee or ethnic minority communities, were often unaware of their rights or too frightened to make a complaint. They feared that if identified they would simply lose their work, and also that employers and subcontractors would dispute their allegations, as they rarely had written evidence and often spoke little English.

The decision to use a code of conduct was a tactical one – the Union decided that rather than pressurize unsympathetic regional governments to strengthen the legislation, a voluntary code of conduct would be a more effective strategy in the short term, but in contrast to most company codes, this was drawn up following the TCFUA's research on home-based work. To push retailers to sign up to this, the union organized a broad-based campaign which highlighted the appalling employment situation of many homeworkers. Women's groups, church bodies and community organizations joined the union in calling for companies to take responsibility for the workers situated at the bottom of their subcontracting chains, and organized media-friendly stunts and demonstrations outside their stores to make customers aware of how their clothes were produced. In so doing they strengthened the position of the homeworkers without requiring them to identify themselves and risk reprisals from their subcontractors. Companies which then sign up to the code are required to demonstrate that they have systems in place to guarantee that any homeworkers producing clothes for their subcontractors are employed legally, and then to provide the union with details of their suppliers so that this can be confirmed. The code also contains detailed provisions for the enforcement of homeworkers' rights – including for example, a labelling system for tracing the origins of clothes and a manual to calculate piece rates that would ensure that homeworkers were receiving the minimum wage.

Annie Delaney from the TCFUA stresses that the code has been used as one tool alongside research and information campaigns, traditional worker organizing and vigorous attempts to pursue companies through the courts where there is sufficient evidence of breaches of existing legislation (culminating in their recent victory against Nike, who claimed that they did not need to sign the code on homeworking as their own code outlawed the practice (Fairwear Campaign, 2001)). To date the campaign has been successful; not only do home-based workers within Australia have a much higher profile and some degree of legal protection but they are also beginning to get some results – for example, the majority of Australian retailers have signed up to the code and some are seeking accreditation and permission to use the union's 'no sweatshop' labelling system. The information from the companies also enables the union to trace their suppliers and to build up a database of information about subcontracting chains and trends within the industry.

Improving conditions for own account home-based workers in craft industries

A contrasting case study comes from the United Kingdom where B&Q, a large home improvements retailer, has taken an innovative approach to improving the employment conditions of workers producing goods in developing countries. They sell many items produced by what they call 'cottage industries' – home-based producers working on an own account basis, often in traditional craft industries which are becoming increasingly commercialized (for example brass door handles, coir door mats, capiz shell lampshades). Although undoubtedly B&Q's interest in the issue has once again emerged in response to the concerns of campaigners and consumers, they have so far resisted the temptation to issue a glossy but unrealistic company code. Instead they begin by stating clearly that they accept both that they are accountable for the conditions under which the goods they retail are produced, and that at present in many cases these are unacceptable (B&Q, 1998, p76). However, they argue that rather than impose high standards that local suppliers cannot meet (with the result that workers' risk losing their livelihoods), they propose a step by step process, supporting local non-governmental organizations (NGOs) who then build alliances with the local producers in order to implement gradual improvements in working conditions in ways which do not jeopardize the competitiveness of their products.

To date they have developed a number of such schemes, several of which involve home-based workers. Thus for example, in the Philippines where home-based assemblers of capiz shell lampshades were earning less than half the minimum wage, provision of training has improved productivity and thus increased homeworkers' incomes (Ferguson, 1998). In Aligarh, India where small producers cast and polish brass products in their homes, the obvious health and safety risks have been reduced by working closely with a local subcontractor to develop small village workshops and also to provide health care for workers (Singh and Kowale, 2000). Both of these schemes are managed by local NGOs, which B&Q claims minimizes the risks of their 'western values being imposed on another culture', and provides third party verification (B&Q, 1998, p77); however, as presumably the NGO's work is funded by B&Q their independence could be questioned. Thus, for example, a report written by the NGO involved in the brassware project in Aligarh does not challenge the manufacturer's opposition to issues of workers' representation, and instead focuses on the less contentious health and safety concerns.

Taking these examples at face value, B&Q certainly seems to be experimenting with an alternative approach to ethical trade which appears to be more appropriate for home-based workers operating in situations where conditions are so far below 'recognized' labour standards. However, at the moment they themselves accept that only a few of their suppliers are covered by such schemes, and say little about the costs entailed and the sustainability of the projects concerned – particularly if they were to be extended to cover all of their suppliers.

Although these different campaigns vary considerably in their approach they both agree on the central importance of involving homeworkers but also recognize that their weak economic position means that a direct confrontation approach is unlikely to be effective and may even harm their interests. Particularly in the Australian example, creative ways of organizing – building broad-based coalitions of homeworkers, women's groups and consumer organizations as well as trade unionists and NGOs – have been used alongside more traditional legal work to put pressure on manufacturers and retailers and bring about improvements in the homeworkers working conditions without jeopardizing their work.

HOW MIGHT CODES OF CONDUCT BE USED TO HELP HOMEWORKERS?

In HomeNet's experience the first step towards improving conditions for home-based workers, be they own account or disguised waged labour, is collective organizing; by bringing the workers together they can identify the critical problems which they face and gain the capacity to strengthen their bargaining power with local traders, money lenders or local government officials. Codes of conduct are merely one tool amongst a range of strategies which could form part of this process – the advantage being that they redirect the focus of the campaign onto more powerful actors in the chain, rather than the home-based workers' immediate employer who may not be in a position to improve the employment conditions of the homeworkers – but they are only likely to be useful if they form part of a campaign which reflects the interests and voices of the homeworkers' themselves.

The first priority for many homeworkers is to guarantee a regular supply of work. Homeworkers are commonly in a particularly weak social and economic position – they tend to be drawn from the poorest social groups (for example, migrants or, in the industrialized countries, ethnic minority communities) and usually have no other source of income. Their work is unprotected and often irregular, which makes it difficult for them to risk taking any action which might jeopardize their work – even in an attempt to improve their situation. In addition, by definition they are isolated in their homes, working for long hours often with the fear that their situation is illegal – all factors that make it difficult for them to organize.

Company codes need to acknowledge that often the gap between local working conditions and accepted labour standards may be vast. Incremental improvements introduced over a period of time may therefore be a more realistic way to bring about change whilst minimizing the risk that the homeworkers lose their work as local suppliers develop alternative production processes in response to the code, because these are more easily monitored. However, such a developmental approach needs to begin with the recognition that current conditions are unacceptable and set out clear but achievable goals, with deadlines, which can be monitored by workers, suppliers and the company. This approach takes time and resources if it is to be effective, especially as in the meantime the risk of adverse publicity remains, but there are some signs that a few companies are addressing the issue in this way.

CONCLUSION

In this chapter I have explored the relationship between codes of conduct and home-based workers – providing examples of their dangers as well as their potential utility. However, at present, the vast majority of codes make no mention of home-based workers – in spite of the accumulating evidence of their involvement in transnational supply chains. This silence is worrying as it inevitably means that their interests are not considered if a code is implemented on the ground. Although this paper includes positive examples of codes which are explicitly designed to protect home-based workers, it is important to emphasize that little is known about the impact of the more general codes on home-based workers, the vast majority of which remain unorganized and largely invisible. We need new forms of research to deepen our understanding of the role of these workers within global subcontracting chains and result in codes which can protect their interests – a process which can only be effective if the workers are able to play a central part in this process. Nevertheless, the reality of the situation is that codes are here to stay, and as such, the challenge is to develop strategies which allow home-based workers and their organizations to use them in ways which can strengthen their position and thus bring about positive change.

ACKNOWLEDGEMENTS

The author would like to thank Jane Tate, HomeNet International Coordinator, for the information and ideas that she contributed to this chapter. However, the author is responsible for the opinions expressed within it.

NOTES

1   Some HomeNet members have used basic research techniques (for example a neighbourhood survey) as a means of both identifying the key issues facing home-based workers in a locality and using the contacts developed as a first stage in organizing (HomeNet, 1999, pp8–9).

REFERENCES

B&Q (1998) *How Green is my Patio? B&Q's Third Environmental Review*, B&Q, Eastleigh

Brill, L M (2000) 'A Study of Homeworking in the NorthWest', unpublished paper

Dayal, M (1997) *From Embroidery to Footballs: Report of a South Asia Workshop on Homebased Work*, HomeNet Report, HomeNet, Leeds

Fairwear Campaign (2001) *Stop the Sweatshops*, http://stopthe sweatshops.com, accessed 4 July 2001.

Ferguson, C (1998) *A Review of UK Company Codes of Conduct*, DfID, London

HomeNet (1995) 'North and South', in *HomeNet Newsletter*, No 1, Summer, pp6–7

HomeNet (1999) *Using the ILO Convention on Home Work*, HomeNet, Leeds

HomeNet (2000a) 'Kilim: an Ancient Craft', in *HomeNet Newsletter*, No 14, Autumn, pp7–11

HomeNet (2000b) *New Ways of Organising in the Informal Sector*, HomeNet, Leeds

Jhabvala, R (1994) 'Self-Employed Women's Association: Organising Women by Struggle and Development' in S Mitter and S Rowbotham *Dignity & Daily Bread*, Routledge, London pp114–38

Mitter, S (1986) 'Industrial Restructuring and Manufacturing Homework: Immigrant Women in the UK Clothing Industry', *Capital & Class*, No 27, pp37–80

Phizacklea, A and C Wolkowitz (1995) *Homeworking Women: Gender, Race & Class at Work*, Sage, London

Rose, K (1992) *Where Women are Leaders: the SEWA Movement in India*, Zed Books, London

SCF (1999) *Child Labour Project, Sialkot*, Social Monitoring Report, SCF, Sialkot, Pakistan

Singh, V and G P Kowale (2001) 'Employment Conditions, Exploitation, Safety, Income in Home Based Enterprises in Brassware Industry of Aligarh', presentation at CARDU Conference on Housing, Work & Development, Newcastle-upon-Tyne, 26–28 April 2000

Smith, S (2000) Untitled presentation at HomeNet Mapping Workshop, Leeds, May.

Chapter 10

'Made in China': rules and regulations versus corporate codes of conduct in the toy sector

Alice Kwan and Stephen Frost

Sometimes it's not hard to imagine that almost everything available on the shelves of your local toy store originates from a factory somewhere else. Pick up any toy and you are more likely to find an inscription showing it was made in Indonesia, Thailand or Mexico than in the United States, Britain or Germany. It is no secret that manufacturing has moved offshore, especially now that the big players in the toy industry are spending large amounts of money and effort trying to convince consumers that toys made overseas are manufactured in fair conditions. As in a number of other sectors, European and North American companies are keen to demonstrate that factories turning out the latest plaything for children are not the contemporary equivalent of the Dickensian satanic mill.

To some extent they have been successful. If they have appeared on the radar screens of workers' rights activists and consumer campaign groups at all, companies have reacted by hunkering down and admitting nothing, or developing codes of business practice designed to prove minimum standards in offshore plants. However, the rise of the code of conduct as the preferred response of larger players in the market to consumer, trade union, activist and other citizen's concerns raises a number of issues. In this chapter we examine those that seem most important from the perspective of two non-governmental organizations (NGOs) in Hong Kong closely involved in researching conditions in Chinese toy factories. China accounts for the greatest single proportion of manufactured toys in the world today (more than 10 per cent of total world production, if video games are not included). The inscription 'Made in China' is found on more toys than any other.

Box 10.1 Hong Kong Christian Industrial Committee

The Hong Kong Christian Industrial Committee (HKCIC) is an independent church-based labour organization which focuses on labour concerns in Hong Kong and China. It has positioned itself as follows: to provide services to workers and their families; to investigate current government policies with regard to workers; to empower workers to fight for their own rights; to promote an independent trade union movement; to preach the gospel to workers and to develop relevant theologies; to serve as a consultant to the Church for its industrial mission.

Hong Kong Christian Industrial Committee
57 Peking Road, 704-5
Kowloon, Hong Kong
Tel: 852 2366 5860
Fax: 852 2724 5098
Email: hkcic@hknet.com
http://www.cic.org.hk/

The words 'Made in China', however, have a double meaning in this chapter. They not only refer to the process of manufacturing, but also the rules that we believe really matter for workers. In this chapter we suggest that for Chinese workers the rules that matter are not found in industry or company codes of conduct which are formulated by teams headquartered in North America or Europe. We suggest that, like the toys, the rules that count are made in China, by factory managers and in the context of contemporary Chinese labour practices. Codes of conduct are well-known, often – though not always – freely available to the public, voluntary and general to the point of being vague. Factory rules and regulations on the other hand are generally unknown outside of the factory gates, obligatory and enforced, and highly specific.

Box 10.2 Asia Monitor Resource Center

The Asia Monitor Resource Center (AMRC) is an independent non-governmental organization (NGO) which focuses on Asian labour concerns. The Center provides information, research, publishing, training, labour networking and related services to trade unions, labour groups and other development NGOs in the region. The Center's main goal is to support democratic and independent labour movements in Asia. In order to achieve this goal, AMRC upholds the principles of worker's empowerment, gender consciousness and follows a participatory framework.

Asia Monitor Resource Center
444 Nathan Road, 8-B
Kowloon, Hong Kong
Tel: 852 2332 1346
Fax: 852 2385 5319
Email: admin@amrc.org.hk
http://www.amrc.org.hk/

In this chapter we examine the gap between corporate codes – in this case all 'Made in America' – and the rules that matter – 'Made in China'. We examine the issue with regard to three giants of the toy world; Mattel, Disney and McDonald's (whose link to the sector consists of its vast array of popular promotional toys). We conclude that if the rules that really count are made in China, then codes of conduct in and of themselves may offer little to workers in the way of addressing issues related to their conditions of employment.

MAKING TOYS IN CHINA

Toys are big business. If we include computer games, the industry accounts for over $71 billion[1] annually in retail sales (ICTI, 2000b). This is the equivalent of every child on earth spending $34 per year on toys – ranging from a high of $372 in North America to a low of $1 in Africa (ICTI, 2000a). In the United States, where over 40 per cent of all toys are consumed, retailers shift over 3 billion units per year comprising over 125,000 separate designs.

Manufacturers located in China now dominate this sector. It is a complicated picture, and generalizations are impossible. Nevertheless, companies located in China exported toys – calculated at manufacturers' prices – to the value of approximately $6.3 billion dollars in 1999 (Nuremberg International Toy Exhibition, 2000). It is impossible to know what this figure might translate to in retail terms, and thus to determine Chinese output as a percentage of a global market worth $71 billion. As a starting point, however, the United States alone imported – at retail prices – $10.7 billion worth of toys from China in 2000 (TMA, 2001). The picture is even more intricate if we take into account statistics published by the Hong Kong Toy Manufacturers Association which indicate that toys exported from mainland China by Hong Kong-based manufacturers stood at around $15.48 billion for the year 2000 (China Online, 2000).

However, despite the complexity of data, we know that toys account for around 3 per cent of all mainland Chinese exports. This production is met, according to the China Toy Association (CTA), by around 6000 toy manufactures (Ye, 1999), most of whom are located in Guangdong province in South-East China (abutting the Northern border of the Hong Kong Special Administrative Region (SAR). Just over 75 per cent of the country's toy factories are located here (Wang, 1998), and even as long ago as 1996 employed over 1.3 million people (AMRC, 1996). The output from this area is of such magnitude that a source contends that 'one out of every six toys in the United States is made in China' ('Mainland base', 2000). China has become the single most important manufacturer of toys in the world today, in a sector that is enormous and which, by most accounts, seems set for continued growth in the long term.

MATTEL, DISNEY AND MCDONALD'S:
CODES AND MONITORING

Of the three companies, Mattel, Disney and McDonald's, only Mattel is solely dedicated to making and selling toys. Despite their other interests, however, Disney and McDonald's are significant players in the market. Disney manufactures and markets an extensive range of toys and games, covering dolls, collectable bean bags, plush toys, musical toys, playsets, electronic games, party sets, stationery and so on. Linked with well-known cartoon characters and Disney movies, these items are often best sellers and trade the world over. McDonald's is best known for its burgers, not toys. None the less, it is one of the largest manufacturers of toys by virtue of its promotional toys that are often released to coincide with Disney movies.

Each company has a code of conduct, but only Mattel has publicly disclosed theirs in full (Mattel, nd). Both McDonald's and Disney have in private meetings or under pressure allowed us to see their codes, or part thereof. The Disney code is published in full in the HKCIC recent report on factories subcontracting for the company (HKCIC, 2001, pp36–7). However, even Mattel, which has issued a detailed list of what it calls 'global manufacturing principles' (GMP), still resists total transparency by keeping secret the standards suppliers are required to meet. For instance, in an independently monitored report on its factory in Chang'an (in the province of Guangdong), monitors were able to state on several occasions that specific facilities (such as dormitories) were 'within GMP standards' (Wong and Frost, 2000, p25). However, without quantifying those standards, we can never be sure whether they conform to standards we ourselves (consumers, activists, trade unionists and so on) consider fair. In the toy industry, Mattel is regarded by some as being the leader with regard to the quality of its code of conduct and its monitoring by an independent team referred to as MIMCO (the results of which are detailed in MIMCO, 1999).

Most companies have not sought to involve as many actors as Mattel, nor have they been as public in the monitoring process. Indeed, if toy companies request that suppliers comply to any code at all, it is most likely that they conform to the industry code; the International Council of Toy Industries (ICTI) Code of Business Practices (ICTI, 1998). The ICTI code presents less challenges for suppliers than does the Mattel code, particularly as it mentions nothing about the right to free association and is designed to be monitored professionally by Intertek Testing Services (ITS), a market leader in the testing, inspection and certification of consumer goods. As with all commercially driven monitoring, the results of the monitoring are a private and confidential matter between the client (the toy company and factory) and the monitoring company. Monitoring is then simply a commercial arrangement whereby a client seeks to pass an audit for the sake of certification.

In an off-the-record conversation, one experienced social auditor in the employ of an auditing firm with a global presence (who must remain nameless to protect her identity) has told us of her experiences in China. She spoke at length about the psychology of the audit; of the battle between the auditor and management. In all cases, she assumes that the factory management is attempting to cheat on the audit and thus sees her job primarily as catching them out. She assumes the presence of a second set of accounts, and accordingly sets about seeking to determine how to best expose the company books in front of her as fake. Tactics include requesting workers to sign their names during the course of interviews so as to provide authentic signatures against which to compare pay records. In more than one instance she has ascertained entire payrolls comprised of employee signatures falsified by management. The falsification of hours worked can be uncovered by comparing data regarding factory output with the output of workers observed over a number of hours. In a number of instances she and her team have been able to verify that employees working legal hours could not produce items in the quantity exported by the factory. In an instance where a factory failed to receive certification, the auditor in question subsequently discovered that another auditing firm was engaged with more positive results.

Given that commercial audits in all cases are announced beforehand, it is unsurprising that few companies fail to receive the certification they desired. As ITS made clear at the Hong Kong Toys and Games Fair, certification for the ICTI Code of Business Practices involves an initial visit to determine areas requiring rectification, and then a future visit to satisfy the auditor that changes have been made. Garret Brown, an Industrial Hygienist with the Department of Industrial Relations for the State of California, and a veteran of over 500 factory inspections, believes that unannounced visits are critical in ensuring that inspectors are able 'to observe (as best as can be done) normal working conditions in the workplace' (Brown, 2000). Brown notes that under both state and federal US law, it is 'illegal [for inspectors] to give employers prior notice of inspections'. It is 'critical' he says, that the first visit be unannounced. He thinks this system should be a part of providing effective enforcement in China too. However, it is not.

Factory management has more than adequate time to prepare for auditing visits, both initial and follow-up. HKCIC researchers have routinely talked to workers producing for Disney and McDonald's who have been coached on the 'correct' answers to give visitors, have participated in factory clean up, and have been given personal protective equipment for the first time on the eve of a social audit.

The failure to comply with either national law or a company or industry code is not uncommon, but in the case of a toy factory subcontracting for McDonald's the result was beyond our worst expectations, and perhaps worse than the violations outlined above. In August 2000, the HKCIC determined that a factory producing toys for McDonald's restaurants in China had engaged several hundred underage workers. HKCIC researchers learnt that the workers were students from high schools recruited to work during their summer holidays, some as young as 13. Subsequent investigations by a journalist from Hong Kong's *South China Morning Post* led to a headline story and worldwide media publicity (Wong, 2000). In the context of this chapter, the salient point to note is that the factory, referred to in the media by name, had been 'evaluated against the McDonald's Code of Conduct for Suppliers in October 1999' (SGS, 2000). The auditor in question was Société Générale de Surveillance (SGS), the 'largest verification, testing and certification organisation in the world [and] global benchmark for the highest standards of expertise, quality and integrity' (SGS, 2001).

With a global public relations nightmare on its hands McDonald's acted swiftly. The following day McDonald's teams were on the spot inspecting the factory. However, investigations by HKCIC established that the factory (owned by Hong Kong interests) had beaten the auditors by sacking workers immediately the story broke. No underage workers were found on site, and workers told HKCIC that underage workers had been sent home. McDonald's, with the assistance of Simon Marketing, the organization responsible for contracting facilities to produce the toys, publicly stated their intent to conduct a thorough review of the factory. Successive statements revealed that McDonald's was satisfied that no underage workers were employed by management. However, on 7 September McDonald's announced that it would terminate the contract with the factory in question, not as a result of the unsubstantiated stories regarding underage workers, but for other problems. Simon Marketing announced that 'the audit revealed certain violations of the code of conduct for suppliers adopted by McDonald's and Simon Marketing, including incomplete employment records. As a result, Simon Marketing has halted all current and future production of McDonald's toys at City Toys' ('McDonald's toy maker sacked', 2000). The future of all workers was cast in doubt.

The incident raised the question for us of whether the code of conduct was more a tool designed to head off adverse publicity than a mechanism devised to protect workers' rights and conditions. The following and final section of this chapter suggests the answer.

'MADE IN CHINA': THE RULES THAT COUNT

As the independent monitoring team in Mattel's Chang'an plant – along with HKCIC in their research into factories subcontracting for Disney and McDonald's – demonstrates, codes of conduct are often poorly known or understood by workers. As the MIMCO Report stated: 'where workers were able to explain elements of the GMP [Mattel's code of conduct], it was more what appeared to be memorization of certain facts' (MIMCO, 1999, p63). In our experience, workers may be ignorant, or confused, about codes of conduct

– their contents or the relevance for their lives – but they have no uncertainty with regard to the rules that matter. Codes formulated, implemented and monitored by outsiders (in these instances all 'Made in America'), are of consequence only in extreme instances and then detrimentally. The real code, the rules that matter, are 'Made in China'.

Workers in Chinese factories producing toys for Mattel, Disney and McDonald's not only understand the rules that matter, but perceive the impact on their lives all too clearly. All of the workers we talk to are acutely aware of the rules by which they must live their lives; the fines and punishment for transgressing them often means the difference between a pay cheque that is meagre and one that is below survival level. Often the rules are unwritten, or not codified, and workers learn them from line supervisors, other workers and by experience. However, HKCIC and AMRC researchers have visited some factories which publish booklets listing rules and regulations. These booklets are handed out to all workers and offer valuable insights into factory life. They also offer an interesting comparison to the often vague codes of conduct.

For instance, Mattel's Code of Conduct – made in America – runs to two, single-spaced pages of A4 paper. However, the Chang'an plant factory handbook – made in China – which lists rules, regulations, pay rates, management systems and so on runs to 11 chapters and 90 pages (*Dongguan Chang'an*, 1999). There are few areas of life untouched in this document. They include: tips for new workers on how to adapt to their new life in Guangdong (most employees are migrants from other provinces); the rights and obligations of the enterprise and workers; how to earn money and become a good citizen; the need to safeguard public order and traffic safety; the terms of recruitment; and information on Mattel's adherence to high quality products. Most interesting for us here, however, is the chapter entitled 'Factory discipline and regulations'.

Here we find the real code of conduct. The chapter is divided into sections, with 26 rules for working on the factory floor, 19 for life in the dormitory, and 9 for the canteen. Factory rules are wide-ranging, and do not include specific occupational health and safety instruction which are covered in a later chapter. Under factory rules, Rule One sets the tone with a grandiose sweep. All staff shall:

> Uphold the legal rights and interests of factory personnel, establish and uphold the socialist market economy's enterprise system, promote economic growth and social progress, and on the basis of national laws and regulations formulate one's own rules (Dongguan Chang'an, 1999, p7).

This goes beyond the most comprehensive of Mattel's GMP, and establishes that workers have commitments to the company, the state, the economy and the success of all three. Other rules are more mundane but nevertheless as thorough.

Rule Three covers a wide range of issues:

Anyone who applies to work in the plant must provide authentic and valid documents. If documents are falsified, you will be held fully responsible. In the case of serious infractions, guilty persons will be handed to the local public security bureau. A worker's probation period is for three months. If during this period, the management ascertains that communication with any worker is impossible, or determines that the worker has a physical problem, or that the employee is not suited to the work assigned, the plant has the right to propose that worker's dismissal (Dongguan Chang'an, 1999, p7).

Rule Seven sets very strict guidelines for worker behaviour. In full it states:

During work hours the following behaviour is prohibited: leaving one's work station to meet with friends and visitors; reading magazines and books; eating, laughing and shouting; leaving one's work station without permission; or preventing others from carrying out their work (Dongguan Chang'an, 1999, p7).

Fees and wages are the subjects of several other chapters. In the chapter entitled 'Recruitment terms and related matters', workers are informed of the fees which will be deducted from their wages. For instance, every worker must pay:

- RMB 4 per month for the electricity and water they use in their dormitory;
- RMB 5 for their factory ID card;
- The cost price of the handbook (that is, *Dongguan Chang'an Meitai wanju erchang: jianjie*, 1999);
- A deposit for equipment provided by the management; and
- RMB 2 per month for the medical fund (*Dongguan Chang'an*, 1999, p48).

It is clear that these are the rules and regulations that matter. Other factory handbooks are less expansive, but are much more detailed than the codes imported from outside.

For instance, in two factories that supply to Hasbro and Disney we can see the same level of detail, if not on the same scale. In Zhongshan Toy Factory Number 1,[2] workers receive a nine-page booklet when entering the workforce. The introductory comments set the tone of the relations between management and workers:

Welcome to [Zhongshan Toy Factory Number 1]. This is a big family. From now on you are in an even better place to work and live. Please read the following by-laws carefully so that you understand and observe them. (Zhongshan Toy Factory Number 1, 2000, p2)

The by-laws are not extensive, but cover day-to-day procedures, personal regulations, welfare facilities and health and safety. In a section entitled 'Procedures for entering the factory', the fees workers are charged for the right to work in the factory are listed:

> New workers arriving at the factory should report to the Administration Section to undergo all formalities. There is a charge of 77 yuan to enter the factory (which consists of a fee of 36 yuan for a temporary resident certificate for six months, 5 yuan for the cost of production for the factory certificate, 8 yuan for your photograph, and 28 yuan for a medical examination). (Zhongshan Toy Factory Number 1, 2000, p2)

Unlike the codes of conduct that grace company reports, these are the rules which bind workers. These rules are not negotiable, and are not the result of activism or corporate responsibility. These booklets, increasingly common, set out point by point the costs, rules and punishments by which workers must abide.

In Dongguan Toy Factory, punishments for infringing rules are more clear. For instance, the factory's Hygiene Charter – a single-page document – specifies a strict regime relating to cleanliness. The first rule states the rules, and spells out in no uncertain manner the cost of infractions:

> Rule 1: Do not spit anywhere, and do not litter. The punishment for your first offence is to copy the hygiene regulations in their entirety 30 times.[3] If you offend again the punishment will be to copy the hygiene regulations in their entirety 100 times. If you offend a third time, you will be expelled from the factory. ('Weisheng gongyue' [Hygiene Charter], 2000).

Infringing the second rule (in fact, a set of by-laws) invites fines up to as much as 20 per cent of a monthly wage or expulsion:

> Rule 2: Keep the toilets clean. It is imperative you keep the toilets clean, cherish the facilities, obey management, and adhere to regulations. If you damage the facilities, you will be required to compensate according to the cost. If you intentionally damage them, then severe punishment will result. If you violate any of the following items whatsoever [the five items cover the use of toilet paper, disposal of sanitary napkins, flushing of toilets, the washing of hands, and prohibitions on defacing the toilet facilities], you will be fined between 5–50 yuan. In addition, you will be required to clean the toilets for a day (the time for which will be arranged by the general services section). Disgusting violations will be punished by expulsion from the factory.

The five by-laws are not in themselves prohibitive. However, the punishments for – for example – substituting newspaper for toilet paper, or failing to wash hands after using the toilet, appear extreme. There are no education and training programmes designed to facilitate the hygienic use of facilities in a large plant. Instead, management simply institutes a table of fines (or expulsion) for transgressions. It is small wonder that Disney's code of conduct has little impact, be it mentally or physically, on workers' lives in this factory.

Space prohibits us from including more examples, but suffice to say that the regulations included above are representative of many we have seen. They are always much more detailed and punitive than the official codes of conduct, more immediate in the lives of workers and, ultimately, more important.

CONCLUSION

Codes of conduct, as we have shown in this chapter, are not formulated, implemented and monitored by the people they are designed to protect. Codes are made elsewhere (in America or Europe), and have little relevance to workers (even if they are aware of them). In fact, we think that workers' lives are ruled by another set of regulations that bear little resemblance to codes of conduct, and are designed and made in China. In no arena, however, are workers themselves able to negotiate for themselves. Whether it is the code of conduct or factory rules that dictate their lives, workers are a silent and invisible stratum with no bargaining rights or ability to determine their conditions. Codes fail to provide workers with any means by which they might effectively make a difference in the way the factory is managed. Until workers are in a position to help write the rules or codes, and are able to directly speak to consumers in North America or Europe – either directly or indirectly – they will remain voiceless. To move beyond codes of conduct is to move into an arena where those concerned do more than interview workers and promote training programmes based on the answers. It may require us to actively engage workers in more creative and long-term relationships than we have envisaged, and to listen to workers so that we may act with them, and not on their behalf.

NOTES

1   Unless otherwise stated, all figures refer to US dollars.
2   Please note that this and Dongguan Toy Factory are pseudonyms. Unlike the Mattel plant, neither the management nor the TNCs involved in either of these plants has shown any evidence of transparency or of engaging with outsiders. Mattel's Chang'an plant is in the public domain at Mattel's bidding; we do not wish to name the other plants for fear of recrimination against workers.
3   Note that the Charter is about 350 Chinese characters in length, and would take perhaps 10–15 minutes to copy by hand. Even allowing 10 minutes per copy, the first offence would occupy a worker for 6 hours (assuming no breaks).

REFERENCES

AMRC (Asia Monitor Resource Centre) (1996) *Labour Rights Report on Hong Kong-Invested Toy Factories in China*, Asia Monitor Resource Centre, Hong Kong

Brown, G (2000) Personal communication, email to Stephen Frost dated 31 July

China Online (2000) 'World's largest exporter of toys, Hong Kong, has few self-owned brands', http://www.chinaonline.com/industry/consumer/News Archive/Secure/2000/October/c00100406.asp, accessed 18 April 2001

Dongguan Chang'an Meitai wanju erchang: jianji (1999) [Mattel's Number 2 Toy Factory at Chang'an, Dongguan: A Brief Introduction]

HKCIC (Hong Kong Christian Industrial Committee) (2001) *Beware of Mickey: Disney's Sweatshop in South China*, Hong Kong Christian Industrial Committee, Hong Kong

ICTI (International Council of Toy Industries) (1998) 'International Council of Toy Industries, Code of Business Practices', http://www.toy-icti.org/mission/bizpractice.htm, accessed 15 February 2001

ICTI (International Council of Toy Industries) (2000a) 'Key figures, 1999', *World Toy Facts and Figures, March*, http://www.toy-icti.org/publications/wtf&f_2000/03.html, accessed 29 November 2000

ICTI (International Council of Toy Industries) (2000b) 'Total toy markets, including video games', *World Toy Facts and Figures, March*, http://www.toy-icti.org/publications/wtf&f_2000/03.html, accessed 14 November 2000

'Mainland base for Santa crew'(2000) *South China Morning Post*, 26 December

'McDonald's toy maker sacked', (2000) *South China Morning Post*, 8 September

MIMCO (Mattel Independent Monitoring Council) (1999) *Global Manufacturing Principles: Audit Report 1999*

Mattel (nd) *Responsibility*, http://www.mattel.com/corporate/company/responsibility/, accessed 15 April 2001

'Nuremberg Int'l Toy Exhibition Expects Chinese Toy Manufacturers' (2000) *People's Daily*, 30 October

SGS (Société Générale de Surveillance) (2000) Extract from SGS ICS press release, 27 August

SGS (Société Générale de Surveillance) (2001) *About us*, http://www.sgsgroup.com/sgsgroup.nsf/pages/about.html, accessed 15 April 2001

Toy Manufacturers of America (TMA) (2001) 'US imports of toy products: Statistics', http://www.toy-tma.co.m/industry/statistics/imports00.html, accessed 18 April 2001

'Weisheng gongyue' [Hygiene Charter] (2000) (Dongguan: Dongguan Toy Factory)

Wang Rong (1998) 'Guandong toy makers buck glum trade trend', *China Daily*, 13–19 September

Wong, M (2000) 'Childhood lost to hard labour', *South China Morning Post*, 27 August

Wong, M and S Frost (2000) *Monitoring Mattel: Codes of conduct, workers and toys in southern China*, Hong Kong, Asia Monitor Resource Centre

Ye Yongjian (1999) 'Chinese toys popular in US, Europe', *China Daily*, 25 February

Zhongshan Toy Factory Number 1: Worker Regulations (2000) Zhongshan: Zhongshan Toy Factory Number 1

Chapter 11

The contradictions in codes: the Sri-Lankan experience

Kelly Dent

SPOTLIGHT ON SRI LANKA

Sri Lanka was the first South Asian country to change from import substitution, which included protective tariffs, and import controls to an export-oriented economy. In 1977, under then President Jayawardena, regulations protecting local industry gave way to regulations for the protection of foreign investors. This economic policy implemented under the guidelines of the International Monetary Fund (IMF) and the World Bank placed greater emphasis on direct foreign investment in achieving the objective of export-led growth, with numerous more than attractive concessions being offered to foreign investors (Heward, 1997). The first free trade zone (FTZ) was established at Katunayake (near to the airport and capital Colombo) in 1978.

Today the garment industry is one of the fastest growing industries in Sri Lanka. Since 1989 exports have increased six fold to a value of 3 billion US dollars in 2000. Garments account for 52 per cent of all exports from Sri Lanka. According to the Ministry of Industrial Development, at the end of 1998 there were more than 280,000[1] garment workers employed in 890[2] factories producing for export across Sri Lanka. This figure does not include workers in the informal sector or those working for factories producing for domestic consumption; 34 per cent of garments produced for export are sent to the European Union (64.2 per cent to the United States). It is worth noting that codes do not apply to factories producing for domestic consumption.

Garment factories are located both inside the various FTZs, industrial parks and estates, and outside in the villages and districts. In 1992, President Premadasa declared the whole of the country an FTZ and simultaneously set

---

BOX 11.1 TRANSNATIONALS INFORMATION EXCHANGE-ASIA (TIE-ASIA)

TIE-Asia is a non-profit, politically independent, regional labour network, founded in 1992 in Asia to encourage and support the development of democratic workers organizations, new forms of organizing and broader social coalitions in the export-oriented industries of South and South-East Asia. Its aim is to promote and implement the rights of mainly women workers and to bring about improvements to the livelihoods of women workers, their families, communities and to society.

TIE-Asia's vision is achieved through:

- encouraging women into leadership positions within the broad labour movement at the local, national, regional and international levels;
- identifying, documenting and analysing new issues, trends and developments including the changing processes of production of transnational corporations (TNCs) and their impact on workers and the labour movement;
- ensuring information is accessible to workers, activists/leaders and organizers in their own languages;
- extensive training programmes;
- regional and national seminars;
- supporting and initiating campaigns from the factory floor and broad labour issues at the national, regional and international levels;
- facilitating (in workers' own languages) the sharing of information, experiences and strategies through focused regional exchange programmes;
- re-establishing links between urban and rural workers through internal exchange programmes;
- networking with other labour and related organizations.

TIE-Asia Regional Office
141 Ananda Rajakaruna Mw
Colombo 10
Sri Lanka
Phone and Fax: +94 74 617 711
Email: tieasia@sri.lanka.net

---

up garment factories in each of the districts, including the war-affected eastern districts, under the Garment 200 Factory Programme.

Inside the FTZs over 75 per cent of workers are single women. These women have migrated from their villages in rural areas to work in the zones, and are mostly aged between 20 and 29 years. Women are preferred as workers in the FTZs as they are seen as a more flexible workforce for employers, easily manipulated and less likely to demand their rights. Women working in factories have a poor image and marriage advertisements in major Sri Lankan newspapers often state 'no factory girls'. They are also largely unorganized.

Some examples of conditions for workers inside the zones include:

- being forced to work long hours of overtime to reach unrealistically high production targets;
- denial of legal entitlements, with leave being extremely difficult to take;
- excessive fines and penalties: ranging from being late; sick; not reaching production targets and refusing compulsory overtime – bonuses, fines and penalties are complex and workers frequently cannot calculate how much they will earn each month;
- repression of the right to organize, form a union or bargain collectively;
- poor or non-existent occupational health and safety practices;
- frequent sexual harassment and imposition of inhumane restrictions such as a time limit per week for going to the toilet;
- lack of transportation, especially after late night shifts;
- misrepresentation by the Board of Investment (BOI) of labour law and frequent attempts to circumvent the law or to make it more 'flexible' for employers.

Conditions outside the factory in the FTZs are no better. There is a lack of adequate infrastructure and housing, transport and medical facilities remain poor. Sexual harassment is also an issue. Workers live in a single cramped room, in a boarding house, often 10 or 12 women share a 10ft x 12ft (3m x 3.5m) room, and cook as well as sleep there (AMRC, 1998, p141). Frequently there is no electricity and a shortage of fresh water. Ventilation and sanitation systems are usually inadequate.

Outside the FTZs, conditions for workers are poor and wages are often lower than in the FTZs; however, there is more freedom for unions to be formed and the living conditions are generally better as workers tend to stay within their village community.

Workers' wages are spent on survival: food; accommodation; transport to and from the factory; and a small amount remitted to their family; sometimes, over several years, workers save some money for marriage. Pay levels are based on the minimum wages concept and are between US$1.04 to US$1.49 per day, these are further reduced by remittances and the continual devaluation of Sri Lanka's currency, the rupee. The World Bank defines extreme poverty as US$1.00 per day.

In the eastern district town of Batticaloa workers can earn as little as US$5.70 per month (19 US cents per day). Anton Marcus, Joint Secretary of the Industrial Transport and General Workers Union (ITGWU) visited Batticaloa and learnt that a substantial number of workers were being paid this training wage for up to one and a half years.[3] In Myhayanganar, a remote area of Sri Lanka, workers are regularly paid below the legal minimum wage.[4] These two examples are typical of an emerging trend in Sri Lanka where major brand labels are being produced for export in remote or isolated areas, where workers are unaware of their basic rights or how to organize, unions are non-existent, there is no knowledge of codes and few job opportunities. This trend presents serious challenges for monitoring supply chains and codes in the garment industry.

CODES AND THE RIGHT TO ORGANIZE: WHAT TO DO?

Codes can be an important tool to use when campaigning for the right to form unions and have them recognized. This is only effective if it is a central focus of campaigning around the code and only if campaigns recognize the need for democratic unions (as difficult as this is to achieve) as an essential prerequisite for all other worker developments. To relegate freedom of association to the 'too hard' basket is not only rendering codes ineffective, it is a violation of basic human rights.

The formation of the Free Trade Zone Workers Unions (FTZWU), established in January 2000, is the result of over 20 years of organizing in the FTZs by the Industrial Transport and General Workers Union, the Women's Centre and the Joint Association. It is the first independent and democratic union to be formed for FTZ workers. Since its inception it has formed 11 branches, six in the garment industry, of which only one has been recognized legally and by the employer. Following the example of the FTZWU other democratic unions have formed in the FTZs.

Recognition for the remaining FTZWU branches is being pursued through the courts and through campaigns. Despite the union following legal processes, the Cosmos Macky factory has stated in writing that the company follows the rules and regulations of the Department of Labour and the BOI, 'and not instructions from any Trade Unions, because trade union activities are prohibited by the BOI [Board of Investment] in the zone.'[5] The union has written to the BOI asking them to clarify their position, but they have not yet responded. Letters have also been sent by the union to the Minister of Labour and to the ILO Office, Colombo, asking them to intervene and ensure that the laws of Sri Lanka are upheld. Cosmos Macky is a Korea/Sri Lanka joint venture company, producing sports- and skiwear for export, under the Cosmack trade mark, located in the Katunayake FTZ.

Of the ten FTZWU branches awaiting recognition, four have been smashed. In the case of Fine Lanka Luggage Ltd, 858 workers lost their jobs for forming a union and the factory closed in March 2000. The factory reopened in May 2001, employing a smaller number of non-unionized staff and 60 of the original and unionized employees under stringent conditions. The conditions were that they withdraw their names from the current court case against the factory, agree to a probation period and do not claim backpay for the period that they were locked out of the factory. Fine Lanka produced labels for: Federated Department Stores (Charter Club and Metopolis labels); Sears Roebuck (Forecast Mendocino); J.C.Penny and Co (Protocol and Support Tech); R.H.

Macy & Co Inc; High Sierra Sports Co (High Sierra); additional labels included Travel Gear, Atlantic, Jeep and Sports Plus.

The FTZWU launched an international campaign including a solidarity appeal to support Fine Lanka workers. As part of the campaign, letters were also sent to owners and buyers of the brand labels above in October 2000 explaining that their codes had been breached and requesting them to intervene and force the management of Fine Lanka to resolve the dispute in accordance with the labour laws of Sri Lanka and their code. To date no response has been received by the owners or buyers.

At Joy Lanka Pvt Ltd 107 union members lost their jobs for forming a union. The company sought permission from the Department of Labour to terminate these workers on the grounds that the company was losing profits.

On 6 September 2000, 410 workers of Venture International in Kotmale (located approximately 125km east of Colombo) producing for major brand labels – Marlboro Classics; AE77 Performance; Mountain Trek Sport & Athletic; Old Navy; Etam; Gap DPP; Marks and Spencer; Catalina and Outdoor Wear – were dismissed under emergency regulations for taking strike action. The strike, banned under emergency regulations, was in support of worker demands for a pay increase, awarded under the same emergency regulation and because their employer had failed to deposit money forcibly deducted from their wages into a savings account, as promised. Again a mass campaign and a court case were launched, however workers remain unemployed.

Using codes as a tool to pressure companies into respecting and implementing the right to organize, freedom of association, collective bargaining, labour laws and ILO conventions has not, in the experience of TIE-Asia in Sri Lanka, been successful yet. This strategy also relies on unions and activist organizations in developed countries being prepared to make these rights central to any campaign. Unions and campaign-based organizations in developed countries – whilst agreeing with this position – express difficulties in gaining popular support for a campaign of this nature.

The Clean Clothes Campaign strategy and evaluation meeting held in Barcleona in March, 2001, attended by unionists and activists from over 29 countries overwhelmingly agreed to a major campaign on the right to organize, form and join unions using codes as a tool. This is an exciting development.

CAMPAIGNING FOR EFFECTIVE CODES

There have been successful campaigns around codes of conduct that have benefited factories, regions or groups of workers. But there are millions of workers worldwide who have not benefited. As mentioned previously, in Sri Lanka alone 750,000 precariously employed women workers stand to be disadvantaged through the misuse of codes.

For majority world countries effective campaigning requires links internationally with unions and well-organized campaign groups in developed countries. However, campaigns devised in developed countries around a specific company or companies, designed to assist workers in producing countries, without consultation with those that they are likely to affect, are problematic. Unions and worker organizations are frequently left to deal with the often disastrous results of these campaigns on the ground, without an awareness of the campaigns nor any input into their implementation. Effective campaigns also need to be long-term and sustainable.

TIE-Asia believes organized workers need to both generate and understand campaigns, including the role and possible positive and negative consequences that information provided by them will play. This is critical if workers are to be empowered. Without this, improvements, if there are any, will be eroded away as TNCs continue to find a way around codes.

MISUSE AND MANIPULATION OF CODES

As described above, buyers, suppliers and investors of the major brand labels often choose to overlook blatant and repressive violations of codes with respect to the formation and operation of unions. However, they are quick to force other provisions of codes on factory-based management and governments if it benefits production and profit. This manipulation of codes by TNCs on governments and workers of producing countries and the manipulation of codes by government to reduce workers' entitlements under the law can be illustrated through the prevailing situation with regard to overtime in Sri Lanka.

The current legislation in Sri Lanka for the private sector states that the maximum number of overtime hours women can work is 100 hours per year. Within this legislation no more than six hours per week should be worked. The total number of weeks that overtime is worked should not exceed 25 per year. There is no corresponding legislation prescribing overtime limits for men.

In July 2000, the government of Sri Lanka sought to amend the overtime legislation to 100 hours of overtime per month. This was subsequently reduced to 80 hours per month. In media releases the chairperson of the BOI, Mr Thilan Wijesinghe, claimed these changes needed to be made so Sri Lanka would remain internationally competitive. He claimed it would be necessary especially when quotas under the Multifibre Arrangement (MFA) are removed in 2005. Wijesinghe inferred the changes were also needed to conform to the codes of major brand labels/retailers who do business in Sri Lanka. This is contrary to most codes that recognize that the labour law and/or a stipulated number of hours should prevail, whichever is better.

Most codes state that overtime should be voluntary. This is not reflected in the proposed changes to legislation nor in statements made by the BOI. A newspaper article by Wijesinghe (2000) announcing that Marks and Spencer was creating a South Asian distribution hub in Sri Lanka appeared at the same time as the changes to overtime legislation, submitted by the Presidential Secretariat (to whom the BOI report), were being considered by the labour department. The FTZWU and TIE-Asia believe that major brand labels were behind these amendments. Marks and Spencer have denied any involvement in the proposed amendments. However, when asked to reaffirm their commitment to the labour laws of Sri Lanka, including freedom of association and the right to organize, they refused to do so.

Employers, investors and the BOI of Sri Lanka justify legislative changes on the basis that workers want extra overtime, citing as evidence the high number of overtime hours that are worked, albeit that these are often forced. Yet workers constantly say that, although they need to work long hours to earn enough money to survive, they still want some control over the overtime hours that they work. In addition, if they received a living wage they would not need to, nor want to work excessive hours of overtime.

The overtime amendment was eventually postponed in Parliament due to pending elections in October 2000, but with elections over the issue will be raised again. The main reason why democratic and independent unions protested against the overtime amendment is that the law as it exists, although routinely violated, offers some protection for workers if they need to refuse overtime work, as should be their right for whatever reason. The very real fear is that if overtime hours were increased to 80 hours per month, then 80 hours would be the amount of 'compulsory or forced' overtime that women workers would be required to work.

This fear is reinforced by a number of judgments from the Supreme Court of Sri Lanka, which state that in certain circumstances overtime is not voluntary. These judgments have applied to the need to meet production orders. Other judgments recognize that an employer has a right to ask an employee to do overtime for a reasonable reason and that the employee has the right to refuse overtime for a reasonable reason.[6]

Positions vary among unions on the provisions that should be contained within the overtime legislation. TIE-Asia's position is that there must be real consultation and discussion with unions before changes are made. Any changes must reinforce the position that all overtime is voluntary and will be remunerated at overtime rates.

Technically, forced overtime would be a violation of most codes, but how can this violation be dealt with? There is no mechanism apart from 'naming and shaming' through protest campaigns and actions to deal with violations. If this amendment is passed, government and the BOI will have succeeded, by using codes to satisfy local and foreign owned suppliers, major retailers, buyers and investors, in reducing the entitlements of an estimated 750,000 women workers. Workers have virtually no redress through a legal system that is already biased against them when it is legal to force extra overtime hours on workers and where precedents support this.

A major campaign is currently underway opposing these changes. The campaign involving unions, labour organizations and women's groups in Sri Lanka so far has obtained the support of the ILO, which has written to the government. Separate letters have also been sent to government and major retailers. Unions and NGOs internationally have responded to urgent appeals by sending protest letters to the Sri Lankan government and solidarity messages to workers.

On 19 March 2001 the government of Sri Lanka signed a memorandum with the International Monetary Fund covering economic and financial polices and technical aspects, without any parliamentary debate or public consultation, committing Sri Lanka to various reforms including reform of the labour market designed to 'facilitate greater labor mobility' (IMF, nd). This agreement was signed in order to receive additional loans. Concurrently relevant government authorities are examining documents recommending changes to labour legislation, including overtime legislation, that are regressive for workers.

MAKING CODES WORK

Training programmes and access to information are central to raising awareness. They enable workers to participate in the debates around codes and to decide for themselves whether they are a relevant tool to use in their strategies for bringing about change in the workplace and society.

TIE-Asia has conducted leadership training programmes for factory floor leaders and organizers in Sri Lanka for the past four years. Topics covered include: labour laws; organizing (includes campaigning and networking); negotiation and grievance settling; health and safety; women in the workforce and labour movement (including barriers to participation) and globalization. Participatory methodologies are used including a mix of presentation, questions, small group discussions and problem solving. For the past two years information and analysis of codes has been included in these programmes, focusing on using codes as a possible tool in the context of organizing, negotiation, campaigning and globalization.

The Women Working Worldwide (WWW) information and education packs on codes and related issues, developed and trialled by WWW with organizers using a participatory approach in Sri Lanka in 1999, have been invaluable resources for training programmes, and taught two important lessons (WWW, 1998). First monitoring and evaluation has confirmed that training related to codes is best located within broader programmes on workers rights. Often separate training on codes makes it seem as if codes are something different to, rather than complementary to, labour rights/organizing. Second, TIE-Asia Training Programmes have been successful in educating workers on their rights and how to obtain these through organizing as well as improving general knowledge on issues such as globalization. They have also led to an increased number of democratic trade unions that have women taking an active role in leadership positions. The Industrial Transport and General Workers Union (ITGWU), FTZWU and TIE-Asia all have 50 per cent or more women on their Executive/Board.

However, despite being well organized and initiating campaigns, it is still not uncommon for these unions to be crushed and workers left unemployed. If the factory reemploys workers there is a huge disincentive to organize another union. Likewise dismissed workers, if they are lucky enough to find work, are often discouraged from organizing. This reinforces the need for campaigns and codes to deliver on freedom of association, the right to organize and collectively bargain. Union leaders in Asia also need education on codes. Many unions are active in organizing workers, but have not had access to information and training on codes, which they in turn can use to educate their members and develop positions and policies.

The complexities of the codes debate are perhaps most apparent in the monitoring and verification processes. Central to effective monitoring and verification is: worker involvement through unions; transparency of the supply chain, including the disclosure of suppliers; and transparency in the audit reports of factories. However, monitoring activities around codes involving either private companies or company employed compliance officers vary in their degree of effectiveness (see O'Rourke, Chapter 16 in this volume, for more discussion of this issue).

Another worrying trend is auditors becoming involved in worker education and competing with unions and/or non-government organizations (NGOs) for involvement in worker training. Late in 1999 a US-based audit company identified the need for combined training of both workers and management (including supervisors) in preventing sexual harassment in the workplace at a factory producing for Tommy Hilfiger in Sri Lanka. The auditor then approached several NGOs, seeking their involvement. Unions were not allowed to contribute. At this time there was an active union in the factory and a major campaign by unions, women's and human rights groups on harassment in the workplace was gathering momentum, both of which the audit company were informed about. Unions pointed to the dangers of combined training of workers and management, and also that training alone would not address the serious issue of sexual harassment in the factory.

CONCLUSION

It is often stated that as labour laws, ILO conventions and constitutions are routinely violated a new approach is necessary. Essentially, regulation has not worked. While to some extent this is true, TIE-Asia does not believe the answer lies in abandoning regulation. After all, if these regulations are mandatory and are not enforced, what hope is there that voluntary legislation will be? Self-regulation or regulation outside existing frameworks (such as legislation, laws, constitutions and so on) can lead to the privatization of labour standards. Voluntary regulation focusing on a specific area, such as clothes, has its uses in spotlighting particular abuses and raising awareness. Where it can reinforce or strengthen existing mandatory regulation its uses are obvious. However, it is doubtful that this will occur on any widespread scale in Asia in the foreseeable future. It may be more productive to ensure that regulation is effective and applies to everyone. This should be done through strengthening existing regulatory mechanisms.

Transnational corporations, as well as speculative investment, need to be regulated and binding. Governments worldwide, in both the developed and majority world, should be pressured to implement ILO conventions that they have signed and – where they have not signed – be pressured to do so. The enforcement capacity of the ILO needs to grow to develop the capacity to force governments and TNCs to implement ILO conventions. Some UN agreements exist that have the potential to rein in global corporations, but these too are under attack by corporations and the US government (Karliner, 1999).

The UN needs to maintain its role as a watchdog and remain an independent enforcer of human rights, including workers' rights. It cannot do this if it is in partnership with TNCs. Governments should also be pressured to implement existing labour legislation in its entirety and, where necessary, for improvements to be made to existing legislation. National labour law and ILO conventions need to be extended to cover areas of the workforce that are not covered at present.

Codes may have some relevance to the workers of Sri Lanka if they can deliver the right to form and join unions, organize, collectively bargain and strengthen existing regulatory frameworks. If codes can assist the mostly women workers of Sri Lanka's FTZ, currently struggling to have their unions recognized at the factory level, then codes will be relevant. Unions, once established and recognized, can then address the multitude of other issues such as the implementation of labour law, a living wage and ILO conventions.

Where strong organization of workers exists at the factory level then codes can be an effective tool for workers to use when putting forward demands for improvements to their wages and conditions. This requires education on codes to be situated within locally conducted broad worker training programmes. Our most important efforts and energy must go into this and continuing to build genuine international trade unionism and real solidarity at the factory floor level.

ACKNOWLEDGEMENTS

This chapter could not have been written without the support from and willingness of workers, worker activists and their unions/organizations to share stories of their struggle and experiences. The author would like to acknowledge their contribution to this chapter.

NOTES

1   The numbers employed in the largest FTZs are: Katunayake (60,409), Biyagama (24,432) and Kogalla (14,000).
2   There are approximately 84 industrial parks in Sri Lanka.
3   This visit took place in February 2001 as part of a TIE-Asia and CWGW District Leadership Training Programme.
4   Information collected during a TIE-Asia District Level Leadership Training Programme in Myhayanganar, August, 2000.
5   Letter dated 12 March 2001 on Cosmos Macky letterhead and signed by a Company Director.
6   Conversation with Attorney at Law, Mr S. Sinnathambi (Sri Lanka).

REFERENCES

Asia Monitor Resource Centre (AMRC) (1998) *We in the Zone*, AMRC, Hong Kong
Heward, S (1997) *Garment Workers and the 200 Garment Factory Programme*, Centre for the Welfare of Garment Workers, Colombo, citing Fernando, L (1988) 'The Challenge of the Open Economy: Trade Unionism in Sri Lanka' in R Southall (ed) *Trade Unions and the New Industrialisation of the Third World*, Zed Books, London, pp 164–81
IMF (nd) 'Sri Lanka Letter of Intent, Memorandum of Economic and Financial Policies and Technical Memorandum of Understanding' http://www.imf.org, accessed 14 May 2001
Karliner, J (1999) *Kofi Annan's Corporate Gambit*, http://www.corpwatch.org, accessed 28 June 2000
Wijesinghe, T (2000) 'We Should not Fear the Crisis of Garment Quota in 2005', *Lanka Deepa* Daily Newspaper 10 May, Colombo, Sri Lanka
Women Working Worldwide (WWW) (1998) *Company Codes of Conduct: What Are They? Can We Use Them? – An Education Pack for Worker Activists*, WWW, Manchester

The potential of codes as part of women's organizations' strategies for promoting the rights of women workers: a Central America perspective

Marina Prieto, Angela Hadjipateras and Jane Turner

The appearance of Free Trade Zones (FTZs) in Central America dates back to the 1970s.[1] However, due to instability throughout Central America during the 1980s, development was slow and in some cases truncated. At the end of this decade there was a steady rise in the number of factories established in the region. The maquila sector employs approximately 400,000,[2] mostly female workers, in 'maquiladora' or assembly factories, some located in FTZs and others outside, taking advantage of a range of fiscal and other incentives offered by the governments to attract foreign investment. In Central America, a high proportion of the maquila industry produces garments, in many cases for big brand names such as Gap, Levis, Nike, Adidas, Docker and Liz Claiborne.

The majority of workers are young women, many single mothers with children and other family members to support on the meagre salaries they earn in the factories. With limited alternative employment opportunities owing to high levels of unemployment in most of the countries in the region, there is widespread exploitation of workers. Long hours, forced overtime, lack of basic health and safety conditions, physical violence, denial of social security and employment rights, lack of access to healthcare and maternity rights, and sexual and psychological harassment are among the many forms of abuse that have been widely documented by women's groups and others concerned with the situation of women workers in factories (Flores and Kennedy, 1996; Kennedy

---

BOX 12.1 CENTRAL AMERICA WOMEN'S NETWORK (CAWN)

CAWN was set up in 1990 by a group of women activists based in the UK with lived experience of, and interest in, the women's movements in Central America. Over the years, it has worked in different ways to raise awareness of, and support for, the work of women's groups in the region in areas such as domestic violence, reproductive health rights and political representation. Alongside this objective, CAWN seeks to promote North-South linkages and solidarity through organizing study tours and exchanges, the production of newsletters and other forms of information dissemination. Currently, CAWN's main focus is on women's labour rights and gender-based violence. Through dialogue and systematic consultation with partners in Central America, CAWN is developing an advocacy role in the United Kingdom in particular to influence campaigns and initiatives on labour rights to include a crucial gender and Southern perspective in their work.

Since 1998, CAWN has also been a member of the Ethical Trading Initiative (ETI) and has played an active role within its non-governmental organization (NGO) caucus. CAWN has two part-time paid workers and relies heavily on the voluntary input of members and supporters.

CAWN
c/o OWA
Bradley Close
White Lion Street
London N1 9PF, UK.
Tel: 020 7833 4075.
Email: cawn@gn.apc.org

---

and Cardoza, 1995; MEC, 2000a; Oxfam-Solidaridad, 1997). Women's courage and determination has also been the focus of different studies (STITCH and Maquila Solidarity Network, 2000).

In recent years, an increasing number of companies supplied by factories operating in Central American FTZs have adopted company codes of conduct. This has partly been brought about by pressure from human rights organizations, women's organizations and trade unions in Central America who have campaigned and raised workers' awareness of their rights. Consumers have also been mobilized by US campaigns to provide proof of ethical sourcing in line with a more generalized global trend emphasizing corporate social responsibility. None the less, the conditions for women in factories still leave a lot to be desired.

Against this background, and in the context of a burgeoning women's movement in Central America[3] and severe limitations faced by trade unions, women's organizations have been founded with a focus on the promotion and defence of women workers and human rights in the maquila sector. Many of these organizations have been set up by women who have come out of the trade union movement.[4] As autonomous organizations working within a feminist and/or gender-aware framework, the approach of these women's organizations differs from that of trade unions and others in that they place women's interests and priorities at the heart of their political strategy (see Box 12.2 for a description of some of the main groups).

While views and experiences vary from country to country, and from one individual to the next, there is widespread consensus among women's organizations throughout Central America as to the value of codes of conduct in terms of their potential to enforce the implementation of national and international labour legislation, and as part of a wider strategy aimed at improving women workers' rights and conditions in the factories.

In the wider debates about codes, the views of women workers and women's organizations tend to be marginalized (Bickham Mendez, 1999; Bickham Mendez and Köpke, 2001). In this chapter, we look at how women's organizations in Central America are responding to codes. Whilst recognizing many inherent problems and limitations with codes, they are finding creative ways of using codes and developing alternative approaches to monitoring as part of their overall strategy for raising awareness and mobilizing women to demand improvements in their working conditions. The views presented in the chapter are based on interviews carried out with representatives of two women's organizations, CODEMUH from Honduras (Colectiva de Mujeres Hondureñas), and MEC (Movimiento de Mujeres Trabajadoras y Desempleadas María Elena Cuadra) from Nicaragua. The chapter also draws on data compiled from personal communications and secondary sources from the region, such as workshop reports and research conducted involving women workers.

APPROACHES AND STRATEGIES OF WOMEN'S ORGANIZATIONS

Awareness-raising with gender sensitivity

The fundamental goal of most women's organizations is to promote women's empowerment and active participation in the defence of their rights. Information is power, and a key strategy for attaining this goal is through awareness-raising, worker training and the development of networks of 'promotoras' or women workers who have received sufficient training to be able to advise other workers on their rights. The promotoras advise workers in their communities as well as on the factory floor (see Box 12.2).

In line with their feminist or gender-focused framework, women's organizations take a holistic approach to training, based on the recognition that women's work-related needs cannot be isolated from their needs as individuals, women and mothers. In short, work in the reproductive sphere is as important as that in the workplace. Women's organizations provide a wide range of training and services including legal and psychological support for women survivors of domestic violence, and information on sexual and reproductive health, as well as training on labour rights and health and safety at work. As such, they respond

BOX 12.2 WOMEN'S ORGANIZATIONS

El Salvador: Movimiento de Mujeres Mélida Anaya Montes, MAM

A feminist organization focusing on gender training, literacy, and promoting human rights among women maquila workers.

Email: melidas@netcomsa.com

Guatemala: Mujeres en Solidaridad: Women in Solidarity

Aims to promote women's rights, with special emphasis on sexual, reproductive, and labour rights and the right to live a dignified life without violence.

Email: gmes96@guatenet

Honduras: Colectiva de Mujeres Hondureñas, CODEMUH

Involved in training and education with women maquila workers from a feminist perspective, through a network of 'promotoras'. A member of the Honduran Monitoring team (EMI).

Email: corcodemuh@globalnet.hn

Nicaragua: Movimiento de Mujeres Trabajadoras y Desempleadas María Elena Cuadra, MEC

A national autonomous women's organization working on campaigning, lobbying, training on human and labour rights, and extensive research into working conditions.

Email: mec@ibw.com.ni

Dominican Republic: Centro de Investigación para la Acción Femenina, CIPAF

A feminist NGO that was directly involved in monitoring Levis factories in 1998. A key player in the Central American monitoring initiative.

Email: cipaf@tricom.net

Mexico: Casa de la Mujer Factor X

A feminist women's collective, promoting organization for the defence of women's human rights, particularly those of maquila workers.

Email: factorx@mail.tji.ceyts.mx

Costa Rica: Asociación de Servicios de Promoción Laboral, ASEPROLA

Provides services in training, research and advice to the region's labour sector with part of their work focused on women workers in the maquila sector. Indirectly linked to the ETI Costa Rica Pilot Project.

Email: aseprola@racsa.co.cr

to women's needs for support in dealing with problems in the home as well as the workplace. The underlying rationale is that women must be empowered to challenge oppression wherever it is, not only the violence or abuse they may face in the workplace.

Openness: seeking cooperation and alliances

The political strategy adopted by women's organizations is to promote communication and dialogue and use tactics based on negotiation and conflict resolution in order to enhance the level of cooperation between themselves, the employers and the state. In the case of Nicaragua, MEC has succeeded in transforming its relationship with the FTZ authorities in Managua from one initially characterized by deep mistrust to one based on mutual respect and cooperation. The pay-offs have been considerable. Currently, MEC can negotiate entry into factories and their legal advisers are permitted to enter the grounds of Las Mercedes, the largest FTZ in Nicaragua, where they provide advice and support to workers. In addition, MEC has started to have monthly meetings with the heads of human resources of three of the factories in order to discuss, and find solutions to, problems faced by women workers.

Similarly, women's organizations are increasingly open to working with trade unions by identifying common issues and respecting differences, and by seeing their respective roles as complementary, rather than antagonistic. One of the main strengths of trade unions is that they are recognized by the state as official representatives of workers with the legal remit to negotiate collective bargaining agreements on their behalf. Women's organizations do not have this recognition, nor do they seek it. On the other hand, trade unions have been widely criticized for their lack of gender awareness and failure to represent the gender-specific interests of women workers, which is the specialism of women worker's organizations (Bickham Mendez and Köpke, 2001).

By contrast, collaboration between women's organizations in the region constitutes a vital component of their strategy. A prime example is the Central American Network of Women in Solidarity with Women Maquila Workers (the Network), which brings together women's organizations involved with labour rights issues from four Central American countries. The Network itself and individual members within it are also building alliances with other sectors of civil society, both nationally and internationally, in order to increase the level of support for change in the maquila sector.[5]

WORKERS' PERSPECTIVES ON CODES AND THEIR USE BY WOMEN'S ORGANIZATIONS

Perhaps the most salient finding to emerge from the regional workshops that took place in Central America[6] was the very low level of awareness of the existence or purpose of codes among workers in all the countries involved. The majority of workers had never heard of codes of conduct and had no idea, therefore, whether the company employing them had signed a code. In the few cases where workers knew that their factory had a code of conduct, it had often not been translated into Spanish and/or it was just pinned up on the wall with no explanation of its purpose. Moreover, many workers expressed fears that any action to defend their rights could lead to dismissal or result in factory closures and companies leaving the country.

Despite these limitations, many of the workers consulted felt that codes could be useful if supplemented by training on how to use them effectively. Training provided by women's organizations, which includes information about codes and a focus on gender awareness-raising and empowerment, has resulted in an increase in workers' levels of awareness of their rights and also their willingness to report abuses. In a workshop in Honduras, women workers reported that whereas before the code was only a piece of paper stuck to the wall with no obvious significance for them, now they have begun looking out for codes in their factories and seeking out information about how they can use them to defend their rights.

None the less, to date, there is little documented evidence of improvements in working conditions resulting from codes. One positive example is that of four factories in the Dominican Republic that applied the Levis code of conduct and were then monitored by a multidisciplinary group in 1998. Magaly Pineda from CIPAF concludes that the factories applying the Levis code had better working conditions than other factories in the same FTZ (Pineda, 2000). Moreover, they offered workers social and health care programmes. The evidence that exists in Central America originates from reports on code compliance in specific factories by Independent Monitoring Groups.[7] For example, in the case of the Commission for the Verification of Corporate Codes of Conduct's (COVERCO) monitoring of a Liz Claiborne factory in Guatemala, after constant complaints from the workers of the abusive and intimidating management style of a particular supervisor her contract was not renewed (COVERCO, 2000). In the experience of Equipo de Monitoreo Independiente's (EMI), who briefly monitored the Kimi factory in Honduras, some of the positive changes noted were a reduction in sackings, unjustified punishments and verbal abuse (Paredes, 1998; Köpke, 2000). The Honduran women's organization CODEMUH has reported some improvements in factories supplying to more than one company, where better conditions were noted in the parts of the factory supplying to a company where a code existed, compared with those where there was no code. A specific example cited by the same organization was the provision of drinking water in a factory where this had not previously been available. Another improvement in the same factory was the relaxation of strict controls on toilet use.

MAKING CODES GENDER-SENSITIVE

One of the major weaknesses of company codes of conduct is that the supposed beneficiaries, in this case mainly women workers, have not been involved in their development, and the codes do not deal with many of the most commonplace abuses in the sector (see Pearson and Seyfang, Chapter 4 in this volume). However, the case of Nicaragua shows how, by involving women workers themselves, it is possible to overcome these weaknesses and ensure that the specific needs of women workers are addressed.

When MEC decided to develop its own Ethical Code (see Box 12.3), the first step was to organize a far-reaching consultation with women workers in the factories to find out from them first-hand what they would like to see included in the code. As a result, the Ethical Code incorporates many of the women's specific demands, such as protection against physical, mental or verbal abuse and respect for women's maternity rights. MEC campaigned actively to get the code accepted and women workers themselves were directly involved in the parliamentary lobbying. In February 1998, the code was signed by the Ministry of Labour and adopted as a Ministerial Decree, and it was subsequently signed by employers in the FTZ in Managua. The code has proved a useful tool, both for lobbying purposes and for training and awareness-raising among women workers and the wider public. While, in general, progress is slow on making codes gender-sensitive, it is encouraging the incorporation of some of the women's specific demands, such as sexual harassment, in multi-stakeholder codes and standards like SA 8000 and the ETI base code.

USING CODES TO COMPLEMENT NATIONAL LEGISLATION

By and large, women's groups in Central America share some of the concerns of many of the trade unions, that codes risk undermining national and international labour legislation and its enforcement. However, they are also aware of the potential of codes as a means of reinforcing and strengthening the implementation of national and international labour standards.

One of the most fruitful ways in which the Ethical Code in Nicaragua has been used by MEC is as a basis for campaigning for the reform of national labour legislation to bring it in line with women workers' demands. In the words of MEC's Director, Sandra Ramos: 'For us, codes are ... an instrument for raising awareness and highlighting what is contained in our national legislation'. She adds that in Nicaragua the experience has been very positive because the Ethical Code placed the issues that concerned women workers on the public agenda.

Women's groups in other countries in the region also concur that the main priority is the enforcement and improvement of national legislation, which is more comprehensive than the provisions of codes. In Honduras, for example, the labour code says that every factory with more than 20–30 workers must have a nearby crèche where women can go and breastfeed their children. It also includes maternity rights, such as the right to pre- and post-natal care. However, the main problem is enforcement. The priority of the women's organizations is to improve the implementation of national legislation. However, this is a big

---

BOX 12.3 THE NICARAGUAN ETHICAL CODE

A Ministerial Resolution adopted in February 1998 by the Nicaraguan Labour Minister, this code applies to all established free trade zones in the national territory.

Art 1 – Employers must ensure that employment of all workers is under the same conditions, without discrimination on the basis of pregnancy, race, religion, age, disability or political belief.

Art 2 – All employers will guarantee job security to their employees without denying their rights, particularly in regard to pregnant women. Women cannot be fired during pregnancy nor during the post-natal period, as is guaranteed by law.

Art 3 – Employers have the obligation to show consideration and respect in the workplace, abstaining from physical, mental or verbal abuse. This includes all acts or omissions which could affect the dignity and self-worth of the workers.

Art 4 – Employers must create working conditions that guarantee physical integrity, observe health and safety, and minimize work-related risks in order to ensure the occupational safety of the workers. This will be done through the following:

- Medical examinations, both regularly scheduled and those specifically prescribed for the particular job;
- Ongoing health education and training designed to prevent occupational accidents and illnesses, and common illnesses which affect the population;
- The implementation of policies designed to improve general safety conditions related to sanitary facilities, buildings, lighting, noise levels, food quality and other related workplace issues;
- Regular reports which could permit both employers and workers to overcome any problems encountered in complying with the measures listed above.

Art 5 – Employers must register their workers in the national social security system in order to guarantee full protection and means of subsistence in the case of disability, old age, occupational injuries, illness, maternity, and, in the case of death, that benefits be directed towards the family or in accordance with the law.

Art 6 – Employers are obliged to guarantee their workers wages and social benefits in compliance with the laws.

Art 7 – All employers must respect the established workday and overtime pay in accordance with the law.

Art 8 – All employers must allow workers to organize in the various forms laid down by the law, including the right to negotiate collective bargaining agreements.

Art 9 – Employing minors under fourteen years of age is prohibited.

Art 10 – This Ministerial Resolution is effective from the date of first publication, regardless of its later publication in the Official Gazette.

---

challenge in the context of limited state regulation and the weaknesses of labour and health ministries. As has been widely reported, there is also a prevailing culture of state corruption, for example labour inspectors are easily bribed by employers and the state is often used by powerful political groups for their own ends. Along with other forms of pressure, codes can serve as a tool or new form of leverage for enforcing these rights.

MONITORING CODES

Simply having a code of conduct is clearly meaningless unless mechanisms are in place for ensuring its implementation. Questions, such as who does the monitoring, how it is done, the transparency of the findings and the involvement of workers in the monitoring process, are of critical importance in determining the value and authenticity of the exercise.

Social auditing

Firms may use a variety of internal and external monitoring procedures and auditors, and a number of issues are raised about their effectiveness (see O'Rourke, Chapter 16 in this volume). Participants at the regional workshops held in Nicaragua in 1999 and 2000 to compare experiences with codes in Central America and the Caribbean felt strongly that workers should be directly involved in monitoring. It was argued that forms of monitoring, verification and certification should be carried out by local organizations familiar with the living and working conditions in the country involved.

Independent monitoring

Central America has seen the emergence in recent years of several independent monitoring initiatives, which have developed alternative monitoring models that address some of the above concerns (see Box 12.4). Some companies, such as Gap and Liz Claiborne, are contracting local independent monitoring groups in countries like El Salvador and Guatemala. Meanwhile, negotiations are underway to allow this system of monitoring to be extended, to be used in more factories and to be adopted in other countries as well. However, the number of factories monitored by independent monitoring groups in Central America is still very small.

   The involvement of women's organizations in such initiatives is of crucial importance in ensuring that the monitoring reflects women workers' particular concerns. Several women's organizations in the region are involved with independent monitoring groups. Their participation takes different forms. In some cases, they have been consulted by monitoring groups, in others they have provided training on rights for the workers, and in the case of CODEMUH in Honduras they actually form part of the independent monitoring team. In Nicaragua, MEC are planning to establish an independent monitoring group. For them, the composition of the monitoring team is absolutely critical in terms of the outcome, so they plan to use multidisciplinary teams of researchers and monitors with expertise in areas such as sexual and reproductive rights, trade

---

BOX 12.4 MONITORING GROUPS

El Salvador: El Salvador Independent Monitoring Group, GMIES

GMIES was set up in 1996 to monitor the resolutions that were negotiated to resolve labour conflict with Gap suppliers, and now monitors for several MNCs.

Email: gmies@amnetsal.com

Guatemala: Guatemalan Independent Monitoring Group, COVERCO

COVERCO's work has focused on the garment and agricultural export industries, as well as the privatized electric power industry.

Email: coverco@infovia.com.gt

Honduras: Independent Monitoring Team, EMI

EMI monitored for Kimi specifically on pregnant women workers and is in negotiation with several MNCs to monitor factories.

Email: Jesuitas@hundetel.hn or corcodemuh@globalnet.hn

---

union issues, and occupational health and safety. Gender balance and gender expertise in the monitoring team will also be ensured to enhance gender-sensitivity in the monitoring methods applied. A key feature of the involvement of women's organizations revolves around their close relationship with women workers. They not only talk to them in the factories and in the streets, but in some cases, they live in the same community, gaining trust and a real understanding of the workers' daily reality.

NEW REGIONAL INITIATIVE

An exciting new initiative bringing together women's organizations with experience of developing gender policies, lobbying, campaigning and research (MEC, CODEMUH, CIPAF), the labour rights NGO ASEPROLA and independent monitoring groups from several countries in the region (see boxes for definitions), is in the making. This initiative seeks to create a new space for lobbying and influencing monitoring practices building on shared experiences and common approaches from a clear gender perspective. The power of such a grouping lies in the combination of women's organizations with their understanding of the needs and priorities of women workers, and the independent monitoring groups with their experience in the development of sound monitoring methods. The credibility of women's organizations and their potential for influence is based not only on their work with women workers, but also on their track record of lobbying both the government and business sectors. There are still many hurdles to overcome and doubts about the genuine commitment of companies to improve their monitoring practices, but, if successful, this could provide a model for the region and beyond.

THE ROLE OF INTERNATIONAL CAMPAIGNS AND SOLIDARITY

Women's groups in Central America fully recognize the vital role played by international campaigns and solidarity in pressurizing companies to adopt codes and conform to minimum labour standards in their factories. However, they are also very critical of the way in which many campaigns have been conducted.[8]

Lack of Southern consultation and gender perspective

Workers and their representatives are very worried that any action taken in the North to defend their rights could lead to dismissal or result in factory closures and companies leaving the country. Job losses are a key concern among workers and they strongly disapprove of actions, such as boycotts, that lead to factory closure. Thus, among the main criticisms is the lack of consultation with groups in the South and with the workers themselves. Northern campaigns tend to view problems in factories solely from their own, predominantly male, perspective, which bears little relation to women's vision. Women's organizations in the region are hardly ever approached, which seems paradoxical considering that around 85 per cent of the workers are women. In Sandra Ramos's words referring to the ETI: 'You need to be present in these spaces so that the voices of women in the South are not left out'.

CONCLUSION

This chapter has tried to make visible the efforts of women's organizations in the region to bring into the debate and practice around codes of conduct an often-excluded gender and Southern perspective. The function and legitimacy of their role in the development and monitoring of codes of conduct stems from their general approach and, more specifically, from their role in facilitating the direct participation of women workers in the design and implementation of codes. Overall, the experience of some of the key women's organizations in Central America suggests that compliance with codes of conduct can potentially promote the interests of women workers in the maquila sector. However, codes of conduct are one of several tools that women's organizations use to improve the implementation of national and international labour legislation.

Their experience also highlights the fact that the potential benefits of codes can only be fully realized if certain key conditions are met. First, it is crucial for workers to be aware of their rights as contained in the company code of conduct, and national and international labour legislation. Second, women workers and/or their representatives must be actively involved at all stages of the process including the design, communication, monitoring and implementation of codes. Assuming these basic conditions are met, codes can be used as a tool by women's organizations as part of their broader strategies to improve the lives of women workers.

However, there are still a great many hurdles to overcome if the potential benefits of codes are to be realized on any significant scale. First and foremost, the importance and value of the contribution and perspectives of women workers in the South must be recognized by all the individuals and institutions involved in the process, including the organizations promoting ethical trade, such as the ETI, campaigning organizations in the North, and trade unionists in both North and South. International solidarity has an important role to play, but this must be based on a two-way exchange of information, including consultation with women workers and women's groups.

In addition, the business sector must prove its commitment to fair and equal treatment of workers by supporting independent and transparent forms of monitoring and the involvement of civil society organizations, including women's groups, in the monitoring process. Resources are also needed for documenting, comparing and evaluating the impact of codes and monitoring processes in a range of different contexts so as to highlight both the strengths and limitations of codes and build these insights into future policies and approaches.

Many aspects of the approach and strategies adopted by women's groups in Central America can, and should, serve as a model for others seeking to promote the interests of women workers in export-processing zones around the world. MEC's success in getting its own Ethical Code approved and adopted in Nicaragua, CODEMUH's use of codes as a tool for empowering women workers in the domestic, as well the employment, sphere, and the use of effective negotiation and alliance-building strategies by both groups, are just a few examples. Recent and ongoing initiatives involving these women's groups and others in the Central America region may also provide a valuable model for the development of transparent, independent and gender-sensitive forms of monitoring. It is up to all those genuinely committed to the advancement of women's interests to learn from and act upon these examples and provide their support in ways that enhance, rather than undermine, the efforts of women's organizations in Central America and beyond.

ACKNOWLEDGEMENTS

We would like to thank Ronald Köpke, Sandra Ramos and Maria Luisa Regaldo for their comments on an earlier draft, and Megan Caine for assistance with the editing.

NOTES

1   In El Salvador the first FTZ appeared in 1974, in Honduras 1976, Guatemala 1978, Nicaragua 1976 and in Costa Rica 1975 (OIT, 1996).
2   Numbers employed in the maquila industry and number of factories are as follows: Nicaragua: 24,000 in 38 factories with plans for expansion over the coming years (La Prensa, 2000); Honduras: 125,000 in 250 factories; Guatemala: 115,000 in 280 factories (ILO, 1999); El Salvador: 79,000 in 220 factories (USAID/SETFE/MTPS, 2000); in Costa Rica: 49,000 in 188 factories (Quinteros, 2000b). There is also evidence that these factories subcontract out their work to small workshops. In Guatemala, for example, up to 50 per cent of the work can legally be contracted outside the factory.
3   From the mid-1980, and into the 1990s, the women's movement in Central America went through a period of intensive development and expansion. New women's organizations appeared with diverse identities, many with a feminist background creating spaces for women's increasing participation and organization around a wide range of issues.
4   For women's participation in trade unions see Naranjo Porras (2000) and Quinteros (2000b). For an analysis of different 'actors' working on labour issues in the maquila in Central America see Quinteros (2000a)
5   Members of the Network have contacts with women's organizations internationally, particularly in Canada, the United Kingdom, Spain and, more recently, in Asia. For example, in February 2001, MEC hosted an Asia-Latin America Exchange workshop in Nicaragua attended by women from several Asian countries to exchange experience and discuss successful strategies (report available at http://www.maquilasolidarity.org)
6   As part of the effort to inform debates in the North on codes as a means for improving worker conditions, and to generate debate in Central America, several initiatives have taken place. These include two regional workshops with the participation of women workers, representatives of women's organizations and trade unions in the region to discuss their views on codes of conduct and monitoring (MEC, 2000b; CAWN and WWW, 1999).
7   Independent Monitoring Groups in the region: El Salvador (GMIES, the Salvador Independent Monitoring Group), Honduras (EMI, the Independent Monitoring Team), and Guatemala (COVERCO, Guatemalan Independent Monitoring Group).
8   For North-South relations and Codes of Conduct, see CODEMUH (2000)

REFERENCES

Bickham Mendez, J (1999) 'Creating Alternatives for Resistance: Gender and the Politics of Transnationalism in Nicaragua' unpublished dissertation. University of California, Davis

Bickham Mendez, J and R Köpke (2001) *Mujeres y Maquila. Respuestas a la Globalización: Organizaciones de Mujeres Centroamericanas en medio de la Competencia y Cooperación Transnacional en la Industria Maquilera,*2nd edn, Ediciones Heinrich Böll, San Salvador

CAWN (Central American Women's Network) and WWW (Women Working Worldwide) (1999) *Women Workers and Codes of Conduct: A Central American Workshop Report,* Nicaragua (Spanish and English versions)

CODEMUH (2000) *Memoria Evento: Solidaridad Norte/Sur, Códigos de Conducta y Monitoreo Independiente,* San Pedro Sula, Honduras

COVERCO (2000) *2nd Public Report, Independent Monitoring Pilot Project, Liz Claiborne Inc,* August

Flores, M and M Kennedy (1996) *Trabajadoras de las Maquilas en Villanueva: Mujeres jóvenes, familia y vida cotidiana,* CEM-H, Tegucigalpa, Honduras

ILO (International Labour Organization) (1999) *Project for Women Workers in the Maquila,* Guatemala

Kennedy, M and M Cardoza (1995) *Mujeres en la Maquila: el caso de la ZIP Choloma,* CEM-H, San Pedro Sula, Honduras

Köpke, R (2000) Las experiencias del Equipo de Monitoreo Independiente de Honduras (EMI), unpublished, Honduras

La Prensa (2000) '*Cae Industria Nica y crece la maquila*' by Gabriela Roa Romero, 18 June, 2000, http://www-ni.laprensa.com.ni/cronologico/2000/junio/18/nacionales/ nacionales-20000618-06.html

MEC (Movimiento de Mujeres Trabajadoras y Desempleadas María Elena Cuadra) (2000a) *Diagnóstico sobre las condiciones socio laborales de las Empresas de las Zonas Francas,* Managua, Nicaragua

MEC (Movimiento de Mujeres Trabajadoras y Desempleadas María Elena Cuadra) (2000b) *Memoria Taller Regional: Responsabilidad social de las empresas, códigos de conducta y monitoreo independiente,* Managua, Nicaragua (Spanish and English versions)

Naranjo Porras, A V (2000) *Participación Sindical de la Mujeres en Centroámerica,* ASEPROLA, Costa Rica

OIT (ILO) Organización Internacional del Trabajo (1996) *La Situación Laboral en las Zonas Francas y Empresas Maquiladoras del Istmo Centroamericano y República Dominicana.*

Oxfam-Solidaridad (1997) *Las Repúblicas Maquiladoras: las zonas francas en El Salvador, Guatemala, Honduras y Nicaragua,* Oxfam, Brussels

Paredes, M (1998) *Informe sobre Experiencias y Reflexiones del Equipo de Monitoreo Independiente (EMI) en la Empresa KIMI de Honduras.* San Salvador

Pineda, M (2000) 'Monitoreando el Monitoreo: El caso de Levis Strauss & Co. en la República Dominicana' in R Köpke, N Molina and C Quinteros (eds) *Códigos de Conducta y Monitoreo en la Indústria de Confección. Experiencias Internacionales y Regionales,* Ediciones Böll, San Salvador

Quinteros, C (2000a) Resistiendo creativamente. Actores y acción laboral en las maquilas de ropa en Centroamérica, unpublished, Tesis Maestría, Universidad de Costa Rica

Quinteros, C (2000b) *Mujer, Maquila y Organización sindical en Centroamérica,* ASEPROPLA, Costa Rica

STITCH and the Maquila Solidarity Network (2000) *Women Behind the Labels: Worker Testimonies from Central America.*

USAID/SETFE/MTPS (2000) *Informe del Monitoreo de la Maquilas y Recintos San Salvador,* July.

Chapter 13

The fox guarding the chicken coop: garment industry monitoring in Los Angeles

Laura Dubinsky

INTRODUCTION

In 1992, with great fanfare, Guess? Inc became the first American clothing manufacturer to sign an agreement with the Department of Labor (DOL) whereby contractors would be monitored for compliance with labour standards. The agreement between Southern California's largest clothing employer and the Department of Labor was hailed by the government and the press as a blueprint for corporate responsibility. The Guess-DOL monitoring format has since been replicated with enthusiasm, first in other agreements between the DOL and garment manufacturers to cover domestic contractors, and more recently through the international monitoring initiatives of the Fair Labor Association. Yet the Guess monitoring programme failed catastrophically to improve working conditions for contract workers. In 1996, after the exposure of widespread continuing violations including child labour, illegal industrial homework, unpaid overtime and sub-minimum wage labour in Guess contract shops, Guess was suspended from the DOL's Trendsetter list of responsible manufacturers. Guess also, while implementing its monitoring programme, ran a virulent anti-union campaign, including mass firings and overt intimidation. In 1997, Guess moved much of its garment manufacturing work to Mexico.

   The failure of the Guess monitoring programme raises troubling questions about the proliferation of new self-policing monitoring schemes, both in the United States and internationally. If corporate codes are to be effective, particularly in complex international supply chains, one would surely expect that

---

Box 13.1 Union of Needletrades, Industrial and Textile Employees (UNITE)

UNITE, a trade union known for its aggressive organizing tactics, represents around 250,000 workers in the United States, Canada and Puerto Rico. UNITE was formed in 1995 from the merger of the textiles and garment unions, the Amalgamated Clothing and Textile Workers Union and the International Ladies' Garment Workers' Union. Around half UNITE's members work in textile and garment manufacture: UNITE also represents workers in many other industries, including warehousing, industrial laundries, retail and nursing homes. UNITE is committed to improving working conditions, particularly for low-wage workers, through organizing and collective bargaining, through political and solidarity campaigns; and through its 'Stop Sweatshops' campaign.

UNITE
1710 Broadway
New York, NY 10019
USA
Tel: 212-265-7000
http://www.uniteunion.org

---

a monitoring programme for domestic contractors, under the scrutiny of a US government department, would be properly enforced.

This chapter suggests that two points about monitoring are illustrated by the Guess experience. The first is that self-monitoring is dangerous: it is risky to allow manufacturers, who profit from lower labour costs, to control the policing of working conditions in their contractors. The manufacturer may establish an ineffective monitoring programme, allow abuses to continue; and *still* reap the public relations bonanza of a seal of approval from a respected body such as the DOL or Fair Labor Association. The existence of a monitoring programme thus provides the manufacturer with a form of immunity from further criticism.

The second point is that unless monitoring is focused upon freedom of association, monitoring (even when overseen by independent organizations) may not help, and may in fact hinder worker organization. The DOL agreement did not oblige Guess to stay and improve the situation at contractors found to be violating labour standards: on the contrary, the agreement required Guess to sever relations with abusive contractors. When workers complained of substandard conditions, Guess could throw up its hands in horror, cite its responsibilities and move on. Contractors used this to threaten union activists in their shops: they repeatedly warned their employees that speaking out could lead to loss of the Guess contract and factory closure.

In addition, while monitoring has the potential to help workers to organize by shining a spotlight on particular workplaces, the presence of a monitoring programme can also have the opposite effect, deflecting criticism of anti-union policies, and convincing observers that all is well.

GUESS IN THE GARMENT PRODUCTION CHAIN

In 1992, Guess employed over 3000 workers in greater Los Angeles, most of them Mexican and Central American immigrants, in over 100 contract shops. Established by the Marcianos, four Algerian-born brothers in 1981, Guess expanded from its initial designer jeans niche into other lines of clothing. Annual global sales in 1992 topped $700 million. Until 1997, over 75 per cent of Guess' production was done in Los Angeles. Guess prided itself on being able to place 'Made in the USA' labels in its clothes.

Guess is a 'manufacturer' in that it cuts and designs its own clothes and arranges production: it also does some of its own retailing in its own retail outlets, and controls distribution and merchandizing. However, the 'manufacturer' term is a misnomer: like most large garment manufacturers, Guess has contracted out its manufacturing operations to multiple small 'contractor' firms, some of which in turn subcontract out overflow work.

As a large manufacturer that does some of its own retailing, Guess is near the top of the garment production hierarchy. Large manufacturers and retailers are able to dictate the price they will pay for goods from contractors. Through their control over pricing, retailers and large manufacturers shape the working conditions in the contract shops, even though they do not directly employ the garment workers. Contractors will often accept unprofitable deals to retain the work of a manufacturer, and then will try to lower labour costs, often by breaking wage and hour laws or by subcontracting to a firm even lower down the chain that is willing to lower labour costs further. Meanwhile, the contracting relationship provides a convenient shield for large manufacturers and retailers. To the public they can plead ignorance of shopfloor abuses and, to the courts, because there is no direct employment relationship, they can deny legal liability. In this way, the risks of breaking the law are passed on to contractors.

THE LOS ANGELES GARMENT INDUSTRY

The Los Angeles garment industry is ripe for this type of abuse. Los Angeles has a burgeoning informal economy staffed largely by immigrant workers, many of them undocumented, marginalized by language difficulties and their precarious legal status. According to the most recent Immigration and Naturalization figures available (1996) 40 per cent of the US undocumented immigrant population, or over 2 million, are thought to live in California. In the garment industry, where small, low-capitalized factories can shut down and reopen the next day two streets away under a new name, it is especially easy to fall outside the net of government inspections and labour standards.

The Los Angeles clothing industry has undergone a remarkable period of growth. Bonacich and Applebaum (2000) have described the conditions that have allowed the Los Angeles garment industry to thrive: a symbiotic relationship with the local arts and entertainment industry; the quick turnaround needs of women's clothing manufacture; and the role of immigrant workers in providing cheap labour and immigrant entrepreneurs in running the contract shops. In 1997, Los Angeles had 118,000 garment-industry jobs, second only to high-technology employment in manufacturing (California Economic Development Department figures, summarized in Quinones (1997)). This was a national anomaly: the rest of the US garment industry was at this time suffering dramatic job losses.

Sweatshop labour is endemic in the Los Angeles garment industry: in 2000, 98 per cent of the Los Angeles garment industry was estimated to be violating health and safety laws, and 66 per cent wage and hour laws (Cal/OSHA 2000, cited in Esbenshade (2001)).

THE DOL ATTEMPTS TO CLEAN UP THE LOS ANGELES GARMENT INDUSTRY

Given its structure, the only effective way to regulate the Los Angeles garment industry is to target manufacturers. If government inspectors focus their enforcement efforts solely on raiding and fining individual contractors, they risk simply driving the problem of abusive workplace practices further underground. Targeted contractors are likely to close down and manufacturers will move work to new and less visible contractors (or the same contractor now operating under a new name) in search of cheaper labour.

The DOL could not hold manufacturers liable as joint employers for labour violations in the contract shops: successive Republican governors had vetoed joint employer liability legislation. Instead, the DOL resurrected Section 15 of the 1938 Fair Labor Standards Act (FLSA) which allows the government to prevent the shipping across state lines of 'hot goods' made in violation of federal laws. The DOL used the threats of hot goods seizures and litigation to lever manufacturers into agreeing to monitor their own contractors.

Guess? Inc. was picked as the DOL's first target. In investigations dating back to 1989, the DOL had discovered serious violations at Guess contractors, including child labour. Under the threat of DOL hot goods litigation, Guess signed a memorandum of agreement with the DOL. The DOL agreed not to sue for the violations it had found in the contractors. In return, Guess would pay the $573,000 of backwages owed in those shops and require that its contractors sign Employer Contracting Compliance Agreements committing to obey the Fair Labor Standards Act (which covers wages, hours, record-keeping and child labour). Guess would initiate a worker education programme at the contractors regarding FLSA rights; set up a toll-free (freephone) number for workers to call to report abuses; and train its own quality control personnel to monitor for FLSA violations. Contractors would either have to take on a payroll service, or be audited by Guess for wage and hours every 90 days (if violations were found, audits would be stepped up). If a contractor was unable to pay any backwages due, Guess would cover the cost, and Guess would pay a sufficient price to its contractors to allow workers to earn the minimum wage and, if necessary, overtime. Guess would notify the DOL of violations found in the contract shops, and if Guess found evidence of underage employees, sub-minimum wage pay or unpaid overtime, Guess would stop doing business with that contractor.

Over the next six years, another 62 California apparel firms (all but two based in Los Angeles) signed similar Augmented Compliance Program Agreements with the DOL. Hundreds of other Los Angeles apparel firms voluntarily undertook to monitor their contractors. A lucrative compliance consultancy business was spawned in Los Angeles, with compliance firms charging an average of $300 to $350 per contractor visit (Esbenshade, 2001). In 1995, a consortium of Los Angeles apparel manufacturers signed a similar agreement with the Department of Labor and launched the 'Los Angeles Compliance Alliance' with its own label. In the same year, the Department of Labor launched the Trendsetter list, a national roster of apparel firms that had committed to obeying US labour laws.

GUESS MONITORS ITS CONTRACTORS

The agreement between Guess and the DOL did not specify who should do the monitoring on Guess's behalf. Guess hired an internal director of compliance, Connie Meza – who had administrative experience, but no experience of monitoring or of the apparel industry – and two inspectors. After Connie Meza left in 1993[1] her job was eventually taken over by her former secretary. The quality control staff were also to watch for labour law violations. In addition to the internal monitoring, outside firms were taken on to help: Stonefield Josephson, and Cal Safety, California's largest compliance firm. During audits, which were, in principle, to take place at 3-month intervals, Spanish-speaking internal inspectors and compliance firm inspectors checked time cards, the payroll journal and interviewed a random selection of 5–10 per cent of the workforce, usually at their machines.

In 1997, during litigation by Guess workers and UNITE over wage and hour violations, many of Guess' monitoring records became available. The documents provide an extraordinary insight into the Guess monitoring programme. Fundamental flaws in the monitoring programme are apparent from the documents: violations were frequently overlooked; when violations were found, remedial action was rarely taken; and when Guess *did* respond to violations in the contract shop, the measures taken might have adverse consequences for workers.

Contractors violate US wage and hour laws through a variety of schemes. Very commonly, contractors are able to avoid paying the minimum wage and also the legal overtime premium by telling workers to punch in for fewer hours than are actually worked. Piece workers are especially easily cheated: even if the worker is punching in for correct hours, a fictional piece rate may still appear on the paycheque which falsely suggests that the rate was multiplied by the mandatory one and a half times for overtime hours. More rarely, contractors may use homework: workers do work at home on their own machines, often with the unpaid help of family members. Industrial homework is illegal in the United States because it allows the evasion of any regulation of hours, wages, health and safety, and child labour.

At A&R for example , a denim shop which employed around 35 workers, cash payment and industrial homework went unnoticed for years by Guess inspectors; meanwhile, child labour and off-the-clock work were noticed but went unremedied. In July 1996, an internal Guess auditor found '22 employees on the floor and only 14 time cards punched' and a 13-year old working with her mother (US DOL document GU0019). The DOL agreement had laid down the prescribed response for child labour violations. Guess was to pay a scholarship for the child and sever its relationship immediately with the contractor. However, there are no records of any follow up by Guess to the child labour violation at A&R and Guess continued to send work to A&R. The Guess inspectors did not report finding any evidence of illegal industrial homework or payment in cash. However, in November 1996, workers were found by a DOL investigator to still be working off the clock; certain workers were being paid in cash; piece workers were not being informed of their piece rate until after the completion of work; and there was an illegal homework operation being run from the shop.

At Buzz, which had a workforce of around 150 working exclusively for Guess, an illegal payment and off-the-clock-work scheme *was* noticed by Guess inspectors but none the less continued for over two years (US DOL documents GU0303; GU0161; GU0272). In December 1993, Guess auditors reported that Buzz workers were being told to punch out early and keep working. They were paid in chits for the extra hours worked, and could only cash the chits at a truck outside the factory for a fee of $2.00 for every $100.00 of wages. Yet Division of Labor Standards Enforcement hearings in 1997 found that the chit-cashing operation had continued at Buzz until the summer of 1996 (California State Case No. 35-12194-188/172). Buzz also had an illegal homework operation which had not been mentioned by the auditors and which was discovered in August 1996 by TIPP, the joint federal and state governments' Targeted Industries Partnership Program. However, the DOL's own lack of resources meant that even when, as at Buzz, violations were discovered by government inspectors and backwages were assessed for workers, workers rarely received the money. Under the Guess-DOL agreement, backwages owed to workers that were collected from Guess would be held by the DOL for six months, and, if the DOL did not locate the workers, the monies went back to Guess. In 1997, for example, UNITE discovered that only 13 out of an estimated 150 workers from Buzz had been paid the backwages owed to them. Little effort had been made to reach the other workers and the remaining money was about to be returned to Guess.[2]

At Infinity Jeans, employing around 130 workers in Vernon, where between 50 and 80 per cent of the work in the shop was for Guess, discovery of minimum wage violations resulted in work speed-ups and firings. In June 1993, 11 piece-work trimmers told a Guess inspector that they were working extra hours in the mornings and on the weekends off the time clock, meaning that they were not earning the minimum wage nor were they receiving the mandatory overtime premiums. The inspector calculated that the 11 workers were earning an average of $2.88 per hour (the minimum wage being $4.25) (US DOL documents GU 0522; GU 0444; GU 0519). In response, rather than increase the *rate paid* per piece of work to bring piece workers' hourly earnings up to the minimum wage, or guarantee a minimum of $4.25 per hour, Infinity exerted additional pressure on the workers to speed up and *produce more* pieces per hour. In September 1993, the contractor wrote to the Guess inspector to tell him that measures were being taken to ensure compliance with the law (US DOL document GU 0514). These included appointing a new supervisor who would report daily on workers whose hourly piece rate production fell below the minimum wage, and firing workers who were not working fast enough for their piece rate to match the minimum wage. One of the trimmers who had initially complained to the Guess inspector was among those fired. This was still not the end of working off the clock. In June 1996, a worker reported to Guess that she was working eight-hour days but only punching in for three hours, and was working entirely off the clock on Saturdays: she had an average wage of $2.59 per hour (US DOL document GU0467).

When a *New York Times* reporter questioned Guess's General Counsel, Stan Levy about Guess's dealings with repeat violators of labour laws, 'he said Guess cut off business with repeat offenders, while pressing large factories with violations to comply with the law. Guess, he acknowledged, hesitated to cut off big contractors for fear of throwing scores of employees out of work. "Guess had a lot of sympathy for the workers," he said, "As a result, sometimes you give more than three strikes [from three-strikes-and-you're-out baseball rules]. Sometimes you'll give companies four strikes."' (Greenhouse, 1997)

GUESS CONTRACT WORKERS SPEAK OUT

However, this sympathy dried up when workers attempted to speak out. When workers from Kelly's and Jeans Plus attempted to organize a union in 1996, and workers from Kelly's cooperated with the Department of Labor Standards Enforcement's (DLSE) investigation of homework in their factory, Guess withdrew its work from the shops. The contractors, which had employed over 450 workers between them, subsequently closed down. The ostensible reason for withdrawing the work was because of multiple violations found in the shops. However, as seen, Guess continued to do business with other contractors after violations had been found, including those types of violations (employment of minors, minimum wage and overtime violations) which were supposed to lead to automatic withdrawal of work according to the agreement with the DOL.

The Guess-DOL agreement covered Fair Labor Standard Act rights (minimum wage, overtime pay, no child labour) but did not cover workers' rights to take collective action, organize a union or bargain collectively. This appears to be typical of apparel monitoring in Los Angeles. Jill Esbenshade's study of compliance monitoring firms in Los Angeles found that none of the firms surveyed examined freedom of association in their audits (Esbenshade, 1999). Richard Reinis, a prominent attorney for the Los Angeles apparel industry who heads the Compliance Alliance, told her: 'Through self-policing, my monitoring, the workers are able to improve their standard of living, their wage level, without organizing in effect … the workers don't need to organize, they don't need to pay dues to Jay Mazur [President of UNITE] in order to obtain the benefit because they have stronger forces than even the union in order to compel payment in accordance with the law.'

While its monitoring programme was ongoing, Guess was cracking down on worker attempts to organize and speak out. In 1996, Guess's direct employees at its warehouse tried to organize with UNITE: after 20 union activists were fired, Guess was ordered by the National Labor Relations Board to pay $113,000 in backpay.

In August 1996, Guess contract workers had launched a class action suit against the contractors and Guess over wage and hour violations. Guess and the contractors worked together to pressurize workers to drop the case. Guess sent members of its compliance department to the contract shops to ask workers to sign forms opting out from the lawsuit. Two workers from the Pride contractor were locked into a room with Guess compliance officials and told to sign the form to drop out of the lawsuit. In at least two shops, the owner-contractor first met with the workers to warn them that if the lawsuit continued, the factory might close leaving the workers without jobs (California State Case BC 155 165 1997). The judge examining the opt-outs decided that they were invalid; and the class action suit continued.

GUESS FALLS FROM GRACE

Meanwhile, investigators from the Department of Labor and the California Division of Labor Standards Enforcement continued to find Guess contractors violating labour standards. Between January 1996 and January 1997 alone, the DOL and DLSE found violations in 20 different Guess contractors, owing a total of $244,580 in backpay (US DOL quarterly No Sweat Reports for 1997, DLSE Targeted Industries Partnership Program Reports for 1997). In July and

August 1996, the DLSE found that Guess clothing was being sent out from three contractors for illegal industrial homework. In July 1997, more evidence of industrial homework by Guess contractors was found.

In November 1996, the DOL suspended Guess from its Trendsetter list citing 'lack of attention to obtaining back wages for contractor employees, as required by [Guess'] agreement with the department, and systemic failures of monitoring practices.' (Letter from Suzanne Seiden, Director of Special Projects, Department of Labor to Glenn Weinman, Guess General Counsel, November 26 1996). Guess, however, continued to refer to its trendsetter status in publicity for its clothing and in its response to allegations of abuse by workers.

In 1997, Guess placed advertisements about its sweatshop-free status in the *Washington Post*, the *New York Times*, *Newsday* and the *Los Angeles Times*: 'Guess? is proud of its labour record during this season of conscience. Guess supports workers' rights ... manufacturers' voluntary monitoring programs work!!' said one Guess advertisement. Another advertisement declared that: 'After review by the state and federal Departments of Labor during the last 12 months, Guess? contractors are 100% guaranteed sweatshop free and in full compliance with fair labor standard laws.' The DOL sent Guess a sharp letter of protest: 'the Trendsetter list ... is not intended to serve as an endorsement of the companies that appear on the list. Moreover, Guess? was placed on probationary status with respect to the list one year ago ...' (Letter from Marvin Krislov, Deputy Solicitor for National Operations, Department of Labor, to Glenn Weinman, Guess General Counsel on December 8 1997).

GUESS MOVES PRODUCTION TO MEXICO

In January 1997, Guess? Inc announced that it would move 40 per cent of its production to Mexico. Richard Reinis, head of the Compliance Alliance, suggested that the move was a response to pressures to comply with labour laws: 'We're experiencing tremendous pressure from a very effective Department of Labor Wage and Hour division. ... The conditions here are making it inhospitable' (Kanter, 1997). Guess simply stated that it was moving to remain competitive.

Guess continued its monitoring practices in Mexico, at a safer remove from the eyes of US government inspectors, journalists and UNITE. In 1998, the National Interfaith Committee for Worker Justice (NICWJ) investigated conditions in maquiladoras in Tehuacan, Mexico. The NICWJ reported multiple abuses, including child labour, unpaid overtime; and armed guards preventing workers from leaving the factory during their shift, and concluded that in Tehuacan, 'worker rights are not respected and codes of conduct are not enforced' (NICWJ, 1998). Guess, a major customer for the Tehuacan maquiladoras, dismissed the allegations, pointing to the fact that it had an 'extensive monitoring program in Mexico' and that Cal Safety and its own compliance director paid regular visits to the Mexican contract shops (Smith, 1998).

Guess's remaining US workforce is still non-union. In July 1999, Guess agreed to settle out of court the class action suit by the Los Angeles contract workers, paying up to $35,000 per worker, to a total of up to $1 million.

Meanwhile, despite the loss of the programme's poster child, the DOL's attempts to encourage corporate self-policing in the Los Angeles apparel industry initially appeared to be making an impact. In 1996, the DOL's Survey of LA garment shops showed that overall compliance with wage and hour laws in Los Angeles was up to 39 per cent from 22 per cent in 1994. They also found that 58 per cent of monitored shops were in overall compliance with labour standards laws, compared to 22 per cent of non-monitored shops. (Of course, this still meant that over 40 per cent of all monitored contractors were not in compliance.)

More recently, the DOL's programme has suffered setbacks. By 1998, the DOL found that the prevalence of monitoring had risen sharply: 77 per cent of Los Angeles garment contractors were now being monitored, up from 48 per cent in 1996. Yet overall compliance rates for Los Angeles were disappointingly unchanged since 1996 at 39 per cent. The latest figures, for 2000, have cast more doubt over monitoring in Los Angeles: compliance rates are now falling, with a dramatic drop in compliance rates for monitored shops. Overall compliance rates for 2000 were at 33 per cent. Less than half of the monitored shops were now in compliance: compliance in monitored shops was at 44 per cent, compared to 11 per cent compliance in non-monitored shops (US DOL 2000).

CONCLUSION

The monitoring programme at Guess was a disaster. The intended beneficiaries of the scheme, the workers, enjoyed no material improvement in their working conditions and were threatened and penalized when they dared to speak out. According to a former high-level Guess compliance official interviewed by Edna Bonacich, prices paid by Guess to contractors for garments *fell* while the monitoring programme was being implemented (unpublished interview, Bonacich, 1995). Most disturbingly, the lessons of Guess have not been learnt. The monitoring model that underlay the Guess scheme is being replicated on a far larger scale, generally in the form of increasing numbers of self-policing corporate codes of conduct and more specifically in the form of recent US government-sponsored initiatives such as the Fair Labor Association.[3]

The failures at Guess indicate clearly the pitfalls of corporate self-regulation. The apparel industry attorney Richard Reinis justified the contradictions of this type of monitoring by saying that: 'it may be a fox in the chicken coop, but at least the fox has to pay attention' (Bonacich and Applebaum, 2000). Reinis' words were somewhat nonsensical: foxes, and multimillion dollar corporations, usually have a very good idea of what they are doing. Placing responsibility for inspection and correction in the hands of those who have an interest in the continuation of violations is a recipe for ineffective monitoring.

The curious Guess combination of virulent union busting with a programme to 'protect workers' rights' also points to the ambiguous relationship between monitoring and worker organization. There is a risk that establishing monitoring programmes may become, for certain employers, a publicly palatable substitute for allowing workers to organize. Obvious though it may seem, it is worth reiterating here that workers need to be centrally involved in the improvement of their workplaces. Without the participation of workers, the finer devices by which contractors circumvent minimum requirements are difficult to spot. Many 'paper rights' are unenforceable without an organized workforce: one can prohibit forced overtime on paper, but this will be meaningless if workers are too frightened to refuse overtime. Most importantly, workers unionize in order to go above minimum standards and to be in a position to negotiate at regular intervals for further improvements; workers also unionize in order to deal with the non-economic, relational aspects of their jobs, and take some control over their working lives. Effective monitoring can play the vital role of enforcing minimum standards, and clearing a space within which workers are able to organize in safety, but monitoring in itself does not give workers power.

Effective monitoring, then, is only a first step. Monitoring without a focus on freedom of association risks at best relegating workers to the sidelines, a passive audience to the struggle by outsiders to raise their working conditions. At worst, sophisticated employers will seek to use monitoring as a new form of company unionism: rules negotiated and enforced by others, on workers' behalf, with the participation of a few hand-picked workers. Where there is a possibility of workers forming autonomous unions, the goal of monitors must be to render themselves superfluous by enabling workers to form their own organizations. After all, the basis for trade unionism and collective bargaining is that workers must be allowed to negotiate workplace rules, enforce them and spot violations: workers if allowed to organize and speak freely, are the best monitors.

ACKNOWLEDGEMENTS

This chapter represents only the views of the author.

NOTES

1   In a subsequent interview with *Fortune* magazine, Meza said that she had been forced out when she attempted to deal with contractor violations and exposed a system of kickbacks from contractors to Guess production managers (Behar, 1996). In 1997, Meza repeated the accusations to the *New York Times*, saying that

Guess had been engaged in 'window dressing' and had told her to stop making surprise inspections on large factories on which production managers depended (Greenhouse, 1997).

2 Buzz had closed down. UNITE reached workers who were owed money through newspaper and radio advertisements and leafleting contract shops.

3 See Chapter 2 by Jenkins for a discussion of the Fair Labor Association.

REFERENCES

Behar, R (1996) 'Guess What's Behind this IPO?' *Fortune* 14 October

Bonacich, E and R Appelbaum (2000) *Behind The Label, Inequality in the Los Angeles Apparel Industry*, University of California Press, Los Angeles

Esbenshade, J (1999) 'Monitoring in the Garment Industry: Lessons from Los Angeles', paper for the *Chicano Latino Policy Project*

Esbenshade, J (2001) 'The Social Accountability Contract, Private Monitoring from Los Angeles to the Global Apparel Industry', *Labour Studies Journal*, Spring

Greenhouse, S (1997) 'Sweatshop Raids Cast Doubt on Ability of Garment Makers to Police Factories', *New York Times*, 18 July

Kanter, L (1997) 'Guess Defection Unlikely to Spark Garment Exodus', *Los Angeles Business Journal*, 20 January

Case No. BC 155 165 (1997) Brenda Figueroa et al. vs. Guess? Inc et al, in the Superior Court of the State of California, Report of the Referee, Judge Jack M Newman Sept 10

NICWJ (1998) *Cross Border Blues; A Call for Justice for Denim Workers in Tehuacan Maquiladoras* (pamphlet), National Interfaith Committee for Worker Justice, Chicago

Quinones, S (1997) 'Garment Industry Thrives on Continental Drift', *United States/Mexico Business Observer*, October

Smith, J (1998) 'Garment–Textile Boom Brings Wrenching Change to Mexico', *Los Angeles Times*, 27 September

State of California, Employment Development Department, 'Los Angeles County Historical Monthly Labor Force Data, 1983-Current', http://www.calmis.cahwnet.gov/htmlfile/subject/indtable.htm, accessed 25 July 2001

US Department of Labor (1992) *Press Release*, 5 August

US Department of Labor *No Sweat Quarterly Reports*, http://www.dol.gov/dol/esa/public/nosweat.htm, accessed 25 July 2001

US Department of Labor (2000) *Compliance Surveys in Garment Manufacturing*, 25 August

Chapter 14

Working with codes: perspectives from the Clean Clothes Campaign

Nina Ascoly and Ineke Zeldenrust

INTRODUCTION

Since the main demand of the Clean Clothes Campaign (CCC) is that retailers and the major brand-name companies live up to their responsibility to ensure that garments are produced in decent conditions, it has always been important for us to be clear about how we define good working conditions. The principles that have guided the CCC are the conventions issued by the International Labour Organization (ILO), and these figure prominently in our 'model code'. Compared to just five years ago, the number of codes of conduct today is astonishing and the amount of time spent discussing their pros and cons is perhaps disproportionate to their usefulness. How and why did the CCC enter into this 'code debate', as it has come to be called within the movement, and what have codes really done to bring us closer to our goal?

ARTICULATING OUR DEMANDS

In January 1992 the CCC (just a Dutch campaign at the time) organized a study day to broaden the coalition inside the Netherlands. Following this, a working group, later called the Fair Wear Charter working group, was set up consisting of the CCC, FNV (trade union federation), and NOVIB (Oxfam Netherlands) to further work out these ideas. Drafts of the Fair Wear Charter, as it was starting to be called, were sent around to workers' organizations and women's groups in Asia and representatives of the campaign took drafts with them to discuss during visits to the Philippines, Hong Kong, Indonesia and India. One of the main points raised at the time was that the five basic ILO labour conventions –

Box 14.1 The Clean Clothes Campaign (CCC)

The CCC is a network of coalitions – made up of non-governmental organizations (NGOs), trade unions, human rights organizations, solidarity groups and researchers – that aims to improve working conditions in the global garment industry. The Campaign began in the Netherlands at the end of the 1980s. There are now CCCs in ten European countries, supported by a wider, global network. The strategies we use to achieve our goal fall into four broad categories: solidarity work, pursuing legal possibilities, working with consumers to raise awareness and press for change, and putting pressure on companies.

Clean Clothes International Secretariat
Postbus 11584
1001 GN Amsterdam
The Netherlands
Tel: +31-20-412-2785
Fax: +31-20-412-2786
Email: ccc@xs4all.nl
http://www.cleanclothes.org

---

the starting point of many other codes and charters – did not cover the needs of garment workers. Without standards for wages, hours of work and health and safety, the real problems of the majority of the workers remain unaddressed. As these discussions were taking place, the CCC started an English newsletter to keep groups informed. In 1994, the working group presented the text of the 'Fair Wear Charter for Clothing and accompanying documents'[1] to the Dutch retailers' association.

Going European

The next step for the campaign was unclear. Industry accused the campaign of making impossible demands. They refused to enter into a real debate on the issues, arguing that it was the job of governments, assisted by the ILO, to work this out. The Dutch coalition decided to make an all-out large-scale effort to 'go European', to show that there was widespread support for these demands. The 'Euro project' as the CCC started to call it, started in 1995 with workshops in the UK, Germany, France and Belgium and material produced in local languages. Parallel to this, meetings and research were organized in eight Asian countries, culminating in 1996 with a month-long tour throughout Europe of six Asian guests from different countries, together with people from the Dutch CCC, for public debate, street actions and visits to garment companies.

The potential for building this type of coalition was a real incentive for many organizations to become active at their national level. Unions as well as development NGOs, and those with a background in the solidarity movement, felt a real decline in membership, mobilizing power and public attention. This had been going on for years, but had reached a stage where it was so serious that people were willing to try new approaches and form new alliances.

The Eurotour

The 1996 tour generated unexpected levels of interest and resulted in a future planning meeting and establishing a system for European coordination for the campaign. One of the main issues raised was the threat of a proliferation of codes and of systems for monitoring their implementation. Companies had started developing their own in-house codes, and we ourselves were working with different sets of demands. The Dutch Fair Wear Charter had been translated and discussed in Europe during the course of the project, but unions in other European countries, for example, worked only with the five basic conventions. Extensive discussions with our Asian partners took place, especially on the issue of monitoring (CCC, 1996, 1997a). The first step, it was decided, should be to develop a joint model code, for the European and Asian groups to speak with one voice to the companies and to show that a large number of people *do* agree that workers have these rights.

It was agreed that this model code should set a standard to prevent company in-house codes from being accepted. Ideas on independent monitoring should also be discussed and outlined in the model code. Asian organizations, international union organizations, and other relevant NGOs should be part of the process, in addition to the CCC member organizations.

It was also made clear that addressing the retailers and big producing companies (the 'Northern' companies), was the job of the NGOs and unions in the North. Both the access and the responsibility for that end of the production chain lies here. In the current context of the debate on codes of conduct this may sound strange. At that time, the choices in solidarity work for NGOs and unions were between promotion of fair/alternative trade, promotion of social clauses in trade agreements, or pressuring companies. The mandate for the European CCC was largely to lobby companies, whilst also promoting fair trade

---

BOX 14.2 THE CCC MODEL CODE

The CCC model code, the ICFTU model code, the SA 8000 standard and the ETI base code all contain the following standards:

- freedom of association
- right to collective bargaining
- no forced labour
- no child labour
- no discrimination
- maximum hours of work
- health and safety
- a living wage
- security of employment

as an alternative for consumers. What companies should be pressured into doing was still open to debate. In our view, it was clear that they should be made responsible for a whole package of labour standards – not just child labour, and not just the five basic ILO conventions.

In February 1998 the model code was finally unveiled, supported by the CCCs, international union federations, and a number of regional and national organizations in Asia (CCC, 1997b). Since that time the CCC standard has continued to gain support.

WHAT'S IN THE MODEL CODE?

Section one of the CCC code (see Box 14.2) sets out everything that it's *not* intended to be. That list is quite long, and it appears first because it was considered essential to make it clear that codes are *not* meant to replace collective bargaining, for example, or national legislation, and should *not* be implemented only among the first tier of subcontractors. We find that this needs to be continually emphasized. Section one of the code also outlines the scope and says something about the context and our own expectations. For us, the code is just one tool out of a toolbox, whose value is dependent on the other tools in that box. As campaigners we can never forget that any code is merely a list of standards – what is done (or not done) with that list is open to a range of possibilities.

The second part of the model code lists the labour standards, the five basic conventions (child labour, forced or bonded labour, discrimination, freedom of association and the right to collective bargaining) plus provisions on hours of work, living wage, health and safety, and job security. Today there is a high level of consensus among activists that these are our demands, and that company codes (and others) not mentioning these fall short of the mark. In that sense, we accomplished one of our goals. Increasingly, we saw the use of codes as a way of entering into a political debate, forcing companies to talk about the notion of a living wage and of job security, and forcing authorities to react to violations of the right to organize. At the same time it enabled campaigns to be much more effective watchdogs using either our own or the companies' code as the standard against which 'reality checks' take place.

The third part of the model code lists the tasks of a company to implement the code. For example, they must translate it into local languages and distribute it to workers. Implementation is as crucial as independent monitoring, though less talked about.

The fourth section lists principles for independent verification, and is the least specific. It is loosely based on the Dutch idea for a foundation, but opens the door for other models. Despite the unformed nature of our ideas, it was felt that we should put them forward. To oppose one must propose, and in our direct surroundings others were developing their own systems at high speed, for example via the US Apparel Industry Partnership and SA 8000.[2]

In the CCC 'foundation model' monitoring can be based upon a two-track system: one track includes the use of accredited agencies and organizations, who can gather a certain type of information via the methods open to them; the other track includes information gathered by local-level worker organizations, for example via complaints, who have access to different kinds of information and use different methods. Pressure must be applied to maintain a balanced interest in the pursuit of both tracks. Input from trade unions and NGOs at the local (production) level needs to be fully integrated into methods of implementation, verification and monitoring. In discussions about monitoring systems, access by local-level organizations is often mentioned as important, but it remains a highly complex issue for all and more work is needed to see how we can guarantee quality, confidentiality and credibility. Only more participatory forms of monitoring can make this process one that really helps to address problems in the workplace.

With a certain level of consensus achieved on the content of model codes, the focus of debate has now shifted to the implementation of these standards and the need to develop procedures for independent monitoring and verification of such codes. Monitoring systems that would continue to put all the responsibility for upholding good working conditions with suppliers, and exempt their clients who set the actual wage norms for example, are clearly not acceptable. Sourcing guidelines should in no way facilitate a 'cut and run' approach – in which a company, seeking to cut their losses and keep their brand from being tainted by scandal, cancels their contract with a factory in which labour rights violations have been exposed, and transfers their production to another facility, possibly in another country – and instead should call for a commitment to help those without access to resources to improve conditions over time.

Meanwhile, the backdrop to these CCC activities has been the emergence of company codes and other corporate initiatives[3] that have been adopted by major garment and sports shoe companies. Their priorities and agendas, of course, can be quite different from ours. We believe that these differences are also reflected in the content and modes of implementation and verification they use in relation to their own codes of conduct. Highlighting the differences between the standards and the quality of implementation and monitoring is an important activity that campaigners have taken up – it has meant raising awareness among all stakeholders as to the distinction between sincere and superficial attempts to empower workers (see Box 14.3).

INVESTIGATING POSSIBILITIES FOR MONITORING AND VERIFICATION

As clear as the CCC is in its critique of company codes, we are admittedly less clear on the way our own proposals can be put into practice so that they yield

---

Box 14.3 The CCC on company codes

Over the years CCC has criticized company codes on four counts: for being

1   vaguely defined;
2   incomplete;
3   not implemented and monitored; and
4   not independently verified.

These continue to remain outstanding issues and the CCC code continues to be the standard we encourage companies to adopt as their own.

---

the intended outcomes. Those companies that have committed, after sustained pressure, to the implementation of the CCC model code have started pilot projects with CCC partners in several countries. These projects will test out ideas on implementation, monitoring and verification. They are an important step toward gathering the information we need to make important strategic choices.

These initiatives – involving the CCCs in the Netherlands, Sweden, Switzerland, the UK and France – are at different stages of completion and are testing a variety of models. All involve pilot projects, which are experiments to test our ideas 'on the ground'. The CCC sees pilots as essential because they directly involve local NGOs and trade unions from the areas where the actual production is taking place. A project is underway to specifically facilitate the exchange of experiences related to these five initiatives, improve consistency of terminology, and identify best practices and provide guidance for future national- or European-level initiatives and pilot projects on the monitoring and verification of codes of conduct (Ascoly et al, 2001).[4]

At this time, most of the projects are still incomplete and therefore it is too early to draw any final conclusions.[5] But there are some early lessons that can be acknowledged:

- Worker education on labour rights is crucial, especially where there are no trade unions (where they are banned by law, or by practice – this is precisely the context in which codes are meant to apply). Some organizations at the local level where garments are produced feel so strongly about this issue that they see the provision of worker education as a prerequisite for their own participation in the pilot projects. Tools for worker education (for example cartoon books) have been developed as a result of pilots in Guatemala and Bangladesh.
- Labour-related NGOs and trade unions have to be involved at the local production level if good quality monitoring and credible independent verification is to take place. This is something that the CCC has always believed, but the pilot projects have enabled us to gather concrete evidence

to support this belief – something which is helping companies to begin to accept this position. The precise role which these groups should play in monitoring and verification systems is still something that needs considerable attention, as the varied contexts found throughout the global garment industry means that what works or is appropriate in some situations might not be feasible in others. For example in some cases local NGOs do not want to enter garment factories and talk to management because they feel it would compromise their independence and their position (e.g. workers would lose their trust in them if they were seen with management).

* Unless workers themselves are somehow involved in monitoring systems (for example, by providing information and feedback to factory auditors via confidential off-site interviews, or via a complaints system) there will continue to be concerns about the quality of the information derived from the monitoring/verification process.
* Organizations at the local level where production takes place (unions, NGOs or even industry) need to have much more capacity, knowledge and a sense of 'ownership' of the code and its provisions before they can really take it up, whether in a pilot project or in any other way.
* Who pays for the costs associated with the implementation of codes remains a crucial issue. This cost, which we refer to as the 'true cost' generally cannot be met by the suppliers. To do so they will have to be paid more for their services and given other incentives. This means retailers (the 'buying companies') will have to make policy changes (for example, pricing structures) to allow suppliers to achieve the standards outlined in the code. To this end, the CCC projects have also been testing out retailer-level management systems for code compliance. Transparency is also a key characteristic of management systems that take up code implementation and monitoring, and indeed should be considered at all levels.

WORKING WITH CODES IN THE FUTURE?

A survey carried out in 2000–2001 to gather feedback on CCC activities generated responses from Southern partners that indicated that pressuring companies to enforce the labour standards outlined in their codes can be useful, but there was widespread scepticism (from Northern, Southern and Eastern NGO partners) about their usefulness in actually improving working conditions (see Box 14.4).

One respondent from Asia said that there had been better enforcement of labour standards, due to pressure on buyers. One African trade unionist reported that pressure from European consumers on the government and companies was very helpful – the government pressured the companies to talk with the union and to work on a solution to the labour dispute. Another respondent said that while people at the grassroots level do not see any changes

---

Box 14.4 Codes in action

CCC's solidarity work

The adoption of a code by a company is just the start of a process, and ensuring its compliance with that code is the next challenge. CCC's work includes solidarity actions with workers organizations, as illustrated by this example.

In July 1999, the CCC was contacted by SBSI (the Indonesian Prosperity Trade Union) regarding a labour dispute at PT Aneka Garmentama Indah, a clothing manufacturer in North Jakarta producing for Tommy Hilfiger, the Gap, Ralph Lauren, DKNY for export to the United States, Canada, Mexico, Hong Kong, the Netherlands and Italy. SBSI informed us that workers were on strike seeking a salary increase to meet the minimum wage. Management refused to meet with SBSI mediators to negotiate a settlement. The CCC gathered more information on the companies involved (including the content of their codes – which in some cases protected the right to freedom of association and collective bargaining) and forwarded this to the workers.

By August striking workers had been fired and demands for their reinstatement and recognition of the union by management were still being made. In September the CCC heard from the Department of Manpower that factory management had refused to follow their recommendations in this case. In the meantime, few of the companies whose garments are produced at the factory responded to queries about the labour dispute and code violations.

How did the case 'end'? 'In summation, the PT Aneka dispute was a bitter defeat,' according to SBSI representative Paul Keys. Most of the jobs (600) were lost. It was disheartening, he reported, that companies such as the Gap followed the case, and even investigated, but did not interview the union (though when confronted, a Gap representative did admit that the code was violated, 'without a doubt').

Was the CCC campaigning, which included pressuring companies to live up to the promises stated in their in-house codes, of value to the workers? Eventually the company agreed to recognize the union and modify its contracts – but only 30 SBSI members remained at the company. This is the reality of company codes 'on the ground': months go by and international outcry continues, companies claim they are investigating, and workers remain unemployed and often blacklisted from future employment, desperate and without any income (Ascoly and Zeldenrust, 2000a). The Indonesian union reported on the usefulness of the code in their work at a general level, but in the end the battle at PT Aneka was not a victory. Though the dispute 'ended bitterly and too late for most workers,' Keys notes that 'the negative publicity and the letters forced the GAP to take the dispute and our unions seriously. Also the support from abroad was a boost for the workers who would have otherwise felt isolated.' Evaluating the impact of solidarity work carried out through the campaign's Urgent Appeals system is not simple – cases are complex and drawn out over long periods of time.

---

or experience any benefits, at least there is resistance and a way for worker's voices to be heard, and the companies are slightly restricted by the campaigns – 'they are aware of the people and the movements that are watching them'. One respondent said that in situations where the workers were unable and restricted from forming labour unions, the introduction of 'social clauses' by companies due to CCC activities have allowed workers to experience a certain amount of freedom (Ascoly and Zeldenrust, 2000b).

On the occasion of the campaign's tenth anniversary the CCC has been involved in a process of evaluation and strategizing. The survey mentioned above was the first step in a nearly year-long attempt to gather feedback on all the activities which the campaign undertakes, as well as on the CCC's focus and structure. In March 2001, the campaigns and representatives of the wider CCC network around the world participated in a five-day conference in Barcelona to consider the campaign's work in the past and to strategize for the future (Ascoly and Zeldenrust, 2001). Codes and monitoring were some of the topics that received attention, and the following observations were made:

- There were mixed messages on codes all around, as some participants felt they were not appropriate or even a failure, and others felt they were one of the most important campaigning tools and strategically useful for creating space for debate, publicity and enabling pressure. Codes can be a good tool if they include: core ILO conventions; a process of monitoring and verification that includes workers; labour NGOs and unions in the South. They can also be useful if they are seen as a tool to empower workers and are implemented in countries where there is democratic space for independent peoples' organizations to participate in the process. But codes can also involve risks, for example, that company-monitoring usually only goes as far as the first supplier and does not monitor the whole chain and that it is often workers and not companies who pay the cost of the professionalization of monitoring and verification processes by the corporate sector. Finally, our involvement in developing monitoring systems should be based on a perspective of moving out of this work and towards supporting the empowerment process of workers and playing the role of watchdog over companies.
- The interplay between codes (often voluntary mechanisms) and public regulation (local labour law, international legal measures, trade negotiations, national legislation affecting national production) at different levels was mentioned as an area needing more attention. In some countries new laws are being discussed concerning transnational corporations (TNCs) operating abroad. Furthermore, World Trade Organization (WTO) negotiations pose a big danger for the CCC work, for example, in government procurement.
- People are cautious about (but not willing to dismiss) the CCC's strategy of working with codes and monitoring/verification projects. The key is to proceed in a way that takes these concerns into consideration, and ensures that we do not end up spending a disproportionate amount of our resources on this work (just because corporations are giving codes so much attention).
- Related in part to the code work, but more specifically to our involvement in the multi-stakeholder initiatives to learn more about monitoring and verification is the question of reconciling the campaign's two somewhat contradictory roles – campaigns that target companies vs. organizations that

sit down and work with companies (except in pilot projects on monitoring and verification). The CCC, it was concluded, will continue with both methods of engaging the issues.

- Workers' education appears to have emerged as a new category of solidarity work that the CCC is being called upon to take up. Many participants believed that the CCC needs to follow up on the work that the CCC has begun to do in this area. This is connected to the campaign's work on codes of conduct, as it is a step toward the implementation of good labour standards.

Participants predicted that on this controversial subject of codes and monitoring it would be difficult to come to a concrete, common agenda due to the many different experiences participants have, both regionally and according to organizational background. Across regions (85 people, from 35 countries participated in the five days of discussions) the ideas (definitions, perceptions) on what constitutes monitoring and verification differed widely. But there was agreement on what the CCC should be doing in relation to the five monitoring and verification initiatives mentioned above. Working in close cooperation with those concerned with these issues internationally, the campaign should collect and distribute information on the different monitoring and verification experiences, and make comparisons for our own learning and to combat commercial audit systems. Two important points to be kept constantly in mind when doing this work are the relationship with local labour law and the impact on the right to organize and bargain collectively. Additional roles for the CCC are (1) pressuring retailers to examine how their sourcing policies influence the labour situation at their suppliers and define the obligations of 'buying companies' versus suppliers (this means looking at the 'true cost' of code implementation) and (2) continuing 'monitoring the monitors' in light of continued concerns over the competency of commercial social auditors.

CONCLUSION

The 'code debate' became our vehicle for getting the issue of labour rights and TNC responsibility into the public arena. At the same time 'a code of conduct' has come to have different meanings for different people. In our experience it is clear that model codes of conduct, such as the CCC code, can be useful campaigning and training tools, for example in raising awareness among European consumers or among union activists in countries such as Indonesia who make use of these informational materials in their organizing and educational programmes; but a code that is incomplete, doesn't meet the needs of the workers, is not implemented and is without a good monitoring and verification system will never succeed in empowering workers.

As the CCC moves into its next decade of campaigning and strategic decisions are made it will be important to remember the complexity of the role that codes of conduct have played in the struggle to improve working conditions. While company codes do not work and in most cases are instruments of marketing and public relations campaigns, we should not entirely discard codes – ours or the International Confederation of Free Trade Unions' (ICFTU) model code – as tools for positive change. If companies use codes as a tool to prevent the formation of unions it does not follow that campaigns such as the CCC should stop demanding that international companies accept the right to unionize or accept responsibility when that right is violated where their products are produced. Clear thinking went into articulating the set of demands found in the CCC model code and no obstacles, whether the proliferation of company codes or the fatigue induced by the 'code debate', should dilute the vehemence of those demands when it comes to pressing corporations to take responsibility for upholding labour standards in the workplace.

NOTES

1   Reference was made specifically to the ILO tripartite code, which goes much further in detailing TNC obligations to workers, but is limited to subsidiaries, and to the draft UN code of conduct, which has a broader definition of TNCs, and can be read to include subcontracting relationships (FNV, 1994).

2   See Jenkins, Chapter 2 in this volume, for further discussion of the AIP. SA 8000 is a standard for labour practices, similar in content to the CCC model code, which comes with a specific system of verification attached. Supplier companies can request accredited firms (to date mainly commercial quality control firms) to perform an audit to check their compliance with the standard. If they pass, or embark on corrective procedures, they receive a certificate. For more on SA 8000, see CCC (1998). Note that this critique is based on the third SA 8000 guidance document (manual for those carrying out audits), there is now a revised fifth edition of this document available and an updated critique of SA 8000 is forthcoming from the CCC in 2001.

3   This paper focuses on the campaign's experience with codes of conduct, though the campaign has also been highly critical of other corporate activities which have been presented as corporate initiatives to improve the lives of workers. See for example CCC (2000) on the Global Alliance for Workers and Communities, a project that includes Nike, the World Bank and the International Youth Foundation.

4   For more on the five initiatives and the pilot projects, see the website of the SOMO (Centre for Research on Multinational Corporations) project: http://www.somo.nl/monitoring/.

5   In addition to these European projects, similar work is being carried out in Central and South America, where local NGOs have been closely involved in monitoring and verification. It is important that these experiences also be considered when drawing conclusions on the value of different monitoring and verification systems and the possible roles and competency of various actors within such systems. To that end, the CCC has tried to include organizations involved in those initiatives in discussions on these issues (for example Barcelona March 2001, Brussels October 2001).

REFERENCES

Ascoly, N and I Zeldenrust (2000a) 'Clean Clothes Campaign Discusses Disclosure' *Monitor*, No 4, pp10–12.

Ascoly, N and I Zeldenrust (2000b) 'Evaluating the CCC' Clean Clothes Campaign Discussion paper http://www.cleanclothes.org/news/01-01-11.htm

Ascoly, N and I Zeldenrust (2001) 'Clean Clothes International Meeting, Barcelona, March 2001', CCC International Secretariat, Brussels

Ascoly, N, I Zeldenrust and J Oldenziel (2001) *Overview of Recent Developments on Monitoring and Verification in the Garment and Sportswear Industry in Europe*, Centre for Research on Multinational Corporations SOMO, Amsterdam

CCC (Clean Clothes Campaign) (1996) *CCC Newsletter*, No 6

CCC (1997a) *CCC Newsletter*, No 7

CCC (1997b) *Code of Labour Practices for the Apparel Industry including Sportswear*, http://www.cleanclothes.org

CCC (1998) *Keeping the Work Floor Clean: Monitoring models in the garment industry*, Clean Clothes Campaign, Brussels, http://www.cleanclothes.org/

CCC (2000) 'Wages, Hours and Trade Union rights – Still Missing: Research into Nike's Global Alliance assessment study,' *CCC Newsletter*, No 13, November, pp27–8.

FNV (1994) *Het EHH en Bijgevoegde documenten*, Amsterdam

Chapter 15

ETI: a multi-stakeholder approach

Mick Blowfield

WHAT ETI IS AND IS NOT

The Ethical Trading Initiative (ETI) is an alliance of companies, non-governmental organizations (NGOs) and trade union organizations committed to working together to change business behaviour by identifying and promoting good practice in the implementation of codes of labour practice. It is a membership organization currently comprising 33 companies, four umbrella bodies from the trade union movement, and 19 NGOs. Corporate members agree to promote and observe international labour standards in their supply chains, and all members agree to collaborate to achieve this (Box 15.2). ETI's main focus is developing countries, but many members recognize that exploitation of workers is not unique to the South.

For ETI, good practice means: (a) acceptance of internationally-agreed standards; (b) their incorporation into codes of practice used by ETI corporate members; and (c) monitoring and verifying adherence to these codes in ways that are meaningful and credible. The emphasis placed here on internationally-agreed standards and their incorporation into codes of practice is important because when ETI was established in 1998, company codes tended to cherry-pick particular aspects of international standards that had resonance with consumers, the Western media or campaigning groups, and exclude those they disagreed with (Varley, 1998; Ferguson, 1998). Today, although some company codes continue to cherry-pick, incorporation of internationally-agreed standards is much more common. Indeed, anyone familiar with such proprietary standards as SA 8000 will not be surprised by the content of the ETI Base Code (Box 15.3), and may even ask what is unique about ETI.

To an extent, we can understand the uniqueness of ETI by understanding what it is *not*. ETI is not a solution to all of the challenges of corporate social

---

Box 15.1 Ethical Trading Initiative (ETI)

The ETI is an alliance of companies, non-governmental organizations (NGOs) and trade unions, established in 1998, whose aim is to improve labour conditions in the global supply chains which produce goods for the UK market. The desire to improve labour conditions reflects a concern for basic human rights and an intention to contribute to a reduction in global inequalities.

ETI is funded by membership fees paid by its company and NGO members and by a grant from the international development budget of the British Government's Department for International Development.

Ethical Trading Intitiative
2nd Floor Cromwell House
14 Fulwood Place
LONDON WC1V 6HZ
Tel: +44 (0) 20 7404 1463
Fax: +44 (0) 20 7831 7852
Email: eti@eti.org.uk
http://www.ethicaltrade.org

---

and environmental responsibility – it deals with a particular but critical range of all the possible social issues companies are being asked to manage in their supply chains, that is, internationally-agreed labour standards. Unlike accreditation agencies, it does not offer a proprietary code, and unlike certification or auditing bodies it does not pass or fail suppliers. ETI does not offer consultancy services, nor does it offer prizes or labels in recognition of good performance. What ETI does offer its members is a space where they can develop the skills and share the experience of trying to be a responsible company in an era of global supply chains.

Box 15.2 Corporate members' commitments to ETI

ETI members believe that a collaborative approach involving business, trade unions and NGOs provides the opportunity for making significant progress in promoting the observance of internationally recognized standards, in particular fundamental human rights throughout the global supply chains. There are two distinct but inter-related aspects of members' commitment: (1) adherence to core standards, and (2) experimentation in how to implement them:

1 Member companies are expected to adopt the Base Code (or a code that fully incorporates the Base Code), and must require that suppliers meet agreed standards within a reasonable timeframe, and that performance is measured and transparent, and will ultimately become a precondition to further business.
2 Member companies agree to work together with NGOs and trade unions as well as their suppliers to identify the most effective approaches to making codes of practice meaningful and credible, particularly with regard to monitoring and verification (for example through pilot projects).

BOX 15.3 PRINCIPLES OF THE ETI BASE CODE

The ETI is based on the principle of incorporating internationally-agreed standards into codes of labour practice. These are set out in the ETI Base Code under the following headings:

- employment is freely chosen;
- freedom of association and the right to collective bargaining are respected;
- working conditions are safe and hygienic;
- child labour shall not be used;
- living wages are paid;
- working hours are not excessive;
- no discrimination is practised;
- regular employment is provided;
- no harsh or inhumane treatment is allowed.

A second way of understanding ETI's distinctiveness is by reference to its history. Some current members of ETI were also active in developing other initiatives at the time ETI was being set up,[1] and ETI's first chair was an early advocate of multi-stakeholder engagement. Yet ETI was the first concrete example of an alliance where business, trade unions and NGOs worked together from the outset, placing internationally-agreed labour standards at the centre of their work.

Today, ETI could not claim uniqueness on this basis alone as other initiatives, both Northern and Southern, have adopted a similar approach. ETI's value today cannot be divorced from its history, but it is the experience of using a multi-stakeholder approach to promote good practice in implementing international labour standards which is the focus of this chapter.

THE ETI APPROACH

There are three key premises behind the ETI approach: first, that internationally-agreed standards (complementary to national and international regulations and frameworks) contribute to the well-being (the lives and rights) of workers and their families; second, that there may be difficulties in implementing these standards in supply chains; and third, that understanding how to overcome these difficulties can be achieved through a multi-stakeholder alliance of business and civil society. It is this last aspect which separates ETI from much of what is called a partnership approach to corporate social responsibility, because its structure and practices require companies to learn from and with their critics.

ETI has a Base Code which draws on declarations and conventions of the International Labour Organization (ILO) and the United Nations (UN) (see

Box 15.3[2]), and sets out the fundamental rights for workers. ETI companies must enforce this code somewhere in their supply chains, and make this known to other members so that they can verify company claims. It is important to note that although member companies commit to increasing the proportion of their supply chains where the code is applied over time, they are not expected to impose the code everywhere from day one.

The Base Code informs but does not explain ETI's tripartite approach. The tripartite alliance of companies, trade unions and NGOs is reflected in the structure of the ETI Board and every pilot project (the main instruments for learning how to monitor supply chains) requires the three caucuses of the alliance to work together. Moreover, rather than have a large secretariat acting as an executive on behalf of the membership, members themselves take responsibility for much of the work (pilots, working groups and so on). Therefore, the concept of a multi-stakeholder alliance is not just a principle, it is central to the day-to-day functioning of ETI.

Although some may see consensus as a goal of this type of alliance (a view that accounts for some of the criticisms that such alliances can become dominated by one group or another (Zeldenrust and Ascoly, 1998; Stichele and Pennartz, 1996)), a more evident reality is that different groups have separate objectives,[3] and that there is rarely consensus about what has been learned, only a commitment to learning together and sharing that learning within the membership. A cynic would say that the ETI's purpose of identifying and promoting good practice is an implicit admission of defeat – that companies are underachieving in the area of workers' rights and conditions. A more optimistic (though perhaps not contradictory) interpretation would be that companies, trade unions and NGOs recognize that there are no off-the-peg solutions to the challenges of securing international labour standards for a globally dispersed workforce, and that ETI's advantage is to be able to offer a place to experiment, to fail as well as to succeed, and to avoid the spotlight of unrealistic expectation each time one tries to take a forward step. The obvious riposte to this is that by not holding themselves to public account, companies are able to get away with poor performance. To address this, ETI's policy is to test the efficacy and credibility of independent verification of members' performance, but adoption of such verification is at best a long-term goal, and one thing that ETI has learnt since its inception in 1998 is that substantial change takes time. Therefore, in this chapter, I offer some of the early evidence of what differences a multi-stakeholder alliance can make.

MILESTONES AND INDICATORS

The separate parts of the alliance have different reasons for joining ETI. Companies have observed market resistance to products produced under adverse labour conditions when this has been exposed by the media, and they are also concerned to protect their reputations and brand values. Trade union members want to improve global labour standards by fostering the conditions for freedom of association and collective bargaining. NGO members aim to promote a fairer form of economic development around the world. This is not an exclusive list, but it highlights why each caucus will assess ETI's impact in different ways. Moreover, international development agencies (including the Department for International Development (DFID) which has helped fund ETI's work) ultimately regards the impact on eradicating poverty amongst workers and their families as the key indicator.

However, at the present time, three years after being established, the benefits of the tripartite alliance are probably best seen in the learning that has taken place and the changes in member behaviour. Although there is evidence on a case by case basis of suppliers improving their performance in areas intended to benefit workers, the simple truth is that we do not know how many workers are working less hours or how many fewer women are being sexually harassed because of ETI.

Equally important, we do not know enough about the inter-relationships between the different criteria; for instance, whether any reduction in total hours is matched by increases in pay so that net incomes do not decline.

What we *do* know is that more and more corporate members are looking seriously at these issues. Part evidence of this is that in 1999, members monitored over 1500 suppliers or 20 per cent of their supply base: in 2000 that number had grown to over 6700 or 64 per cent. This monitoring takes various forms, but typically includes a mix of desk-based questionnaires leading to factory visits by the buyer or independent auditors.[4] At present, it is not possible to conclude that one system is better at picking up breaches than another, although most observers are likely to be unconvinced by the results of supplier self-audits if they are not verified by other means.

Supply chain monitoring is part of a member company's commitment to ETI, and one area of real achievement in 2000–2001 has been the demonstration of corporate commitment as judged by the growth in auditing programmes, the number of corrective actions *vis-à-vis* non-compliances with the Base Code, and the setting of priorities for future actions. In 1999, about one-third of member companies were judged by ETI criteria not to be demonstrating adequate commitment, as this is defined in Box 15.2. Although these criteria are not easy to meet, other member companies as well as NGOs and trade unions applied pressure to ensure that overall performance improved, and now over 90 per cent of member companies are demonstrating adequate commitment. Of course, all ETI members would like to be able to say that as monitoring increases, the number of non-compliances with the Base Code is on the decrease. However, unacceptable working conditions are a reality, and at ethical trading's current stage of development, it is perhaps a more positive indicator that more non-compliances are being identified rather than less. As Figure 15.1 shows, 23 per cent of total members' suppliers (including

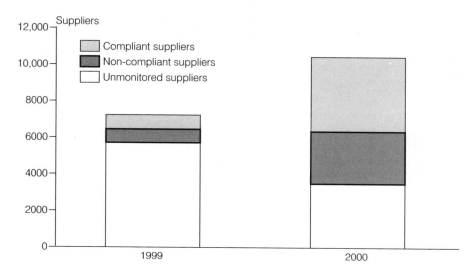

Figure 15.1 *Comparison of corporate members' reporting 1999–2000*

unmonitored ones) had one or more instances of non-compliance in 2000, compared to 11 per cent a year before. That may seem damaging for fragile corporate reputations, but if seen in the light of the number of additional suppliers monitored and, more significantly, the number of corrective actions generated, what we see is a picture of more and more companies identifying and then wrestling with the remediation of complicated issues.

It is important to emphasize that company reports have not necessarily been independently verified, and any figures are those from corporate members. In 2000, these members as a whole reported on significant non-compliances, distinguishing between those where corrective action was and was not taken. The majority of corrective actions (62 per cent) related to health and safety, followed by living wages (15 per cent), working hours (10 per cent) and other aspects of the Base Code (1–5 per cent).[5] Does this mean that health and safety non-compliances are more common than others? Maybe so, and certainly the diversity of health and safety issues makes this possible. But it could also be because it is easier for those carrying out monitoring to identify a missing first aid box or a locked fire exit than it is to recognize discrimination, forced overtime or child labour, for instance. This in turn may reflect the current skills and competencies of the social auditing industry which is still in its infancy and needs to have best practice defined and agreed.

Some will see the above statistics as confirmation that companies are imperfect; others will be impressed at the progress being made. Both interpretations are true and both are to miss the point. What the statistics seem to show is that monitoring is taking place and, moreover, it is detecting non-compliances: given the previous situation this itself is significant progress. The

ETI alliance realizes that it has learnt a lot and has a lot still to learn about how to recognize, correct and report on social performance. Consequently, ETI invests heavily in learning about monitoring (that is to say, understanding what is happening in the workplace), not least because the activity of monitoring is an acceptance of corporate responsibility for the supply chain. Individual members are trying their own approaches, ranging from in-house monitoring by technical advisors to the use of independent auditors, from repeat visits to one-day assessments. ETI runs its own pilot projects, each involving trade unions, NGOs and business, experimenting with different approaches in different countries and with different industries (Table 15.1). One such example is the Zimbabwe pilot on monitoring performance in the horticulture industry. This began in 1998 and got off to a rocky start when producers felt threatened by an ETI delegation trying to explain the pilot's purpose, and local trade unions were not involved in the early stages. Several months of bridge mending followed, and only then could the process of learning more about monitoring begin.

Zimbabwe producers challenged the appropriateness and even the legitimacy of the internationally agreed standards, but the final version of the industry's code of practice met fully the provisions of the ETI Base Code. Although certain ETI members, especially some NGOs, may question the consequences of international standards for improving worker well-being, ETI's approach to worker rights and welfare is not based on cultural relativism. This is not to say that members are unaware that voluntary codes of labour practice could be a 'double-edged sword' which, depending on how they are implemented, may improve or harm their intended beneficiaries. The ETI working group responsible for the Zimbabwe pilot project concluded that involvement of Zimbabwe industry and civil society organizations was not only essential to the credibility of the pilot project, but contributed significantly to learning about monitoring.

Involvement of local and international NGOs and research organizations led to the introduction of participatory approaches to farm and pack-house inspections. This was a direct response to worries about auditing techniques, and is part of an experimentation process to overcome the limitations of commercial auditing companies and company technical staff. According to local participants, the approach developed in Zimbabwe highlights the importance of auditor competencies (for example gender balance, linguistic capacity) and methodology (for example sampling, types of respondent). Furthermore, according to Di Auret, who played a key role in the pilot project, rather than simply checking for compliance, the Zimbabwe approach seeks to measure the behaviour and attitudes of employees at every level of authority, and how these impact on the company's overall social performance. Crucially, it also aims to create awareness and facilitate behavioural change amongst workers and management by identifying why problems arise and how to solve them.

Table 15.1 *Current and past ETI pilot projects*

South Africa: wine Companies (established 1998)		Trade unions	NGO
UK	Sainsbury's Co-operative Wholesale Society (CWS) Tesco Raisin Social (non-member)	Trades Union Congress (TUC) General, Municipal and Boilermakers' Union	Christian Aid Fairtrade Foundation Traidcraft
South Africa	Six suppliers	Food and Agricultural Workers Union (FAWU) General Workers Association (GWA)	Centre for Rural Legal Studies
Costa Rica: bananas (initial discussions: 2000)	Companies	Trade unions	NGO
UK	Sainsbury's Tesco Safeway Asda Somerfield Marks & Spencer (M&S) CWS	International Union of Food, Agricultural, Hotel, Restaurant, Catering, Tobacco and Allied Workers Union (IUF) Transport and General Workers Union (TGWU)	Central American Women's Network World Development Movement
Costa Rica	Corporación Bananera Nacional (CORBANA) (marketing organization) Chiquita Dole (Standard) DelMonte (Bandeco) Asociación Nacional de Productores Bananeros (ANAPROBAN) (national producers' organisation) (Ministry of Labour & ILO as observers)	Coordinadora Latin-americana de Sindicatos Bananeros (COLSIBA) Sindicato de Trabajadores de Plantaciones Agricolas (SITRAP)	Foro Emaus
Zimbabwe: fresh produce (established 1998)	Companies	Trade unions	NGO
UK	Fisher Foods Sainsbury's Tesco Somerfield Waitrose (non-member)	IUF TGWU	Save the Children (SCF) Fairtrade Foundation National Resources and Ethical Trade Programme (NRET) (non-member)

Zimbabwe	Horticultural Promotion Council Hortico Mitchell and Mitchell Baileys	General Agricultural and Plantation Workers Union (GAPWUZ)	SCF Zimbabwe
Sri Lanka: ready-made garments (initial discussions 2000)	*Companies*	*Trade unions*	*NGO*
UK	Littlewoods M&S Lambert Howarth Desmond & Sons Pentland (possibly)	GMB	Oxfam Women Working Worldwide
Sri Lanka	Marsylka (Littlewoods) Hydramani (Desmonds)	To be confirmed	To be confirmed

Participatory appraisal of this kind, is now seen in Zimbabwe as the most effective way of identifying social issues, despite the amount of time required compared to some auditing techniques. What is more, partly because of the credibility that comes from ETI, Zimbabwe's new auditing community is starting to influence the development of methodology elsewhere in Africa and in other international initiatives such as COLEACP (Liaison Committee Europe-Africa-Caribbean-Pacific). Equally, evidence from the pilot that business and civil society organizations could work together in ETI encouraged the Zimbabwe horticulture industry to adopt a similar approach in establishing its own code of practice, one which is now being implemented with the full participation of local trade unions and selected NGOs. Today, the Agricultural Ethics Association of Zimbabwe, a business-NGO-trade union alliance independent of, but with close relations to, ETI, is responsible for fostering the development of ethical trade in Zimbabwe and is also informing practice in other African countries.

Although there is not enough space in the present chapter to describe all of ETI's pilots, some of the lessons from Zimbabwe are echoed elsewhere. The difficult start up in Zimbabwe reflects what has happened elsewhere in different forms – initial confusion seems a rite of passage to a multi-stakeholder approach. The testing of different techniques for auditing, reporting and corrective action has been fundamental to ETI pilots, and while Zimbabwe is an interesting case study, it cannot claim to be the gold standard. Rather, it is an appropriate approach to that situation but worthy of testing elsewhere, and one that has been shown in Zimbabwe to recognize poor social performance more effectively than the auditing approaches certain consultancy companies are offering. According to those in the pilot working group, it also shows the importance of developing monitoring techniques that are relevant to the industrial, social, political and cultural contexts, an opinion increasingly shared by members in other pilot projects. Although as I have emphasized throughout this chapter, the assumption that internationally-agreed labour standards benefit workers and their families is central to ETI, this does not mean that monitoring will be the same wherever the codes of practice are applied. What works in Zimbabwe may not work in Kenya, and certainly will not work in China where there are serious restrictions on trade union and NGO activity.

There is an ongoing debate within ETI and beyond about the balance between local diversity and international comparability and credibility. There is an understandable fear amongst some members that diversity will lead to a neutering of standards, but there is an equal concern in some quarters that failure to recognize differences will make codes irrelevant or even damaging for those they are meant to benefit. In seeking locally relevant approaches to monitoring core labour standards, ETI is not in any way saying that standards should be less than those set out in the Base Code: unlike certain process-based standards, ETI's code sets a global base standard to which all members must commit. However, there is growing recognition that the ways of monitoring labour practices will be affected by industrial, social, political, cultural and institutional contexts.

Learning how to implement core labour standards has led to changes in corporate behaviour, and the relationships between corporate and civil society members of ETI. For example, companies began with grave reservations about how sharing of learning would conflict with the imperative of commercial confidentiality, but now more and more companies realize that exchange of experience and disclosure of performance is a net benefit. Many ETI members and their suppliers have invested significantly in building the capacity to implement relevant management systems, and in some cases have changed the nature of the buyer-supplier relationship. There is evidence from the pilot projects, particularly in South Africa and Zimbabwe, that suppliers have changed their behaviour as a result of ETI's work, not only in relatively straightforward corrective actions such as health and safety, but in more difficult areas such as discrimination.

FUTURE CHALLENGES

Improving the instruments and techniques for managing, auditing, reporting and upgrading social performance in global supply chains has been and will remain at the heart of ETI's work. There are challenges here, both in terms of developing applicable, affordable and effective tools and systems, and in terms of understanding the strengths and limitations of a code-based approach. These are, however, challenges that face any organization pursuing global justice through a unitary code of practice. The multi-stakeholder approach of ETI may prove more efficient in finding solutions, but is that the litmus test of its impact? Some members would argue that the long-term indicator of ETI achievement will be its success in rigorously promoting internationally-agreed labour standards wherever companies in the UK market can effect this. However, in the immediate future, the added value of this approach will be more evident in areas of process and relationships. Therefore, the interim indicators of success could be:

1   fostering a constructive environment where organizations (not least companies) that in other circumstances may be at odds or in competition, are able to collaborate, share and build mutual respect and trust;
2   an environment to catalyse thinking on the challenges of ethical trading;
3   a haven where different types of organization can enter into dialogue, allowing companies to meet with and learn from their civil society critics;
4   a place where both members and non-members are able to experiment and learn about the challenges of implementing core labour standards.

ETI members have identified a number of specific areas where they need to know more. Some of these are already being addressed by parties outside ETI (for example the gender dimensions of labour standards, the issue of marginal producers such as homeworkers and smallholders, the cost-benefit of implementing voluntary codes of practice). These are all areas of work that have relevance for ETI which hopes to become more proactive in commissioning research in the future, including a major piece of work on assessing impact.

There are other issues which have been raised by outside parties but have not been fully explored within ETI. One is that despite ETI's name, it does not deal with trading relationships, even though these can affect the level of supplier social performance. Some ETI members recognize this and have reviewed their practices accordingly, but it is not an issue which ETI as a whole has addressed. A separate issue is that of participation by workers and their families in the South, particularly where they are not part of the trade union movement (for example because free trade unions are outlawed). ETI absolutely believes that freedom of association and collective bargaining are fundamental worker rights, but NGO members have raised the issue that there are many marginal workers who are amongst the poorest and most disadvantaged who will not in the foreseeable future be represented by free trade unions. How are their voices to be represented?

Both of these issues relate to the question, Who is a stakeholder? The notion of stakeholderhood is central to modern corporate social responsibility theory, and ETI is a practical example of turning that theory into practice through a multi-stakeholder approach. For ETI, the primary stakeholder must always be the workers, especially those in developing countries. It is easy on a day-to-day basis to lose sight of this when one is juggling the demands of members, each of whom engage with but none of whom are the poor and marginalized. Yet it is such people's well-being by which the ETI alliance must eventually be measured.

NOTES

1   For example, Neil Kearney of the International Textile, Garment and Leather Workers' Federation was involved in establishing both ETI and SA 8000, and J. Sainsbury which also advised on SA 8000 was one of the first corporate members of ETI. The International Confederation of Free Trade Unions was similarly involved in helping to develop FIFA's code.
2   See www.eti.org.uk for a copy of the Base Code.
3   See Chapter 2 by Jenkins for a discussion of the objectives of different stakeholders in relation to codes of conduct.
4   More details on the types of monitoring will be published in the ETI 2000 Annual Report.
5   The full figures will be published in the 2000 Annual Report.

REFERENCES

Ferguson, C (1998) *A Review of UK Company Codes of Conduct*, Department for International Development, London

Stichele, M V and P Pennartz (1996) *Making it our Business: European NGO Campaigns on Transnational Corporations*, Catholic Institute for International Relations, London

Varley, P (1998) *The Sweatshop Quandary: Corporate Responsibility on the Global Frontier*, Investor Responsibility Research Centre, Washington DC

Zeldenrust, I and N Ascoly (1998) *Codes of Conduct for Transnational Corporations: An Overview*, International Restructuring in Industries and Services, Tilburg

Chapter 16

Monitoring the monitors: a critique of corporate third-party labour monitoring

Dara O'Rourke

INTRODUCTION

One of the key issues surrounding sweatshops today involves the development of systems for monitoring conditions in the thousands of factories around the world which produce garments, shoes, toys and other goods. Governments, non-governmental organizations (NGOs), and multinational firms are all currently working to develop systems and protocols to track production practices and the treatment of workers in far-flung supply chains. Monitoring labour practices and the enforcement of codes of conduct has become a linchpin in efforts to analyse and improve factory conditions around the world.

This chapter presents an assessment of the world's largest private monitor of labour and environmental practices – PricewaterhouseCoopers (PwC).[1] PwC performed over 6000 factory audits in 60 countries during 2000, including monitoring for Nike, Disney, Walmart, the Gap, Jones Apparel and other multinational shoe, garment and toy companies. PwC also monitors for a number of universities and their licensees. PwC is leading the development of corporate monitoring systems and is poised to become one of the main auditors for several emerging monitoring and certification systems.[2] In many ways, PwC is setting the standard for what corporate monitors will do, how they will do it, and how much they will charge.

Until now, because their reports were confidential, no independent analyst had been able to evaluate the monitoring procedures of PwC or any of the other main auditing firms. This chapter presents the first detailed assessment of PwC's monitoring methods and audit tools. It is based on an analysis of PwC's written auditing protocols and a detailed assessment of factory audits conducted by PwC auditors in Shanghai, China and Seoul, Korea. The analysis was conducted while doing research for the Independent University Initiative (IUI), a research project supported by Harvard, Notre Dame, Ohio State, the University of California and the University of Michigan. My conclusions, however, are neither endorsed nor sanctioned by the universities or the IUI.[3]

This analysis provides clear evidence of the limitations of PwC's monitoring systems and methodologies. Oversights and omissions are traced directly to problems in PwC's underlying methods. PwC auditors gathered information primarily from managers rather than workers, depending largely on data provided by management. Worker interviews were problematic. All interviews were conducted inside the factories. PwC auditors had managers help them select the workers to be interviewed, had the managers collect their personnel files, and had them bring the workers into the office for the interviews. The managers knew who was being interviewed, for how long and on what issues.

It should be noted that all of the problems identified during this research occurred while PwC auditors knew they were under close scrutiny. PwC auditors were informed months in advance that I would accompany them on these audits. Presumably, PwC sent their best, most experienced auditors to conduct these inspections. I thus believe that what I observed was representative of PwC's general auditing procedures.

CASE STUDIES OF PwC MONITORING

PwC Monitoring in Shanghai, China

On 15 June, 2000, I inspected a 300-worker garment factory outside Shanghai with two PwC auditors. The PwC auditors were both financial accountants with short-term training in social auditing. The factory included knitting operations, fabric finishing, dyeing, sewing and packing. The factory exported all its output to customers in the United States, Europe and Japan. The factory's main product is knitted apparel.

Opening meeting
The PwC inspection began with an opening meeting with factory managers during which the inspection process was explained. Auditors asked factory managers a series of overview questions on factory practices and compliance with local laws on hours of work, freedom of association, forced labour, wages and so on.

Walk-around

The PwC auditors then conducted a 45-minute walk-around of the factory floor to evaluate health and safety and other issues. This inspection was completely unsystematic, starting at the end of the production line and jumping around from section to section. The auditors did not use checklists and took almost no notes during the walk-around. The auditors clearly had little training on how to do a health and safety audit.

The auditors did note a number of health and safety issues in the factory, many after they noticed that I was looking at a particular hazard. However, they missed more health and safety issues than they found, including:

- blocked aisles in the knitting room and fire exits;
- inadequate worker protection in the dyeing section – unsuitable footwear (flip-flops); lack of respiratory protection while pouring dyes into mixers;
- no machine guarding of large chains and sprockets on a polar fleece machine, and machine guards missing on many sewing machines;
- no information on chemical use in the factory; no labels explaining the contents or health effects of the spot cleaners used in the plant; no evaluation of respiratory protection for workers using chemicals;
- failure to provide mesh metal gloves to workers using hand cutting tools;
- no needle guards on sewing machines;
- over-crowded dormitory with inadequate bathroom facilities.

Worker interviews

PwC auditors selected 15 workers to be interviewed from the factory floor during the walk-around. These were selected based on 'looking young'. PwC then selected ten names from the payroll list, based again on age or low pay. This seemed to be a questionable sampling method, as this selects only the most vulnerable and weakest workers to interview. These workers are less likely to know about general practices or trends in the factory, or to complain about problems. PwC then gave this list of 25 names to the factory manager. The human resources department gathered the workers' contracts, pay-roll and time-cards.

One of the PwC auditors conducted all the interviews, based on a standard survey instrument. Interviews lasted 7–10 minutes per worker. By the end of the 3.5 hours of interviewing, the PwC auditor was extremely tired and asked the questions by rote. She seldom looked up at the workers while reading the questions and recording the answers and made no attempt to build any rapport with workers. She did not ask where they were from or how long they had been in the factory, or even which section of the plant they worked in.

The PwC auditor actually answered some of the questions in the survey without asking the worker, assuming she knew the answer without asking. She did not follow up on uncommon answers and never supplemented the survey with additional questions (as they are instructed to do) to obtain a better understanding of conditions. The auditor was also embarrassed to ask several questions in the survey related to discipline and so skipped those questions.

The PwC auditor recorded one of two answers for every worker regarding working hours – 50 or 60 hours per week. The auditor also filled out the same answer for every worker on starting time and quitting time and required hours of work. She wrote no information on overtime or days off which was clearly inaccurate based on an analysis of worker's timecards which I examined on site.

The health and safety information from the interviews was largely useless. For example, not one worker mentioned a health problem. Workers did not seem to understand the questions about personal protective equipment. The auditor failed to explain concepts that the workers did not understand.

Questions on freedom of association did not address the actual situation in the factory (and in China for that matter). The PwC auditor did not explain what a union is, or what role workers might play in it. Because the factory has a management run union, the PwC auditors found no problems on freedom of association. Questions regarding collective bargaining were skipped entirely.

Payroll analysis

PwC asked the factory's managers to input the data on wages and hours into the PwC spreadsheet. The PwC auditor reviewed one or two months of timecards but did not find any problems. However, even based on a very cursory review, I found a number of significant problems, including timecards that were not signed by workers, timecards that were almost identical, giving the appearance of one person punching in for others, and timecards that were hand-written.

From the timecards reviewed it was clear that many workers were working far in excess of maximum overtime laws. One worker worked 316.5 hours and 20 consecutive days in April, while the legal maximum is 204 hours per month. Another worker worked 303.5 hours and 12 consecutive days. The factory manager explained, 'Timecards are just used to make sure workers show up on time'.

The factory's payment system operates according to a piece rate system. In sewing for instance, the workers get paid according to a production quota, as well as being evaluated by managers on quality, timeliness and extra production. Under the piece rate system, salary has little connection to working hours. By using the piece rate system, the factory was violating local laws and university codes on overtime wages. While PwC did note that overtime pay was 'not properly compensated', they did not analyse the underlying payment system which leads to this, or recommend changes. Under the piece rate system, some workers were also probably being paid below the minimum wage during normal working hours. PwC failed to analyse this. When asked about the obvious solution to the overtime pay problem – paying workers the legally mandated pay rate of 150 per cent – one PwC auditor explained simply, 'It is not possible to multiply the piece rate by 1.5' for overtime work.

Concluding meeting

The PwC auditors ended the day with a meeting with factory managers to discuss the problems identified during the day and to present a list of recommended corrective actions. They noted the most obvious problems and asked the factory managers to resolve these.

PwC found:

- the factory is in 'acceptable' legal compliance;
- 20 cases of overtime violations;
- 20 cases of overtime pay violations;
- cases of exceeding the six consecutive day rule;
- no violations of freedom of association or collective bargaining;
- no violations of child labour;
- no violations of forced labour;
- no cases of discrimination;
- no problems with disciplinary practices;
- a list of minor health and safety issues, including:
    - no emergency lights installed in the workshops or the canteen,
    - no alarm system installed in the facility,
    - some workshops had no emergency evacuation plan posted,
    - locked exits during working hours,
    - several employees sampled were not trained in the use of fire extinguishers,
    - some workshop exits did not have 'Exit' signs installed, some doors not used as an exit were not marked as 'Not an Exit',
    - no water supply in the male washroom near the canteen,
    - no knife guards on the cutting machines,
    - workers in knitting workshop were not provided with earplugs and masks.

As PwC stated in their final report, the factory manager 'accepted all findings and recommendations and proactively expressed his intention to enhance and modify current practices to ensure that all of the findings from the monitoring visit will be corrected in their new facility as a matter of priority'. The PwC auditors then went on to verbally recommend how the factory could circumvent overtime laws, explaining that the factory can apply for a waiver of maximum hours from the provincial government during the peak season in order to legally exceed overtime laws.

PwC monitoring in Seoul, Korea

On 21 June, 2000, I inspected a 60-worker garment factory in Seoul, Korea with two PwC auditors. These two male auditors were accountants with short-term training in social auditing. The factory was primarily a sewing factory for football jerseys and sweatshirts. It had cutting, sewing, cleaning, ironing and packing operations and exported its entire output.

Opening meeting

The PwC auditors asked the manager a list of questions on the factory's production and his treatment of workers. These covered the use of involuntary labour or child labour, cases of harassment or discrimination, freedom of association and the right to form a union and health and safety problems. To each question the manager either answered 'No, of course not', or joked with the auditors about how he likes to oppress the workers.

Walk-around

The factory floor inspection lasted 30 minutes. The factory's president accompanied the PwC auditors around the factory and answered questions. The auditors noted a small number of health and safety issues in the plant, including toilets were not marked 'Gents' and 'Ladies', and a warehouse (actually a closet) that should have been marked 'Danger' on the door and was not.

The PwC auditors missed more issues than they found. They completely overlooked the use of spot cleaners called *Benzol* (a carcinogenic benzene-based cleaner) and *Pull Out #2* which contains methylene chloride and percloroethylene (also carcinogens), which have been banned by the licensee sourcing from this factory. PwC also failed to note that workers were not adequately protected while using these chemicals; inadequate ventilation for the chemical spraying area; inadequate personal protective equipment; and lack of training in chemical handling. In addition, sewing machines lacked needle guards and some sewing machine belts were unguarded.

Interviews

Workers were selected off the factory floor for interviews. The president of the factory actually wrote down the names of the workers and then went and got them. Workers were selected based on looking young or having low wages. Most of the workers in this factory were women between the ages of 30 and 50. Both of the PwC auditors were young men. The interviews were conducted in a hallway just outside the main work room and lasted 15–25 minutes each.

The PwC auditor skipped entirely the sections of the survey on freedom of association and collective bargaining (Section C), child labour (Section D) and forced labour (Section E). He explained 'there is no union in this factory, so I don't need to ask these questions'. The auditors reported that the factory was in compliance with freedom of association and collective bargaining standards. One of the PwC auditors was uncomfortable interviewing the workers and laughed when he asked the questions on disciplinary action and when he asked questions on access to toilets.

The interviews revealed that the workers did not understand the contents of the licensee's code of conduct. When asked what was in the code, workers answered with a range of guesses from 'environment' to 'child labour'. None of the workers knew that overtime should be paid at 150 per cent of normal working hours. Workers explained that this factory does not pay overtime.

The PwC auditor often lumped questions together (such as the entire section on non-discrimination), then marked all of the answers the same. He completely missed the health and safety issues associated with one of the workers interviewed regarding use of the benzene-based spot cleaners. He did not think to ask the woman about the chemicals she uses or the health impacts she has experienced. The auditor also failed to ask about the use of *Pull Out #2*.

Closing meeting

In the closing meeting, the PwC auditors primarily joked with the factory manager and discussed the few problems they identified, including:

- the factory was not paying required medical insurance;
- the factory was not paying required pension;
- the factory needed to install a sign for the storage room with dangerous materials, and signs for the toilets.

The auditors did note verbally several problems with timecards. However, they explained that these inconsistencies 'are not a violation but it should be improved'. The manager explained that 'We don't really use the timecards. So we sometimes fill them out by hand. Sometimes there is an additional 10 or 20 minutes here or there'. The auditors also verbally discussed the lack of records on paying overtime at the required 150 per cent rate. They recommended that 'you pay a "bonus" instead of paying overtime', essentially advising the company on how to circumvent the local labour law by not paying overtime.

A CRITIQUE OF PwC's AUDITS

Management bias

PwC employs a standard audit tool for all of their monitoring around the world (Box 16.1). This is designed primarily to solicit information from factory managers, rather than workers. The programme includes efforts to prepare managers for the process, provides guarantees to managers about confidentiality and even involves sending them a questionnaire beforehand to prepare them for many of the issues that will be evaluated.

Most of the information is gathered from managers. In the Chinese factory, the managers were actually asked to enter wages and hours data into the PwC spreadsheet. Worker interviews were also biased towards management. PwC auditors asked the managers to help them select workers to be interviewed, had the managers collect the workers' personnel files, and then had them bring the workers into the office for the interviews. The managers knew who was being interviewed, for how long and on what issues.

The PwC monitoring system failed to protect against the major challenge of evaluating factory conditions – access to reliable information on normal

---

Box 16.1 PwC AUDIT PROTOCOLS

Two PwC auditors spend roughly one day in each factory. They conduct a walk-through inspection of the factory, interview managers, review payroll and personnel documents, and interview workers (25 per cent of a workforce, up to a maximum of 25 workers in each factory). The audits cover 12 topic areas related to codes of conduct.

1 Legal compliance with the code of conduct
2 Wages and benefits
3 Working hours
4 Freedom of association and collective bargaining
5 Child labour
6 Forced labour
7 Non-discrimination
8 Disciplinary practices
9 Health and safety
10 Dormitory conditions
11 Subcontracting
12 Documentation and inspection

---

operating conditions. To understand normal operating conditions, it is necessary to gather sensitive information from workers and other sources. The PwC auditing methodology largely ignores these crucial, non-management, sources of information. Factory managers have incentives to cover up or hide problems, and they are given ample opportunity to do just that.

Failures to collect information from workers

The PwC programme does not effectively gather information from workers. There is no pre-visit information collected from workers and no opening or closing meetings with workers. There is no protocol to explain the programme to workers. There is no strategy for helping workers collect and then provide accurate, verifiable information. Workers are not given the chance to assemble information before the audit, such as recent pay stubs or records of pieces worked on specific days to compare to management reported hours and wages. Workers do not have records in front of them to compare to management records. Workers are chosen 'at random' throughout the plant. All worker interviews were conducted on-site and inside the factory, which exposes the workers to potential intimidation and reprisals for critical comments.

The weakness of the auditing tool was compounded by its poor implementation. Many questions were skipped during the interview. The PwC auditor decided it was not necessary or useful to ask certain questions. In the Korean case, the auditor skipped the sections on freedom of association and collective bargaining, and often omitted questions on discrimination, forced labour and child labour.

The PwC programme does not attempt to systematically compare what managers say with what workers say. There is no protocol for assisting auditors to compare management and worker statements, impressions and overall analyses of key issues.

PwC failed to take seriously the challenges of interviewing workers or to establish a context within which sensitive issues could be discussed. Little effort was made to establish a relationship or rapport with workers. From my experience inspecting over 100 factories in Asia, interviewing workers in a factory conference room (with managers sometimes within earshot) is very unlikely to elicit honest or critical perspectives. Workers need a reason to be candid. Incentives are currently aligned against workers taking any risks by reporting problems. The challenge of getting accurate information on very sensitive subjects from potentially vulnerable workers should not be underestimated.

PwC made no effort to talk to workers outside of the factory such as in their homes or in local gathering places. No effort was made to get information through intermediaries – people or organizations workers trust – such as NGOs, neighbourhood organizations, church groups, unions, local researchers or newspaper reporters. PwC also failed to use safer means of soliciting information from workers such as anonymous complaint procedures, postage paid mailers or telephone hotlines.

Failures to assess restraints on freedom of association

The PwC programme did not adequately address sensitive issues such as freedom of association, collective bargaining or forced labour. The PwC auditing tools and interview procedures failed to assess the underlying context for workers' rights or organizing. In the seven countries in which PwC conducted audits for the IUI, it found not one case of non-compliance on freedom of association or collective bargaining issues. These inspections included factories in countries in which repression of free trade unions is alleged, including China, Mexico, Pakistan and El Salvador. In their programme, PwC did not evaluate whether a factory in China with a management-controlled union was in compliance with freedom of association codes, or whether a factory in Mexico with a 'protection' union was in compliance.

In the PwC monitoring programme there were no questions asked which would gather information on how workers currently collectively respond to problems. Or what they do if their pay is reduced or withheld or delayed. Or what they do if their managers force them to work overtime against their will. And there were no questions that would get at the atmosphere for worker associations. In the cases where unions did exist, PwC failed to evaluate whether the union was a government-controlled, management-controlled or independent worker organization.

Failures to adequately assess health and safety problems

The PwC auditors did not conduct adequate health and safety inspections. Many developing countries have quite strict health and safety laws on the books. Korea for instance has laws equivalent to US occupational safety and health laws. The PwC checklists were so general that they could not evaluate if a factory in Korea was in compliance with local laws, or whether the factory was even providing a minimally safe and healthy workplace.

Even for low-tech garment factories, the PwC audit programme missed most key health and safety issues such as ergonomics, stress, noise, heat, chemical exposures (from spot removers), blood borne pathogens (from tagging guns), airborne particulates, electrical hazards, or training and hazard communication programmes. Despite widespread availability of effective checklists on all of these issues, the list used by PwC omitted many crucial items.

Interviews with workers also failed to evaluate important health and safety issues. Interviews and walk-throughs did not adequately assess hazards associated with certain jobs, personal protective equipment and training for exposed workers, individual illnesses and accidents, or worker concerns about health and safety issues. PwC did not analyse existing safety programmes, employee training or equipment and facilities.

Failures to adequately analyse wages and hours

PwC's audit methods also failed to adequately analyse wages and hours issues in these factories. As labour inspectors can attest, there are many existing strategies to avoid paying workers their mandated wages. PwC did not attempt to identify whether common strategies for paying sub-minimum wages were in use, nor did they prepare workers to answer questions on which they would have detailed information. The PwC programme is not specific enough to gather information such as the number of hours worked in a recent week or the number of pieces sewn on a given day. If available, these data could be compared with figures provided by management to begin to assess its credibility.

The PwC audit programme also did a poor job of analysing deductions from pay. There are many 'tricks' to deducting fees from wages. The audit programme did not assess whether workers understood all of the deductions on their pay slips, or compare these to what workers believed they were being paid.

The PwC auditors failed to inquire about or explain discrepancies in timecards such as hand-written times for workers in the China factory. The time noted for the start of the shift was recorded by the time clock, but the time-out (when the workers ended their shift) was written by hand for several weeks. PwC did not evaluate how timecards are controlled nor verify that the workers themselves were punching in and out.

As mentioned, in China the PwC auditors actually had the factory managers enter working time data into PwC's spreadsheet. Managers could easily manipulate these data while entering it into the spreadsheets. The auditors did not compare individual worker's timecards to management reported hours. In Korea, the auditors did not use a spreadsheet during the factory visit. Wages and hours were analysed by hand, and similarly depended on management reported information.

Incomplete factory inspection practices

Actual factory walk-through inspections were extremely brief and cursory, lasting only 30 minutes in the Korean case. The PwC auditors analysed only very basic life safety issues, checking fire safety issues, blocked aisles and bathroom cleanliness. The visual inspection was not systematic and factory managers accompanied PwC during the entire inspection.

PwC auditors did not appear to have adequate knowledge of occupational health issues or hazard recognition. The auditors used no monitoring or sampling equipment such as simple sound level meters, tape measures (to check aisle and exit widths), current pens (to assess electrical hazards) or even a temperature gauge. The monitors did not use a checklist for health and safety issues.

Flawed reporting

PwC's system for reporting the findings of its audits also leads to problems. The monitoring summary reports that PwC provides to its clients – in this case the university study team – are too condensed to be meaningful. The reports reviewed for the factories visited in China and Korea do not convey an accurate picture of the conditions in these factories, missing many major issues and giving a misleading impression of the factory's compliance with local laws.

The reports do not provide enough information to seriously assess firms along important performance practices, or to analyse best and worst practices. The PwC reports present a simple analysis of compliance versus non-compliance. The auditing process does not provide enough information to evaluate the complex issues facing workers in different political and economic contexts around the world.[4]

PwC also appears to cut and paste liberally from their reports. Language from reports on two factories in Korea were identical in places, as was language from reports on two different factories in China. Language identical to the Chinese reports was even found in a PwC audit of a shirt printing factory in Wisconsin.

CONCLUSIONS AND RECOMMENDATIONS

Monitoring can be an important component of efforts to enforce labour laws and codes of conduct around the world. Proper monitoring can identify problems in contractor factories, measure and evaluate performance, and help to chart strategies for improving conditions. However, flawed monitoring can also do more harm than good. It can divert attention from the real issues in a factory, provide a falsely positive impression of performance, certify that a company is 'sweat-free' based on very limited evidence, and actually disempower the very workers it is meant to help.

PwC is now one of the key corporate players in labour practice monitoring. However, if the cases reviewed in this chapter indicate the state of their art, there is much reason for concern about PwC's monitoring systems and findings. While the company's auditors were able to find minor problems in the factories I inspected with them, they consistently overlooked larger, more important issues. Audit reports glossed over problems with freedom of association and collective bargaining, overlooked serious violations of health and safety standards, and failed to report common problems in wages and hours.

These problems go beyond the level of poorly trained auditors and flawed audit protocols. The significant and seemingly systematic biases in PwC's methodologies call into question the company's very ability to conduct monitoring that is truly independent. While there is no single perfect way to monitor a factory, there are clearly better and worse monitoring practices. One clear recommendation from this research is that monitoring systems such as PwC's must be much more transparent and accountable. The confidential nature of PwC's audits allows the company to produce reports that exclude many sources of information, cannot be verified by other researchers or NGOs, and fail to support broader public efforts to improve factory conditions.

Universities and corporations implementing monitoring systems should commit to making their factory audits and auditing methodologies public to support transparency and broader accountability. Consumers obviously need to be able to compare factories and firms through harmonized or comparable audits. Procedures are thus needed to compare monitors and their monitoring methods. This kind of harmonization and accountability exists in the financial auditing field, but remains far off in the labour practices arena.

There is also a need to establish systems which insulate against conflicts of interest for monitors. Monitors who have a financial relationship with companies they are auditing – such as through accounting or consulting services – should be excluded from monitoring these same company's labour and environmental practices.

It is also critical that workers be involved more centrally in monitoring practices. Workers are almost always closest to problems in a factory. They should thus play a central role in analysing and reporting on working conditions. Workers should be given clear assurances and protections for reporting problems and local NGOs and worker-support organizations should be involved in monitoring and verifying these conditions.

ACKNOWLEDGEMENTS

The author thanks Garrett Brown and Archon Fung for comments on this chapter.

NOTES

1   PwC recently announced that they were spinning off their labour monitoring services into a firm called Global Social Compliance. As one reporter noted however, the 'new company' will 'still use the same 1000-plus PwC staffers to provide essentially the same monitoring services to the same corporate clients', a move largely 'designed to deflect the intense criticism associated with this kind of work' (Gordon, 2001, 85.)

2   For a good overview of monitoring schemes see: http://www.maquilasolidarity. org/resources/codes/index.htm

3   The Independent University Initiative report is available at: http://www.ucop.edu/ucophome/coordrev/policy/initiative-report.pdf

4   Nike recently made public several PwC audits of its factories (available at http://nikebiz.com/labor/grid.shtml) showing the scope of the information provided in PwC reports.

REFERENCES

Gordon, M (2001) 'PricewaterhouseCoopers: Enough!', *Corporate Counsel*, May.

Chapter 17

Code monitoring in the informal Fair Trade sector: the experience of Oxfam GB

Rachel Wilshaw

This chapter explains why Oxfam embarked in 1997 on a pioneering initiative to monitor its Fair Trade partners in a developmental way, through a framework for documenting and improving labour standards. It gives an account of the monitoring of 75 producer organizations working in the 'informal sector' (producer collectives and small enterprises providing work on a piece rate basis). It identifies the main findings, illustrated with extracts from actual monitoring reports. From this experience, lessons are drawn which are relevant to code monitoring in general, so as to help companies and other organizations address some of the problems which have arisen in code monitoring.

MONITORING STANDARDS IN THE FAIR TRADE SECTOR

Oxfam defines the purpose of Fair Trade as 'to overcome poverty by enabling poor producers or workers to access the market in ways which enable them to obtain a fair return for the goods they grow or make'. In this sense it is core to the organization's mission to finding lasting solutions to poverty and suffering, using trade and capacity building as means. This is significant in the context of this book as it is one of very few initiatives undertaken to monitor labour standards in a social development, rather than purely business, context.

Oxfam has had a Fair Trade programme for over 30 years. This has involved buying crafts, textiles and foods directly from producer organizations in developing countries, and indirectly via other Fair Trade organizations such as Cafedirect and Traidcraft.[1] Most of the food products (for example coffee, tea,

---

Box 17.1 Oxfam GB

Oxfam GB (hereafter Oxfam) is a development, relief and campaigning organization dedicated to finding lasting solutions to poverty and suffering around the world. In the last few decades, Oxfam has recognized the increasingly important role played by international trade in shaping the lives of those living in poverty.

Oxfam's work – whether in development, fair trade or campaigning – is aimed at confronting inequities in the global economic order and promoting economic growth with equity. It has been at the forefront of developing socially responsible trading models, starting its own Fair Trade programme in the 1970s, and working with others to found Cafedirect and the FairTrade Foundation in the 1980s. In the 1990s Oxfam campaigned for improved labour standards in the garment industry via its Clothes Code Campaign, helped set up the Ethical Trading Initiative, adopted an Ethical Purchasing Policy and moved its pension fund into a Socially Responsible Investment fund.

Oxfam GB
274 Banbury Road
Oxford OX2 7DZ
http://www.oxfam.org.uk
Oxfam GB is a member of Oxfam International.

---

cocoa and chocolate) are monitored under the international fairtrade labelling scheme (the Fairtrade Foundation in the UK). However in the case of crafts, textiles and some foods, there are no internationally agreed criteria and so monitoring was undertaken by Oxfam directly, using its general Fair Trade principles and trading agreement as frameworks. These are equivalent to a code of conduct.

The Fair Trade principles are the criteria which have informed Oxfam's selection of trading partners since its Fair Trade programme (known then as Bridge) was established in the mid-1970s. These principles are: fair wages in the local context, participation in decision making, good working conditions and practices, gender equity, protection of children and young workers, and sustainable use of raw materials. These principles are complemented by a trading agreement which covers expectations of the relationship between Oxfam and its trading partners, including purpose of trading, payment of a fair price, part payment in advance, product quality and product development, and transparency.

During the 1970s and 1980s relationships between Northern Fair Trade organizations and Southern producer organizations and non-governmental organizations (NGOs) tended towards the informal, having often developed from personal relationships based on mutual trust. In Oxfam's case there were regular visits by field-based staff, but monitoring of standards was not systematized, not least because measuring incomes in the informal sector is extremely difficult.

Challenges include the fact that most producers are self-employed, generally paid by piece rate and that their livelihoods are a jigsaw puzzle of different income sources, which vary with order levels and seasonal employment. There is no representation by trade unions in this sector, nor is there an employer who can be held accountable for labour standards. In addition, Oxfam deliberately selected groups of poor and marginalized producers, so it was unrealistic to expect good labour standards at the outset. What helped Oxfam initiate the monitoring was the fact that supply chains were short and well understood, and there was a relationship of trust between the different parties.

WHY MONITOR FAIR TRADE STANDARDS?

Oxfam started to tackle the issue of monitoring in 1997, with the main drivers being the need to demonstrate the Fair Trade credentials of its partners, especially to consumers, and the need to assess impact and improve programme planning. Oxfam had been developing participatory approaches to planning, monitoring and impact assessment in its humanitarian and development programmes (see Roche, 1999), and it now sought to apply the learning from this to the management of the Fair Trade programme.

The aim was to use the monitoring of standards *as a development tool*, and to gather data in a way which was inclusive and empowering for producers. In other words, a very different approach from the compliance mindset of many companies monitoring against codes of conduct. In effect the activity was an exercise in appropriate monitoring in the informal sector, and as such provided valuable learning for any organization or company needing to undertake this. The aims could be summarized as helping partners recognize and apply the Fair Trade principles; capturing data to support impact assessment and communications, and supporting learning and reflection by all parties.

WHAT HAS MONITORING INVOLVED?

Indicators to help measure the match with Fair Trade principles were developed by the author (in the role of Fair Trade Monitoring and Evaluation Officer) from 1997–1998 (Wilshaw, 1998; Williams, 2000), with input from locally-based field staff and producer organizations in the Philippines, India and Bangladesh. Between five and eight indicators were developed for each principle, based on the International Labour Organization (ILO) conventions but adapted to the informal sector, and a trial undertaken in Indonesia in October 1998. A further tool was developed to help parties review the relationship between Oxfam Fair Trade and partners and identify areas for improvement.

During 1999 and 2000 monitoring assessments were undertaken with some 75 producer organizations and groups in El Salvador, Guatemala, Mexico,

Indonesia, the Philippines, Thailand, Kenya, Malawi, Swaziland, Uganda, Zimbabwe, Bolivia, Chile, Ecuador, Peru, Bangladesh, India, Gambia and Ghana. They were carried out by Fair Trade Programme Coordinators, based in local Oxfam offices in Asia, Africa and Latin America, generally in the first language of the producers.

The findings of the first 50 reports were analysed and presented at an International Federation for Alternative Trade (IFAT) conference in Germany in June 2000,[2] which provided for a good sharing of experience and lively debates, since the membership comprises one-third Northern Fair Trade organizations and two-thirds Southern producer organizations, approximately 160 in all. The organization had established at its biennial conference in 1999 that cost-effective monitoring and reporting mechanisms were needed throughout the movement to protect the good name of Fair Trade.

At the same time an external global impact assessment study was commissioned by Oxfam, to assess the developmental impact of its Fair Trade programme. Based on a sample of 18 producer groups supported by Oxfam Fair Trade in seven countries of Asia, Africa and Latin America, the report focused on income and livelihoods, capacity building, gender and the environment (Hopkins, 2000). Broadly this found that Oxfam Fair Trade made a difference in the livelihoods of producers, in terms of income and capacity building, and in some dimensions of gender relations the programme achieved significant outcomes. However, it also found that a high proportion of the groups supported by Oxfam had become dependent on its orders and that much had yet to be done to access the mainstream market effectively.

HOW MONITORING HAS BEEN DONE

The basic approach to monitoring of Fair Trade partners by Oxfam was as follows: at the intermediary level (generally an NGO or producer organization), the Programme Coordinator introduced the purpose and proposed process, discussed their experience of monitoring, if any, agreed shared use of the information afterwards, and carried out partnership monitoring (reviewing the relationship between Oxfam Fair Trade and the partner and how it could be improved). Data were also gathered on relevant labour laws and the local cost of living. The documents were translated into the local language, if necessary, and the indicators adjusted if some were inappropriate in the context.

At producer group level, the visit was planned in advance and the monitoring conducted informally, in the local language. There was no audit questionnaire with lists of questions to be gone through in a set order. Some Programme Coordinators chose not to refer to written documents at all (or just used a short checklist). Samples of products helped establish common ground and get a discussion going. Open questions were used, for instance 'What happens next when Oxfam places an order for this?' 'How is the price agreed?'

'Tell us about the payment process?' 'What is the customer looking for?' Care was taken not to interrupt once producers started talking. Sensitive subjects, such as wages and gender-related issues, were approached last. Later that day the forms would be completed, assessing whether each indicator was met, partly met or not met, and giving supporting information. This was shared with the intermediary organization, findings and priorities for follow up discussed, and use of the report agreed on.

Table 17.1 shows a sample extract from a monitoring form relating to a group producing rattan crafts in Java, Indonesia, in December 2000.[3]

WHAT DID WE FIND OUT ABOUT LABOUR STANDARDS?

Based on an analysis of the first 50 completed monitoring forms, complemented by the impact assessment study cited above, the key findings were as follows.

Fair wages

Almost all producer groups were found to record payments to individuals systematically. Wages varied greatly, depending on orders received. Where Fair Trade orders are good, wages were significantly above the going rate (10–30 per cent higher), but many producers had insufficient orders to sustain a regular income, as well as being very dependent on Oxfam Fair Trade or other Fair Trade organizations. Only 25 per cent of producers were seeing an increase in income year on year.

Guaranteed timely payment is a clear benefit of Fair Trade: in virtually all cases, producers reported that they were paid on time, in full and properly documented. This benefit was found to be extremely important to producers and not common in the informal sector.

Too few working hours were of much more concern than too many.

We also know from the impact assessment study carried out, that in approximately one-third of cases wages were supplemented by bonuses or dividends, 40 per cent of producers participated in savings schemes, and some 80 per cent had access to credit/loan schemes.

Participation in decision making

Most groups have some kind of forum in which to raise issues. Sixty per cent of producers have the right and opportunity to participate in decision making. Slightly more have the motivation to do so (68 per cent). Nevertheless many producers were assessed as being insufficiently informed about the business on which they depended, and from an empowerment perspective this is a challenge. In the vast majority of cases producers are free to join a union or other such body, but none exists.

Table 17.1 *Oxfam Fair Trade principles indicators: fair wages in the local context*

Indicators	Met	Partly met	Not met	Current situation	Action required and date
(a) Wages/prices to the primary producers are average or above average for similar occupations in the region	✔			Wage is set up based on a piece rate that is similar to the local wage situation in other workshops, but after completed order all workers will receive bonus	Regular monitoring by field staff of Pekerti, and Oxfam will monitor at least once a year
(b) Where there is a legal minimum, wages meet it		?		On average is higher than local wages, locally is about Rp 7500,00 and workers receive Rp 12500,00	See above
(c) Wages/prices are increased in line with increases in the cost of food and other basics		✔		Generally wages enough to buy food and clothes	Confirm with Pekerti the programme plan to introduce insurance and also saving for education
(d) The trend in the level of wages/prices is upward in real terms, they will buy more than they did a year ago		✔		Price is increasing due to the crisis in the country	
(e) Producers are aware of their rights in relation to wages and terms of employment		✔		Workers usually aware about the wage but not all the terms of employment especially due to weak bargaining power	
(f) Wages are paid promptly and in full and are properly documented	✔			Wage is paid based on the agreement between producer and workers	
(g) Working hours in a workplace other than the home do not normally exceed 40 hours per week		✔		Since works are based on piece rate, it depends on the worker how they do it. Usually workers work around 6–7 hours in day time and around 2 hours in the evening	
(h) Producers have access to at least 3 months pay and free health care if they are sick.		✔		Only support that can be provided by the producers but voluntarily, there is no basis for insurance in the contract arrangement	Pekerti have plan to introduce health insurance scheme – Oxfam to check with Pekerti on follow up

(i) Locally set indicators

(j) Overall, producers
receive fair wages
and employment
terms in the local
context   ✔

Note: The term wages includes product prices, where producers are paid piece rate.
Source: Onay rattan producer group, Cirebon, Indonesia, monitored by Retno Winayhu with
Pekerti, December 2000.

Good working conditions and practices (health and safety)

In general, working conditions were found to be neither very good nor very
bad. Where conditions were poor, this was often because the place of work is in
or near the home. There is scope for improved working conditions and practices
in many cases. However, most producers were less concerned about their
working conditions than about the security of their livelihoods. Some saw this
as a concern coming from the 'North'.

Gender equity

In three-quarters of cases women were assessed as getting equal pay for work of
equal value, however women tend to do work of less value. Some of the tasks
women do are not included in the cost of production at all as they are seen as
part of their domestic responsibilities. The organizations assessed as having a
good framework for women's situation to improve (one-third) tended to be
those with a deliberate approach to addressing gender issues.

Children and young workers

No exploitative child labour was found. This is not to say that children do not
work. In half the cases looked at, children under 15 are involved in production
informally (that is in a helping capacity, not as employees) for reasons of poverty
or culture. However, they were assessed as properly protected – they attend
school, the work is light, for a short time only, takes place near a parent and
does not adversely affect their development.

The impact assessment study found that additional income from Fair Trade
activities was often used by producers, especially women, to enable their children
to go to school.

Protection of the environment

In three-quarters of cases the supply of raw material was judged to be
sustainable, with cause for concern in the rest. Raw materials are often bought in
the local market, so influence over management of natural resources is limited.
Over 60 per cent of groups use recycled packaging (often for cost reasons) and

many use off-cuts and used materials in the production process. The monitoring found a relatively high level of awareness of environmental issues amongst producer organizations but more limited knowledge at group level.

ADOPTING AND ADAPTING THE MONITORING – INNOVATION IN INDONESIA

It took time for the monitoring to get established, but then it started to take on a momentum of its own, which is what we hoped would happen. As the then Fair Trade Programme Manager, Maria Jose Barney, observed, 'What it did was raise awareness in a way which had not happened before. At first there was some resistance, because it was new and because it was from outside. But people are adopting and adapting it, which is fantastic'.

One area where people are 'adopting it and adapting it' is Java in Indonesia. It has taken two years for active involvement in the monitoring process to really develop at this level. 'Producers' first reaction was that it was quite strange because it had never happened with other buyers', according to Retno Winayhu, Programme Coordinator for Indonesia and Thailand, 'but when they got further into it they got more interested, because they realised it is something that matters to them. Some indicators do not fit their local context well. But then they started to think, what would be a good indicator for them?' Retno asked partner organizations for their participation to work on indicators that would be more suitable to the local context.

Staff from each of the organizations, Pekerti, Bethesda, Yakkum and Apikri[4] worked with Oxfam to set up a cross-monitoring trial, in order to fulfil their obligation to report to International Federation for Alternative Trade (IFAT) against the code of practice. They translated the code into Bahasa Indonesia, and built a monitoring team of six people which undertook monitoring visits with producer groups of the different organizations. They then communicated the results back to the producer groups for further dialogue. Evaluation from the trials showed that in this way they are learning from each other, and are more transparent to each other. They have also been forced to think about what is the best role for intermediaries to play within the fair trading relationship.

It was agreed in the discussion that all actors, from buyers down to producers, have to be monitored in the implementation of Fair Trade principles. The Indonesian organizations, therefore, not only reviewed and improved the indicators for the local context, but also, in the course of several workshops, developed indicators for monitoring the intermediary organizations and the Fair Trade Organizations in the North.[5] For instance they debated how the risk of loss on an order should be covered.

Table 17.2 shows a sample of the indicators developed for the different levels in the supply chain by the monitoring group in Indonesia. There are two main types in this instance: (a) buyer-intermediary (NGO)-producer group (collective), and (b) buyer-intermediary-family enterprise (small entrepreneur).

A great deal of valuable learning has come out of the monitoring process, and is continuing to do so at all levels: Oxfam, the NGO partner organization, the producer group level and so on. Other Fair Trade organizations are sharing results and costs in relation to common suppliers. The results have informed debates within the Fair Trade movement about internationally agreed standards for all product types, not just certain foods as at present (IFAT, 2001).

The benefit for Oxfam is that a local resource for monitoring has now been developed with momentum to carry it on. There is still some overview of what happens by the Programme Coordinator who attends at certain points. This is a great step forward in terms of active participation by the people the standards exist for, and is much more manageable and cost-effective for Oxfam.

Of course active involvement by producers/workers in monitoring standards can be uncomfortable. They challenge how things are done and terms of trade in general. In Indonesia, producers wanted to know how their product is priced up, why such a margin must be added to it, was it fair? The intermediary NGO, Pekerti, finally agreed that producers can have access to this information, and have learned to become more transparent. Oxfam Fair Trade was also challenged about its mark-up. But this is healthy stakeholder engagement. Producers are also pragmatic, and recognize the risk that if they expect a higher price, this will impact on future orders. So greater transparency can increase understanding of responsibilities as well as rights.

The initiative has gone further than monitoring, in that it has created a mechanism for communication and accountability up and down a trading chain. This carries potential benefits not only within a Fair Trade supply chain, but within any supply chain. It not only provides a framework for improving standards, but also facilitates dialogue up and down the supply chain. This could help buying companies manage not only ethical risks but also quality and environmental risks in critical supply chains, and improve stakeholder engagement and reporting.

GOOD PRACTICE IN CODE MONITORING, BASED ON OXFAM'S LEARNING

What the initiatives described show is that the 'informal sector' need not be a formidable monitoring challenge. As the trend towards informalization of production increases, almost all companies will have homeworkers, smallholders and other informal sector producers in their supply chains, though they may not know who and where they are. When they find them, they need to know how to deal with them appropriately. Otherwise these most vulnerable people in organizations' supply chains will get no protection from the implementation of codes.

Table 17.2 *Sample indicators developed for the different levels in a supply chain*[6]

Issues	Family enterprise	Producer group	Intermediaries	Buyers
Wage setting	Workers have space to negotiate or workers are involved in the wage determination Wage is above the minimum wage of the same work in the local standard Cash and timely or as agreed Increment of wage regularly in accordance to the local standard Documented and accessible for both workers and owner	Wage is discussed and result of the agreement among the group members Documented and accessible for all members	Monitoring and support to make sure wage is in accordance to the fair agreement and above the local standard, and there is also regular increment Monitoring result documented and accessible for all parties	Monitoring and share information as appropriate
Working conditions	Securing health and safety working conditions There is insurance or allowance for health and safety including allowance for accident in the working place Equipment and tool maintenance are in accordance with the health and safety standard Air circulation and ventilation is good Minimized the use of harmful material Waste is disposed of properly	Securing health and safety working conditions There is insurance or allowance for health and safety including allowance for accident in the working place Equipment and tool maintenance are in accordance with the health and safety standard Air circulation and ventilation is good Minimized the use of harmful material Waste is disposed of properly	Provide necessary information on health and safety standard, and socialize these standards to producers To support provision of health and safe workshop, equipment and tools To provide credit scheme for workshop improvements To help producer to access appropriate technology	To provide grant for ensuring the implementation of health and safety measures in the workplace

Social benefits	At least there is allowance for medical expenses, accident in the working place, and death allowance, and bonus for Iedul Fitri or Christmas	At least there is allowance for medical expenses, accident in the working place, and death allowance, and bonus for Iedul Fitri or Christmas	To support and facilitate the availability of social benefit in the producers' level for workers – from profits?	To support and facilitate the availability of social benefit in the producers' level for workers – from profits?

The learning Oxfam has gained from the monitoring of Fair Trade partners may be adapted by companies and other organizations seeking to apply good practice in code monitoring.

Key lessons to be learned were:

1   The monitoring of labour standards is very sensitive and all too easily feels like policing – as yet another demand from the customer on top of quality, price, delivery times and so on. Top-down approaches to monitoring compliance with codes, designed to meet the need of the party instigating the monitoring, will not be successful. Monitoring must yield benefits for those who are monitored, otherwise it will not be effective or sustainable.

2   Time invested in establishing a good process is crucial, and in a non-formal employment situation a participatory methodology is more likely to be effective than an audit format. This includes ensuring that producers/workers understand the importance of good labour standards, and have the chance to develop for themselves the indicators which most matter to them. Workers' priorities, especially those of women, may be very different from those identified by auditors. The implementation of a code needs to be seen as a long-term process of which auditing (or inspection) is just a part.

3   Intermediaries in positions of power, including managers in supplier companies, need to have bought into the business and the moral case for improving labour standards, and be open to reviewing their practices. Otherwise, even if producers/workers know their rights, the attitudes of management will be a block to progress. Monitoring labour standards must become part of good management.

4   People carrying out monitoring, whether in-house company staff or third-party auditors, need to have received basic training in social development, labour rights and gender issues, and have good interpersonal and facilitation skills, as a minimum. The limit of their competencies needs to be recognized and resources budgeted to access organizations with additional essential competencies, such as knowledge of the local culture, language, regulations and skills in using participatory approaches.

The costs of this type of monitoring are considerable. However, they can be offset by working in partnership with local organizations wanting to improve labour standards, sharing reports between parties, and by prioritizing: working with a manageable number of stable suppliers is more cost-effective than a superficial process with many.

.   Lastly, it should not be assumed that if workers are not unionized they are not organized in any other way. They may belong to community based organizations which could provide a valuable means of consulting on labour standards. NGOs with experience of Fair Trade activities may also be a good starting point for companies wishing to identify local resources since they are accustomed to working in this sector, understand the ways in which people are organized and have, or could develop over time, many of the competencies needed to monitor labour standards.

In conclusion, monitoring labour standards in sectors where there is no formal employment relationship is not easy, but neither are the problems insurmountable. In Oxfam's experience, progress can be helped by an approach based on continuous improvement rather than policing, a readiness to use open, participatory approaches, and very good skills and knowledge amongst those carrying out the monitoring. It is hoped this learning will help companies and other organizations tackle monitoring in this important but often neglected area, and so ensure a voice and a measure of protection to those vulnerable people in supply chains who are most in need of them.

NOTES

1   In early 2001, Oxfam GB completed a review of its work in Fair Trade with the objective of increasing the ability of people living in poverty to earn a sustainable livelihood through trade. The recommendations included that Oxfam should scale up its capacity building and market access work, and separate this from its buying activity. Oxfam's work on monitoring pioneered through Fair Trade is now being absorbed into its wider work on sustainable livelihoods, of which Fair Trade remains a key element.

2   Conference (2000), IFAT European Regional Meeting, Wuppertal, Germany organized by IFAT. Refer to website, http://www.ifat.org or contact IFAT on info@ifat.org.uk

3   Thanks to Pekerti Nusantara and Onay rattan group, Indonesia, for permission to reproduce extracts from monitoring reports.

4   Thanks to Pak Imam Pituduh of Pekerti Nusantara and the other NGOs CD Bethesda, Yakkum and Apikri for giving permission to describe this monitoring initiative. For further information refer to http://www.peoplelink.org/pekerti.

5   Refer to IFAT for the document *Monitoring Indicators* produced in workshops involving the Indonesian NGOs cited above.

6   As in 5 above.

REFERENCES

Hopkins, R (2000) *Impact Assessment Study of Oxfam Fair Trade*, available from Oxfam

IFAT (2001) *Standards for Fair Trade Organisations*, International Federation for Alternative Trade, May

Roche, C (1999) *Impact Assessment for Development Agencies; Learning to Value Change*, Oxfam GB with Novib

Williams, P (2000) *Oxfam Fair Trade Programme Manual*, available from Oxfam

Wilshaw, R (1998) *Tools for Participatory Monitoring by Oxfam Fair Trade and Trading Partners based on Oxfam Fair Trade Principles and Trading Agreement*, available from Oxfam

Appendix 1

Useful web sites

RESOURCES FOR RESEARCH

The New Academy for Business http://www.new-academy.ac.uk
New Economics Foundation http://www.neweconomics.org
Warwick University's Corporate Citizenship Unit
   http://users.wbs.warwick.ac.uk/ccu
IIED's Sustainable Markets Group http://www.iied.org/smg/index.html
Eldis: resource centre on corporate responsibility for development
   http://www.ids.ac.uk/eldis/
Social and Ethical Reporting Clearinghouse
   http://cei.sund.ac.uk/ethsocial/index.htm
Natural Resources Institute http://www.nri.org/NRET/nret.htm

ETHICAL TRADE AND CORPORATE RESPONSIBILITY IN PRACTICE

Ethical Trading Initiative http://www.ethicaltrade.org
ILO standards http://www.ilo.org/public/english/standards/index.htm
SA 8000 http://www.sa-intl.org
Global Reporting Initiative http://www.globalreporting.org/
World Business Council for Sustainable Development http://www.wbcsd.ch/
Prince of Wales International Business Leader Forum http://www.pwblf.org
Fairtrade Foundation http://www.fairtrade.org.uk/

CAMPAIGN GROUPS

Oxfam's Clothes Code Campaign http://www.oxfam.org.uk
Clean Clothes Campaign http://www.cleanclothes.org
Asia Monitor Resource Centre http://www.amrc.org.hk
Hong Kong Christian Industrial Committee http://www.cic.org.hk/
Corporate Watch http://www.corpwatch.org
Maquila Solidarity Campaign http://www.maquilasolidarity.org
Sweatshop Watch http://www.sweatshopwatch.org/swatch/index.html

Labour Behind the Label (UK branch of Clean Clothes Campaign)
http://www.poptel.org.uk/women-ww/labour_behind_the_label_campaign.htm
French garments campaign (L'ethique sur l'etiquette) http://www.crc-conso.com/etic/
Women Working Worldwide http://www.poptel.org.uk/women-ww
Homenet International http://www.homenetww.org.uk

Index

Page numbers in *italics* refer to figures, tables and boxes